# Chapman 100-1

## Centenary Double Issue Part 1

# Editorial

It's hard for me to believe I'm sitting here, gazing over my computer to a grey east Edinburgh New Town back-tenement scene, writing the editorial to *Chapman* 100. I'm nearly 50 now: why have I spent my life doing this? I remember a similar scene, almost 30 years ago, though in a modern flat in Clermiston, west Edinburgh, gazing over a cheap Adler typewriter, in the throes of philosophy finals, thinking: *Chapman*, yes, I think I could do that. I'd already helped produce 15 issues to date, with my then husband, Walter Perrie, co-founder with George Hardie of *The Chapman*, a slim 8 page pamphlet born in 1970 out of vision and frustration in 'The Silver Tassie' in Hamilton. Hardie dropped out, I dropped in, but by 1976 Walter was tiring of it, and I was becoming more enthusiastic. I had no ambition to run a magazine which would reach its 100th issue. I've always said that the moment I felt the project going stale, or ran out of ideas and energy, I would kill it off. That moment has never arrived.

I had strongly entrenched ideas about what was needed then: a magazine which promoted Scottish writing as a priority. Only through editing the magazine and coming into contact with Scottish writers had I gained any knowledge of Scottish literature at all, which, Burns apart, simply didn't exist in Scottish education. Realising what a wealth was there filled me at once with enormous pride, and a burning anger that my generation had been effectively disinherited of our own literature and culture. *Chapman* provided a vehicle which could make some small difference.

A similar fate had befallen both Scots and Gaelic, and direct agitation through *Chapman* on behalf of these languages became a plank of editorial policy. Although not then a nationalist, realising the cultural 'predicament' led to a belief that devolution at least was imperative for the rehabilitation of Scottish arts and letters, asserting the value of "the Scottish accent of the mind". I was not then a 'feminist', though indignant about lack of equality, but I discovered gradually how Scottish women writers had been ignored or buried, virtually without trace, or in the case of pesky Gaelic bardesses with sharp tongues, face down to stop their free spirits from further troubling the living. This fuelled a driving impulse to take on these unjust anomalies. The wisest thing about editing I've ever heard said was from Patricia Oxley, editor of *Acumen*, who appears in these pages, that editing a magazine was like educating yourself in public.

Actually, it's all the Scottish Arts Council's fault. One of the most devastating blows in my editorial career occurred on my first day of teaching, about a year later. A poet friend who was walking my dog had arranged to meet me on the banks of the Tyne, at Haddington, and brought a letter from SAC, thinking it would bring good news. It didn't: it gave me one year's notice of termination of grant. I'd produced only 4 issues, whose contents I'd still defend with my life, and felt bewildered and destroyed.

I decided to fight back, ran a press campaign, got signatures from writers – Norman MacCaig, Sorley MacLean, Iain Crichton Smith, to name but a few, who were happy to aver that I'd had "a raw deal" [MacCaig]. There was a 'sponsor-a-page' appeal. The crisis took another year to resolve. Funds were cut by a third for that 'final' year, but the money raised financed the biggest issue up to that time, No 23-4, an attempt at a comprehensive overview of the state of Scots Language then (1979!). The issue sold out, as did its reprint, and I got my grant back, though at it took another 6 years before a 'reasonable' level of funding was achieved. But for that early fight for survival, I might well have given up years ago. It got my dander up. As someone put it, I'd been bitten by "the rat" – after which there is no going back. That adrenalin-inspired fight, once initiated, remains in the blood.

I liked the original *Chapman* idea of being a thorn in the flesh of the establishment and the commitment to wide-ranging, international contact and influence (prioritising Scottish literature was a response to the lack of cultural resources in Scotland at the time). I had no wish to produce a magazine which simply published poems, but wanted to create a vital forum to push for real change in 'the state of Scotland' culturally and politically. *Chapman* and its attendant activities has played a role, however small, in the improvement in publishing facilities, in education, improving the position of women, in Scottish theatre, even in achieving our own Parliament.

*Chapman* has always tried to be open to new writers, new ideas, wherever they come from. As the years rolled by it became difficult to accept that a young writer, coming, say, from Caithness, might view me with deep suspicion, as one of the Edinburgh literati, a member of 'the establishment' – as inherently unsympathetic to, perhaps even opposed to his/ her aspirations. I don't think 'a name' cuts any ice in our office. Exciting good work by a total unknown is as welcome as ever.

I've also tried to avoid cliquishness, refrained from publishing only a personal coterie – indeed from publishing myself (I do here, for the second time ever). In the '70s the literary magazines were often at each others throats, with destructive effects, but gradually a new mood of collaboration emerged: *Cencrastus* and *Chapman* have organised many joint events; there have been readings with *Rebel Inc*, who expected us to regard them as presumptuous interlopers! I've agitated for improvement of the lot of literary magazines, through SCAMP (Scottish Association of Magazine Publishers) in the '70s and currently ALMS (Assocation of Literary Magazines in Scotland). *Chapman* has been lucky to be around during a period of intense creativity and change in the Scottish arts scene. We've tried to use that, be a central part of it, and an active agent in the process.

There has been a price to pay. The strain of having at least 2 demanding full-time jobs left me over the last 5 years or so with Chronic Fatigue Syndrome, and everything almost disappeared down the tubes. I have recovered to a dramatic extent, and regained much of the physical and mental capability which CFS robs one of. The publication of *Chapman* 100/1, marks an end of all that and a new beginning.

I've always thought of this issue as 'a party between two covers'. The whole point of this landmark is to celebrate the creativity of the many writers, musicians, artists and others who've been involved over the years. The response has been overwhelming, and what we in fact have is an entire year's worth of *Chapman* centenary: the celebrations will be published in 3 parts, continuing with 102 and 103 at least. Among the forthcoming attractions are Liz Lochhead, Tom Leonard, aonghas macneacail, Carl MacDougall; our tribute to William Neill on his 80th birthday, and much else.

Over the years probably about 5000 people have been involved, one way or another, in the production of the magazine – as writers, artists, our many invaluable volunteers, technical advisers, printers ... Goodness knows how many contributions we've knocked back! I'd like to give profound thanks especially to my assistants, starting with Margaret Glen, then Rebecca Wilson, Robert Calder (who's always been 'there'), Peter Cudmore, Mary Gordon, Joy Hare, Sam Wood, Gerry Stewart, and now Edmund O'Connor sees to it that the editorial energies are not allowed to flag. Very special thanks are due to Peter Cudmore, who helped far beyond the job remit for more than 5 years and returned recently to help with this issue, and Gerry Stewart, assistant while I was most ill. Without her, *Chapman* would never have reached its centenary at all. I'd like also to thank John Law for help in many different ways.

I'd like also to thank subscribers and readers for their support and feedback. This issue will be the spearhead of a marketing campaign for which Lottery Funding will be sought. Now especially we must redouble efforts to extend readership, which we do now, starting with our 'free subscription for a friend' scheme – see leaflet. No literary magazine is ever 'safe', however long it may have persisted in publication.

Despite what I said earlier, I acknowledge with deep thanks the moral and financial support of SAC's Literature Department and committee members. All the Directors, Trevor Royle, Walter Cairns and Jenny Brown have been consistently sympathetic and helpful, as have their officers, Sheena Duffy, Shonagh Irvine, Gavin Wallace, Jenny Attala, Catherine Allan. The SAC magazine budget has always been controversial, as Trevor's memoir here shows. In the '70s it consumed a high proportion of the literature budget, about which many felt uncomfortable. Extending (rightly) the provision for writers through bursaries, Writers in Public and other schemes has squeezed the magazines down the priority list and today there is increasing pressure on us to be professional, for editors to be multi-skilled to a ridiculous degree, untrained jack and jackesses of all trades. Nicholas Spice's recent wide-ranging report may enable SAC to approach the Scottish Executive with a strong case for literature overall, and literary magazines in particular. The glaring omission of literature from the Cultural Strategy is surely something our Parliament would wish to rectify. Literary magazines are embedded in the creative loam of their country; editors get their get hands dirty. Our contribution to the life of the nation is perhaps minor in the global view, but our role in nurturing new and sustaining existing talent is vital, as is the freedom of expression, the provision for genuine controversy and debate in our pages. Scottish magazines have been remarkably successful over the years, but how much more could be achieved if we were professionally funded as organisations, able to pay writers (and editors) properly for their work! In the '70s I toted myself and *Chapman* round the country, lugging copies, a typewriter, and a large cardboard box of 'current business'. My office was once the bay-window of my sitting room; now it occupies an entire ground floor flat. For any magazine which wants to last and make an impression, what was possible 30 years ago is no longer an option.

I'd like to thank all the contributors to the centenary celebrations, and am only sorry I can't get everybody into one issue. One or two features from the past are reprised, in particular the essays in *Chapman* 16, my first 'solo' issue (with help from David Campbell) These essays, by Norman MacCaig, Sorley MacLean, Iain Crichton Smith, George Mackay Brown, Tom Scott and Kathleen Raine were written in response to three questions: "What started you writing? What keeps you writing? And what is your relationship with Poetry and 'the Muse'. Apart from Sorley's essay, none have been reprinted, and I thank to the families of the writers concerned.

Four poets have died recently: Hamish Henderson, Rayne Mackinnon, Ken Morrice and Tony McManus, tragically young. George Gunn's poem here is our immediate marking of the enormous loss of Hamish, but more will follow later. Tributes to Rayne, Ken and Tony appear here. Our sympathy goes out to all their families and friends. All of them have given enormously to our world, and left us the richer for their work.

An important part of this issue is the reflections on the genesis and development of *Chapman* and other magazines and I'd like to thank the editors and writers for what I hope will be a larger discussion. I'm also especially grateful for the generosity of Jack Vettriano in giving us unrestricted access to his output over many years, including some paintings previously unpublished. This is also a tribute to W Gordon Smith who died in 1996, and brought together many Scottish writers with Jack in the volume *Fallen Angels*. Gordon did so much for Scottish art and letters, and it's a privilege to be remembering him here in this way. I'd also like to thank Shona Dougall, 'featured artist' in *Chapman* 98, who helped greatly in putting together the selection of Jack's work.

One thing leads to another, and publishing the magazine also led to publishing books, the most successful of which have been our *Wild Women Series*, featuring Janet Paisley, Lydia Robb and Magi Gibson, whose *Wild Women of a Certain Age* was so successful that it had to be reprinted. The *Wild Women Anthology* is forthcoming, as soon as *Chapman* 100 is out. Our latest book is Ian McDonough's *Clan MacHine* – another winner. There will, in the autumn, be a major *Chapman* event, and I hope as many people as possible will join in the celebrations. I'll keep you informed!

But most of all, a magazine is made by those who write for it and contribute to it, and my heart-felt thanks go to all the writers and artists, the world over, who have allowed their work to grace our pages over our 32 years of continuous publication. This centenary edition is a tribute to you.

# The Universal Story

## *Ali Smith*

There was a man dwelt by a churchyard.

Well, no, okay, it wasn't always a man; in this particular case it was a woman. There was a woman dwelt by a churchyard. Though, to be honest, nobody uses that word much nowadays. Everybody says cemetery. And nobody really says dwelt any more. In other words:

There was once a woman who lived by a cemetery. Every morning when she woke up she looked out of her back window and saw –

Actually, no. There was once a woman who lived by – no, in – a second-hand bookshop. She lived in the flat on the first floor and ran the shop which took up the whole of downstairs. There she sat, day after day, among the skulls and the bones of second-hand books, the stacks and shelves of them spanning the lengths and breadths of the long and narrow rooms, the piles of them swaying up, precarious like rootless towers, towards the cracked plaster of the ceiling. Though their bent or riffled or still-chaste spines had been bleached by years of anonymous long-gone light, each of them had been new once, bought in a bookshop full of the shine of other new books. Now each was here, with too many possible reasons to guess at when it came to the question of how it had ended up sunk in the bookdust which specked the air in which the woman, on this winter's day, sat by herself, sensing all round her the weight of it, the covers shut on so many millions of pages that might never be opened to light again.

The shop was down a sidestreet off the centre of a small rural village which few tourists visited in the summer and in which business had slowed considerably since 1982, the year the Queen Mother, looking frail and holding her hat on her head with one hand because of the wind, had cut the ribbon on the bypass which made getting to the city much quicker and stopping in the village quite difficult. Then the bank had closed, and eventually the post office. There was a grocer's, but most people drove to the supermarket six miles away. The supermarket also stocked books, though hardly any.

Occasionally someone would come into the second-hand bookshop looking for something he or she had heard about on the radio or read about in the papers. Usually the woman in the shop would have to apologise for not having it. For instance, it was February now. Nobody had been into the shop for four days. Occasionally a bookish teenage girl or boy, getting off the half past four school bus which went between the village and the town, used to push, shy, at the door of the shop and look up with the kind of delight you can see even from behind, in the shoulders and back and the angle of head of a person looking up at the endless promise of books. But this hadn't happened for a while.

The woman sat in the empty shop. It was late afternoon. It would be dark soon. She watched a fly in the window. It was early in the year for flies. It flew in veering triangles, then settled on *The Great Gatsby* by F Scott Fitzgerald, to bask in what late winter sun there was.

Or – no. Wait:

There was once a fly resting briefly on an old paperback book in a second-hand bookshop window. It had paused there in a moment of warmth before launching back into the air, which it would do any second now. It wasn't any special or unusual kind of fly, or a fly with an interesting species-name – for instance a robber fly or an assassin fly, a bee fly or a thick-headed fly, a dance fly, dagger fly, a snipe fly or a down-looker fly. It wasn't even a stout or a cleg or a midge. It was a common house fly, a *musca domesticus linnaeus* of the *diptera* family, which means it had two wings. It stood on the cover of the book and breathed air through its spiracles.

It had been laid as an egg less than a millimetre long in a wad of manure in a farmyard a mile and a half away, and had become a legless maggot, feeding off the manure it had been laid in. Then, because winter was coming, it had wriggled by sheer muscle contraction nearly a hundred and twenty feet. It had lain dormant for almost four months in the grit round the base of a wall under several feet of stacked hay in the barn. In a spell of mild weather over the last weekend it had broken the top off the pupa and pulled itself out, a fly now, six millimetres long. Under an eave of the barn it had spread and dried its wings and waited for its body to harden in the unexpectedly spring-like air coming up from the Balearics. It had entered the rest of the world through a fly-sized crack in the roof of the barn that morning, then zigzagged for over a mile looking for light, warmth and food. When the woman who owned the shop had opened the kitchen window to let the condensation out as she cooked her lunch, it had flown in. Now it was excreting and regurgitating, which is what flies do when they rest on the surfaces of things.

To be exact, it wasn't an it, it was a female fly, with a longer body and red slitted eyes set wider apart than if she had been a male fly. Her wings were each a thin, perfect, delicately-veined membrane. She had a grey body and six legs, each with five supple joints, and she was furred all over her legs and her body with tiny bristles. Her face was striped velvet-silver. Her long mouth had a sponging end for sucking up liquid and for liquefying solids like sugar or flour or pollen.

She was sponging with her proboscis the picture of the actors Robert Redford and Mia Farrow on the cover of the Penguin 1974 edition of *The Great Gatsby*. But there was little there really of interest, as you might imagine, to a house fly which needs urgently to feed and to breed, which is capable of carrying over one million bacteria and transmitting everything from common diarrhoea to dysentery, salmonella, typhoid fever, cholera, poliomyelitis, anthrax, leprosy and tuberculosis; and which senses that at any moment a predator will catch her in its web or crush her to death with a fly-swat; or if she survives these that it will still, any moment now, simply be cold enough to snuff out herself and all ten of

*Illustration by Shona Dougall*

the generations she is capable of setting in motion this year, all nine hundred of the eggs she will be capable of laying given the chance, the average twenty days of life of an average common house fly.

No. Hang on. Because:

There was once a 1974 Penguin edition of F Scott Fitzgerald's classic novel, *The Great Gatsby*, in the window of a quiet second-hand book shop in a village that very few people visited any more. It had a hundred and eighty-eight numbered pages and was the twentieth Penguin edition of this particular novel – it had been reprinted three times in 1974 alone; this popularity was partly due to the film of the novel which came out that year, directed by Jack Clayton. Its cover, once bright yellow, had already lost most of its colour before it arrived at the shop. Since the book had been in the window it had whitened even more. In the film-still on it, ornate in a twenties-style frame, Robert Redford and Mia Farrow, the stars of the film, were also quite faded, though Redford was still dapper in his golf cap, and Farrow, in a very becoming floppy hat, suited the sepia effect that the movement of sun and light on the glass had brought to her quite by chance.

The novel had first been bought for 30p (6/-) in 1974 in a Devon bookshop by Rosemary Child who was twenty-two, and who had felt the urge to read the book before she saw the film. She married her fiancé Roger two years later. They mixed their books and gave their doubles to a Cornwall hospital. This one had been picked off the hospital library trolley in Ward 14 one long hot July afternoon in 1977 by Sharon Patten, a fourteen-year-old girl with a broken hip who was stuck in bed in traction and bored because Wimbledon was over. Her father had seemed pleased at visiting-hour when he saw it on her locker, and though she'd given up reading it halfway through she kept it there by the waterjug for her whole stay and smuggled it home with her when she was discharged. Three years later, when she didn't care anymore what her father thought of what she did, she gave it to her school-friend David Connor who was going to university to do English, telling him it was the most boring book in the world. David read it. It was perfect. It was just like life is. Everything is beautiful, everything is hopeless. He walked to school quoting bits of it to himself under his breath. By the time he went up north to university in Edinburgh two years later, now a mature eighteen-year-old, he admired it, as he said several times in the seminar, though he found it a little adolescent and believed the underrated *Tender Is The Night* to be Fitzgerald's real masterpiece. The tutor, who every year had to mark around a hundred and fifty abysmal first year essays on *The Great Gatsby*, nodded sagely and gave him a high pass in his exam. In 1985, having landed a starred first and a job in Personnel Management, David sold all his old literature course books to a girl called Mairead for thirty pounds. Mairead didn't like English – it had no proper answers – and decided to do economics instead. She sold them all again, making a lot more money than David had. *The Great Gatsby* went for £2.00, six times its original price, to a first year student called Gillian Edgbaston. She managed never to read it and left it on the shelves of the rented house she'd been living in when she moved out in 1990. Brian Jackson, who owned the rented house, packed it in a box which sat behind the freezer in his garage for five years. In 1995 his mother Rita came to visit and while he was tidying out his garage she found it in the open box, just lying there on the gravel in his driveway. *The Great Gatsby!* she said. She hadn't read it for years. He remembers her reading it that summer, it was two summers before she died, and her feet were up on the sofa and her head was deep in the book. She had a whole roomful of books at home. When she died in 1997 he boxed them all up and gave them to a registered charity. The registered charity checked through them for what was valuable and sold the rest on, in auctioned boxes of thirty miscellaneous paperbacks, a fiver per box, to second hand shops all over the country.

The woman in the second-hand bookshop had opened the box she bought at auction and raised her eyebrows, tired. Another *Great Gatsby*.

Penguin Modern Classics. F Scott Fitzgerald. Now a Major Film. The book was in the window. Its pages and their edges were dingy yellow because of the kind of paper used in old Penguin Modern Classics; by nature these books won't last. A fly was resting on the book now in the weak sun in the window.

But the fly suddenly swerved away into the air, because a man had put his hand in among the books in the window display in the second-hand bookshop and was picking the book up.

Now:

There was once a man who reached his hand in and picked a second-hand copy of F Scott Fitzgerald's *The Great Gatsby* out of the window of a quiet second-hand bookshop in a small village. He turned the book over as he went to the counter.

How much is this one, please? he asked the grey-looking woman.

She took it from him and checked the inside cover.

That one's £1.00, she said.

It says thirty pence here on it, he said, pointing to the back.

That's the 1974 price, the woman said.

The man looked at her. He smiled a beautiful smile. The woman's face lit up.

But, well, since it's very faded, she said, you can have it for fifty.

Done, he said.

Would you like a bag for it? she asked.

No, it's okay, he said. Have you any more?

Any more Fitzgerald? the woman said. Yes, under F. I'll just –

No, the man said. I mean, any more copies of *The Great Gatsby*.

You want another copy of *The Great Gatsby*? the woman said.

I want all your copies of it, the man said, smiling.

The woman went to the shelves and found him four more copies of *The Great Gatsby*. Then she went through to the storeroom at the back of the shop and checked for more.

Never mind, the man said. Five'll do. Two pounds for the lot, what do you say?

His car was an old Mini Metro. The back seat of it was under a sea of different editions of *The Great Gatsby*. He cleared some stray copies from beneath the driver's seat so they wouldn't slide under his feet or the pedals while he was driving, and threw the books he'd just bought over his shoulder on to the heap without even looking. He started the engine. The next second-hand bookshop was six miles away, in the city. His sister had called him from her bath two Fridays ago. James, I'm in the bath, she'd said. I need F Scott Fitzgerald's *The Great Gatsby*.

F what's the what? he'd said.

She told him again. I need as many as possible, she said.

Okay, he'd said.

He worked for her because she paid well; she had a grant.

Have you ever read it? she asked.

No, he'd said. Do I have to?

So we beat on, she'd said. Boats against the current. Borne back ceaselessly into the past. Get it?

What about petrol money, if I'm supposed to drive all over the place looking for books? he'd said.

You've got five hundred quid to buy five hundred books. You get them for less, you can keep the change. And I'll pay you two hundred on top for your trouble. Boats against the current. It's perfect, isn't it?

And petrol money? he'd said.

Included, she'd sighed.

Because:

There was once a woman in the bath who had just phoned her brother and asked him to find her as many copies of *The Great Gatsby* as possible. She shook the drips off the phone, dropped it over the side on to the bathroom carpet and put her arm back into the water, quick, because it was cold.

She was collecting the books because she made full-sized boats out of things boats aren't usually made out of. Three years ago she had made a three-foot long boat out of daffodils which she and her brother had stolen, at night, from people's front gardens all over town. She had launched it, climbing into it, in the local canal. Water had come up round her feet almost immediately, then up round her ankles, her knees, her thighs, till she was midriff-deep in icy water and daffodils floating all round her, unravelled.

But a small crowd had gathered to watch it sink and the story had attracted a lot of local and even some national media attention. Sponsored by Interflora, which paid enough for her to come off unemployment benefit, she made another boat, five foot long and out of mixed flowers, everything from lilies to snowdrops. It also sank, but this time was filmed for an arts project, with her in it, sinking. This had won her a huge arts commission to make more unexpected boats. Over the last two years she had made ten- and twelve-footers out of sweets, leaves, clocks and photographs, and had launched each one with great ceremony at a different UK port. None of them had lasted more than eighty feet out to sea.

*The Great Gatsby*, she thought in the bath. It was a book she remembered from her adolescence, and as she'd been lying in the water fretting about what to do next so her grant wouldn't be taken away from her, it had suddenly come into her head. It was perfect, she thought, nodding to herself. So we beat on. The last line of the book. She ducked her shoulders under the water to keep them warm.

And so, since we've come to the end already:

The seven-foot boat made of copies of *The Great Gatsby* stuck together with waterproof sealant was launched in the spring, in the port of Felixstowe.

The artist's brother collected over three hundred copies of *The Great Gatsby*, and drove between Wales and Scotland doing so. It is still quite hard to buy a copy of *The Great Gatsby* second-hand in some of the places he visited. It cost him a hundred and eighty three pounds fifty exactly. He kept the change. He was also a man apt to wash his hands before he ate, so was unharmed by any residue left by the fly earlier in the story on the cover of the copy he bought in the quiet second-hand bookshop.

This particular copy of *The Great Gatsby*, with the names of some of the people who had owned it inked under each other in their different handwritings on its inside first page – Rosemary Child, Sharon Patten, David Connor, Rita Jackson – was glued into the prow of the boat, which stayed afloat for three hundred yards before it finally took in water and sank.

The fly which had paused on the book that day spent that evening resting on the light fitting and hovering more than five feet above ground level. This is what flies tend to do in the evenings. This fly was no exception.

The woman who ran the second-hand bookshop had been delighted to sell all her copies of *The Great Gatsby* at once, and to such a smiling young man. She replaced the one which had been in the window with a copy of Dante's *Divine Comedy*, and as she was doing so she fanned open the pages of the book. Dust flew off. She blew more dust off the top of the pages, then wiped it off her counter. She looked at the book-dust smudged on her hand. It was time to dust all the books, shake them all open. It would take her well into the spring. Fiction, then non-fiction, then all the sub-categories. Her heart was light. That evening she began, at the letter A.

The woman who lived by a cemetery, remember, back at the very beginning? She looked out of her window and she saw – Ah, but that's another story.

And lastly, what about the first, that man we began with, the man dwelt by a churchyard?

He lived a long and happy and sad and very eventful life, for years and years and years, before he died.

# The Migrant/ Colonist Dialectic

## aonghas macneacail

Every community in the world, more or less, is made up of 'settled peo-ple', sometimes called 'aborigines' or 'natives', even 'locals', with a greater or lesser proportion among them of 'settlers'. The 'settled' represent con-tinuity: they may be able to trace their families back through several, or innumerable, generations, identifiable through a genealogical chain that can stretch into the realms of myth, often tied to the same small parcel of land. Even those we call 'nomadic' peoples, should be counted among the 'settled'. Their travels take place within clearly defines territories, of which they will have intimate knowledge. If the territory occupies a landmass of continental scale, neighbouring communities may represent entirely dif-ferent culture and language groups. Multilingualism will be the norm.

'Settlers' are less easy to define. In more conservative societies, full inte-gration takes generations: genealogy can work against you. There is (probably) reason to relax when the 'badge of origin' begins to be used as a term of affection, though it's reasonable to regard any distinguishing form of address, or nomenclature, with suspicion, as it still contains the potential for exclusion.

The Tutsi and the Hutu in East Central Africa are not, apparently, eth-nically, linguistically or culturally, different from each other. For hundreds of years they co-existed peacefully, living out the Hollywood Musical fan-tasy where 'The Farmer and the Cowboy could be Friends'. Then a third element intruded, coming from elsewhere and drawing attention to dif-ference, while down-playing commonalities. In Cambodia, the Khmer Rouge managed to do for a significant number of their own kin, who hap-pened not to share the same social or educational class with them. Those who accused the 'enemy' of absorbing and propagating 'foreign' values were themselves proponents of an equally 'foreign' ideology.

At the same time, many of the (apparently) more 'settled' societies carry evidence, frequently linguistic, of origins elsewhere than the geographies they inhabit. In naming habitations and distinctive features, the pioneers laid traces for much later scholarship to identify. The more 'central' of the Indo-European languages may be able to relax with their common antiq-uity, but there is evidence that the oldest shared words are found on the outer extremities of the language map, among Indian and Celtic languages.

It's equally true that the cultures commonly identified as 'Native Amer-ican', for example, are less native than might appear. There is evidence that their ancestors crossed over from North-East Asia, over 30,000 years ago, and spread throughout the entire American land-mass, north and south. It would appear that we are all from 'somewhere else'. But whether a linguistic group traces its origins back three, or thirty, thousand years, and whether it numbers its speakers in hundreds or hundred millions, each such community has something distinctive, and essential, to contribute to the world: and, if that premise is accepted, it must surely follow that each such community has the right to establish a place for itself – even if that were only a scatter of crofts in a remote glen or rooms in a building in a large city – where the world can be experienced entirely through the medium of its language, and in terms of all the nuanced values associated with that language. This is where the attitudes of incomers become significant. Although a spectrum of reactions may be identified, they can, essentially, be divided between migrants and colonists.

Those whom recent Home Secretaries have depicted as requiring to be coerced into linguistic and cultural assimilation are, in fact, likely to have good economic reasons for wishing to acquire the communication skills which, inevitably, will accelerate integration. Whether the transition is from Afghanistan or Ardhasaig, and whether the individual is identified as refugee, economic migrant or asylum-seeker, the need to have, or achieve, a working command of the *lingua franca* will be taken for granted. Migrants, whether voluntary or enforced, have deference to the host environment written in to their circumstances. Colonists, on the other hand, travel with the assumption that their needs will, at all times, be accommodated. Professional colonists, of course, run things – usually empires, but there is a more pervasive colonist mentality which can be encountered wherever a vulnerable culture struggles to survive. Environmental protection agencies, for example, specialise in placing experts in control of Sites of Special Scientific Interest without taking any cognisance of the fact that they may also be sites of special linguistic interest. Governments which consider themselves progressive, will often act, in a variety of ways, including their education policies and in the deployment of civil servants, against the well-being of marginalised cultural communities.

Individuals who move from the mainstream into a marginalised community are equally prone to bring the same colonist values with them. Because the host community has itself already been, to a degree, colonised, in the sense that educational policy compulsorily connected it to the mainstream, the 'colonist' incomer sees no value, or necessity, in making any effort to assimilate into the host culture. Because the 'host' citizen, whether defined as settled, native, aboriginal, or whatever, can accommodate the colonist register, that can fairly quickly become the principal register of public discourse within the community, marginalising the marginalised culture even more.

And, whereas Home Secretaries can issue decrees of imposition against migrants into the mainstream, the marginalised will be judged unreasonable, if not downright intolerant, should they dare to suggest that they may have reason to make similar demands of those who enter their society. Being too polite, of course, we don't, and what we have attenuates, dissipates and will eventually, inevitably, disappear, unless …

.... and an afterthought: if Home Secretary Blunkett wishes to insist on 'asylum-seekers' having to learn English, should migrants to Gaelic and Scots heartlands be regarded as 'asylum-seekers' too?

# Janet Paisley

## *Scotland*

she is a harsh mother,
arthritic with hills and crags
cut deeper than crow's feet.

her face is lined with ravines
her voice the roar of spume
on broken brown-toothed rock.

she passes boulders off as breasts,
belts her waist with an industrious past,
in her arms, she gathers firs

a grey and grizzled warrior, she is
bordered by ample hips, her tongue
a lash of thunderous voltage.

no season softens her, she drags
her children up on gorse and whin,
winters them without kindness.

she fires the hearth with ice or hail,
expects snow to pass for gentleness.
spring girdles her old in green.

if she holds you to her rugged breast
it is to pour the white-water scorn
of mountains on your head.

when she croons, she throws up seagulls.
sleeping, she drags a lumpen pillow
over the moon, punches out a few stars.

she'll turn your dreams to Scotch mist,
bone comb your hair with tugging wind
scrub your faces with rain.

in your mouth she lodges a language
no-one speaks, in your heart a stone.
if you go from her

a wild song and dance will follow
to bind you forever son or daughter,
make you sick for home.

## The Hawk Stanes

there is nae stane whaur the gled soars
nae gled whaur the stanes staun

nor at their cobbled feet, nae king
tae reign his high, wide street

whaur only rain croons a castlehill
nae burnin weemin wish they'd drooned

an the shuttered shops will sell nae cloth
while nae tea or snuff is taen in there

yet nae gill bell rings the meridian
only fower hunner year as time turns roon

oan a turnpike stair, Auld Reekie sings
an auld sang tae a newborn tune, an a star

is lit whaur stane mounts stoor
tae raise us up whaur the gled kin soar.

## Dream Catching

hard to find the human heart
disguised among its aching parts

in broken rooms, what shadows cast
in desperate lives, what track

no song is sung inside a fist
stone does not dance, or give

but here is a crumb
and here a touch, a gentleness

we are among the whispered strands
of random kindness

though cracked earth drinks our blood
and the thirsty starve for tears

and the grieving bear what they can't
we have the wings of angels on our backs

hope spooned like honey in our mouths
tongues taste morning wine

the hand is open
the stone a full heart
the crumb a loaf

## Greek

Well, it was never exact
even though Pythagoras lurked
and that was the trouble.
Edges blur with the drawl of bees
when there is too much milk and honey,
so many peak-mirrored ravines.

It might have been the sand and orange
byzantine churches breasting every street
or the cut of grey impossible walls
venetian-castled on every ridge
but the truth is, even overdressed by Rome,
dig deep enough in brick-red earth
and the ancients rise again and again.

It doesn't matter if olive groves
or decorated butterflies or blood-red poppies
or tideless see-through sea, if goat or sheep
or cow bells clank, if trees are lemon, almond, fig
or wet-land impressionist umbrella firs
and who cares how they raised the stone
so long as they did. What matters is

an openness, the easy shallow deepest thrust,
a murmured tenderness, hot kiss of skin,
the touch of words, and wordless,
the too much for five senses taste of a lover's name
that never came, no matter how hot it seemed,
cried out. All that to wonder at, and this:
that I am comfortable with the vast,
unknowing ageless all too human gods
from which we came, and you are not.

## Dust

It was your unhurriedness
walking to a friend's,
and the stick, or maybe to shop,
that way the aged have
of knowing there's no rush.

The man who bumped against you
apologised, no more.

I read his lips.

Puzzled, you didn't hear
nor did you look.
What was behind you
is behind us all
running to catch up.

It stopped my breath, the cloud
that would stop yours.

Go inside, the only words.

## Madness

Today we have microphones for breakfast.
They lurk in smoke alarms, listen in.
We are not alone, nor safe now, at home.

At lunch they watch us, our windows
peepholes scrutinised by us. We are
accompanied by fearsome strangers.

They come in waves through radios
or TV sets. The blank screen gapes
while suspect light bulbs are removed.

Tomorrow it may be the nightmares
or the answerphone's silent calls.
It knows when I go out. The house breathes.

He can hear it. I can hear him scream,
in three hour tirades on my failure
to save his life, for help he will not trust.

My son is falling where I cannot reach.
His demons with craziness in their heads
come when summoned. I have let them in.

## Loneliness

It's when it's a dog,
not nipping at your heels
as it always does,
but when walking back
along Princes Street
from a gig where you've talked
to hundreds and left them dancing,
lads and lassies, while you go
for the train and it gets you
by the throat. That's when.

# Stewart Conn

## *Aftermath*

For weeks now she has cried herself to sleep, and her
small brother still wakens screaming. It began the day
they were told the track to the house was to be broadened,
prior to changes in the surrounding land. They wondered why,

the farm perfectly accessible for their vehicles,
at the head of the valley. Next morning they were warned
to prepare themselves. The more speedily they packed
and left the better: could they move in with friends,

take advice on how to sell? Eventually it had to be spelled
out for them: more cattle were to be slaughtered
than could be disposed of: space needed for the carcasses.
Even then they couldn't take it in. No chance to prepare,

they had the children come in from school weeping,
rumours having reached them. Their peace ruined
in the twinkling of eye. The phone went incessantly,
till it was torn off its hook. Next morning they were ringed

by lorries and diggers passing so close the walls shook.
The barn gable crumbled. Fortunately cousins
nearby offered shelter and kindness. Fenced off
from their own farm, they observed its destruction,

earth removers finally obliterating even its remains.
The workmen went. But no cattle came.
There had been a policy change: "no more contiguous
slaughtering". Again, no-one bothered to tell them.

The pastures are still a morass, lined by acres
of glistening black sheeting. And in the children's
minds, wild-eyed beasts and body-parts writhe
in the waterlogged pit where their home had been.


## *In the Radio Class*

While we are discussing the reading of poetry
and lifting the words off the page (the primary
aim) I stress the importance of conveying
to the listener the shape of the piece as written –
the form the poet has chosen to write it in
no accident, but integral to what he or she is saying.

Sound and sense should not compete
with one another, but act in harmony.
Letting the rhyme-scheme, if there is one,
lend variety. Then comes the trickiest bit:
explaining, then demonstrating the split
line, the rhythmic flow hovering, not breaking ...

Here the visiting actress enters the studio,
briskly finds a light and says hello.
She converses easily and when I ask
if she can enlighten us in our task,
confirms (to my delight) what I've been saying,
even pronouncing enjambment *enjambement*.

Warming to her theme, she homes in on
"The Windhover" – a near-perfect instance:
*"I caught this morning morning's minion, king-
dom of daylight's dauphin"* — so daringly broken
mid-word. As I mull the intricacies of "sprung
rhythm", she comes out with an exit-line

which takes my breath away: "The poet,
when I read him it, was pleased I'd got
it right". She turns and says goodbye
and with a little bob, departs. Leaving me
the dubious guardian of her reputation:
Manley Hopkins died in eighteen-eighty-nine.

# Seneca Comes to the Southside

## *Ron Butlin*

Every so often in his later years Seneca the Stoic found himself consider-ing a move to Edinburgh's Southside. Leaky tenements, student parties, double-parking, Scottish neighbours. Surviving the likes of that would surely secure Stoicism's place, once and for all, as *numero uno* among the world's philosophies. The day he and his retinue turned into West New-ington Place could not have been improved upon. Low cloud covered the stonework like sodden mould, horizontal sleet lashed the aged and infirm on their way to chemist's at the corner; Pizza Hut cartons, screwed-up chip wrappings and spilt carry-out rice filled the gaps between dogshit.

Seneca's life of ease as the second richest man in Ancient Rome was now far behind him – ahead lay the challenge of Scotland in the 21st cen-tury. He stepped out of his sedan-chair and, all by himself, shouldered open the door of number seven. His heart rose at the sight of the paint-peeling walls, the strobe-effect stair lighting, the stack of flyers and uncol-lected mail on the lowest step. He beamed:

"Top flat – and, of course, no lift!"

By teatime he had unpacked and was settled in: canopied bed in the front room, feasting-table and couches in the back, Nubian slaves in the box-room. Behind a screen the dancing-girls were getting changed into their silks and tassels. Outdoors, the sleet had turned to a greyish snow that became slush the instant it touched pavement. "Like so much scraped-out porridge," Seneca observed to himself in a first tentative attempt to take the Scottish viewpoint. He shut the curtains. Cosy. A bowlful of the local wine, suitably warmed, and he'd be ready to resume work on his latest Moral Essay. He'd reached Book IX, 'On Tranquillity of Mind'.

Just then his mobile rang.

When he returned the receiver to Nubian Slave V, it was with a gesture "weighted with sorrow", as Horace himself might have put it.

"Even here in this barbarian desolation, Quintus, Destiny marks me with her favour." He shook his noble head. "Though stripped of wealth and all its trappings, I am Chosen. No man can know what Fate …"

Quintus, being one of the trappings, stopped listening. Hundred-to-one a 'Stoicism' speech was coming up and he intended getting himself com-fortable for the long haul. No shuffling, no smiling, no snoring. He clapped his hands for Scribe I to approach, then put himself into standby mode, staring straight ahead, as ready to help his master to dinner as to honourable suicide. He didn't mind which any more.

Once he got into his stride, Seneca could keep the philosophical one-liners coming for scroll after scroll. Tonight, inspired no doubt by the stim-ulating rigour of his new surroundings, he was quick to hit mid-season form and every so often had to pause in his dictation to let Scribe I unroll a further stretch of parchment, re-ink his quill and catch up. As his philoosophic stride lengthened, there came, from behind the screen where the dancing-girls waited, the increasingly frequent rustle of silks and shake of tassels. Then the sneezes started. Seneca ignored them, naturally.

The downstairs bell rang at 8.30. Thanks to Seneca's extended peroration no preparations had been made to receive their honoured guest. Less than a minute remained, the time it would take someone to trudge up the four flights from the street. These sixty seconds Seneca devoted to considering whether the audience he was about to grant should be public – in the presence of Nubian slaves, scribes, cooks and dancing-girls – or *in camera,* with an attendant scribe to video the event for posterity.

The visitor, a man called Murray who'd come all the way from Portobello, was catching his breath halfway up the fourth flight when he heard the sounds of plucked strings and the delicately chimed *ding* that he knew could only be finger cymbals and ankle bells sounding from above. His first thought was "drugs". Not that he cared. Due to the double-parking he'd been forced to leave his car halfway down Causewayside and was soaked through from hatless head to squelchy shoes – he'd be happy to settle for a blast of something himself, if they were offering. Finally, after hauling himself up the last steps, he found he was expected to ring the bell. To ring the bell and wait. This really pissed him off. He'd buzzed them on the security panel downstairs, hadn't he? That was four flights ago. Couldn't they tear themselves away from the central heating even a moment earlier to be at the door to greet him, or at least have it standing open?

Meanwhile, indoors, the dancing-girls had been ordered into the routine that always got an evening with Nero off to a good start: 'Topless on the Tiber' involved a vigorous rowing action that was greatly appreciated by the young emperor. The least they could hope for here was that it might stave off hypothermia. Scribe II was ready to video, the Nubian slaves to prostrate themselves at a given signal. Seneca, modestly toga-ed and sandalled, waited in patrician silence.

Stepping into the hall, Murray gripped his kitchen-design samples case and stared in all directions at once. His "Good-evening-sir-and-is-this-your-lovely-wife …?" remained unsaid as his gaze followed the chorus-line of topless 'Tiber' girls up the hall, into the front room and back down again.

Seneca stepped forward. *"Salve, amice!"*

Murray took an even tighter grip of his sample case, and held on.

"Good evening sir, and is this is your …?" he managed before falling silent once more. Seneca gave a magisterial clap of his hands. The Nubian slaves prostrated themselves on the lino and the dancing-girls rustled themselves into a semicircle of honour on the far side of the feasting-table. Scribe II zoomed in to catch every detail of their visitor's entry.

Murray edged forward into the kitchen, "Have I called at a bad time?" Having been reassured that all moments in a destined world are equally propitious, he began his customary spiel: laying out the photographs, the sample veneers and mouldings, getting the girls to measure the sink, the cooker, count the sockets, make tea. Involve the customer and they'll feel they've already made an investment in the sale, he'd been instructed during that first training weekend. Murray never really expected to succeed as a salesman, and in this he anticipated wisely. A month of follow-up calls and he'd sold one set of mixer-taps – mixer-taps that had proved faulty and been returned. This Seneca guy was make or break time for Murray.

The signs were hopeful. The presence of dancing-girls, Nubian slaves, scribes and cooks suggested a client not stuck for a few bob – a client to be wooed and won. Murray dished out the glossies, the before-and-after pictures, the testimonials from satisfied customers, the coloured charts and statistics on energy-saving. Toga-man was looking a better prospect by the moment. For once, things were shaping up nicely.

While examining the brochures Seneca reflected upon the unexpectedness of such rewards for moral superiority. Deserved or not, these treasures were being given to him, and him alone. As he knew, the fate of lesser men was not his concern – had he himself not written that "it is an unending misery to be worried by the misfortunes of others?" The Stoic, he reminded himself, should accept good fortune with the same calmness that he withstands sorrow.

"Sign here, please." Murray's hand and voice shook as he pushed the contract across the feasting-table.

Scribe II moved closer to capture the historic event. For Murray the moment seemed to last forever with Toga-man leaning forwards in slow-motion, remaining poised over the dotted line. Then he signed. Abruptly, time jerked forward – and began speeding up. Murray swallowed down a whoop of success. Suddenly his life was success-story in the making. From unpromising start to jackpot in one. From zero to Salesman of the Month. To Salesman of the Year. He was dimly aware of the dancing-girls moving into another routine. They were dancing for him. He relaxed, he smiled. As he tore off the customer's copy he remarked that credit facilities were available, but a cheque would be simplest. He made a joke about cash.

"A cheque? Cash? For what?"

"For – for your new kitchen, of course." He laughed, nervously.

"I have been Chosen."

"Yes. And it's true. But you have to *buy* the kitchen first, Mr Seneca – then you go into this month's special draw."

"I have been Chosen."

Outside, the snow was getting worse. Edinburgh's Southside was rapidly disappearing from view. It was the beginning of the heaviest fall in years: thick heavy flakes tumbled from the darkness onto the double-parked streets below, covering the pavements and communal gardens of Newington. By the time Murray emerges, the entire city will have been brought to a standstill with only a few pedestrians tramping and slithering their way among the abandoned buses and cars. Murray will have to walk all the way home to Portobello.

That period of metropolitan calm was yet to come when, sensing all was not well, one by one the dancing-girls shuffled to a stop. They stood in a nervous line and began to shiver – drops of cymbal and ankle-bell melody trickled off into the embarrassed silence. Scribe II ceased videoing.

"I tell you, I have been Chosen."

Murray stared down at the contract and considered the 'ifs' that suddenly made up his life: *If* he on his part didn't mention the cooling-off period, the company lawyers would do their job and squeeze the money out of Toga-man – and his sale would be safe.

*If* he failed this time he failed for good.

*If* he bent the rules this once, he could look forward to the well-deserved certainty of bending them frequently from then on ...

Later, having closed the door on the salesman, Seneca stood at the window enjoying a last cup of tea before bed. Stoicism had earned him a new kitchen. In the short-term, at least. There was a cooling-off period about which the salesman had muttered something under his breath, but the philosopher had good ears. He would sleep on it, while trying not to let the unfairness of all things temporal get to him. He was the leading Stoic of the Ancient World, wasn't he?

Well, wasn't he?

In years to come Seneca was to die by his own hand, falling onto his sword by order of his illustrious pupil Nero. Standing by the window in that Edinburgh Southside kitchen and watching the snow cover the city, he repeated over and over to himself, "I was Chosen, I was Chosen". It was like feeling again and again the sharpness of his sword as he tests his weight on its tip, before running himself through.

---

CANÔNGATE *Classics*

As Chapman celebrates its 100th issue, so the esteemed Canongate Classic series, created in partnership with SAC, will be 100 in July.

With a new introduction from Janice Galloway and additional material from the author, the 100th issue in the series will be Alasdair Gray's *magnum opus* **Lanark** – returning to Canongate after twenty years.

With the best editions of Grassic Gibbon's **A Scots Quair** and Hogg's **Confessions of a Justified Sinner**; omnibuses of James Kennaway, Nan Shepherd, Robert Louis Stevenson and John Buchan, as well as poetry anthologies from The Makars and the earliest of Scottish writers, the Canongate Classics series *is* the Scottish canon.

**www.canongate.net**

# Edwin Morgan

## *John Hunter*

My dear young man, you must learn to be quick.
If I go off at a tangent, you must follow.
My mind is not a standing loch, it churns,
It throws up roots and vestiges of things
In clutter, tangle, lawlessness –
Or is it cluster: triangle, logarithms?
As I was saying before you raised your eyebrows,
I macerated the Irish giant in my boiler –
You know the copper boiler, would boil a whale
The apprentice said, which was not so daft
As not to give me an idea, but anyhow –
The skeleton would grace my medical school
For both art and instruction, lording it a little
Over albino mavises and fossils –
Don't forget, though, I need fossils,
Medicine can learn from the rocks,
It's not all blawflum, there's a story,
Ammonites will do, keep your eye open –
If you think I am a collector, you are right –
And so is my brother William, there's no shame
In a Hunterian Pandora's box: it will go
To Glasgow, to that University
Where William studied theology five years,
Came out sane and did obstetrics, what a man –
Anyhow, I am glad you have kept in touch,
Your dogfish arrived in reasonable condition
(My wife nipped her nose, but she understands),
A large porpoise would go down very well now
If you still have sea friends, and oh yes
What the devil becomes of eels in winter,
I don't want eels, I want information,
If you know any skippers, trawlermen –
What's that? – yes yes, you have things to do,
But just if you can, if you can – the mind
Can be stretched like cahootchy, it's magic
If you want it to be – don't frown man! –
It isn't every day you get someone like me
To unsettle you. – Congratulations, by the by,
I hear you got married, she has money too? –
Well, all the better! – But remember our cuckoos:
I want to know far more than I know:

Shoot an old one, send me its gizzard in spirits.
– It is getting dark. Let's light a lamp.

A good time this twilight, when the bats come out.
If you catch any, let me have some.
I need to count their pulse, their breath.
And do you know I am hedgehogless?
You sent me two for my garden –
One an eagle ate, a ferret the other –
More please! You see how greedy I am!
And now I am into vegetables:
Would you guess that the energy of a vine –
Think of it pulsing away, sap for blood –
Can raise a column of fluid five times higher
Than a horse can do it – green muscles eh?
Is it one world? Of course it is!
Think crystals. Regular? Dead?
But some are irregular as trees.
Deviation is as good as law.
No wonder William dropped divinity!
I see you are not shocked: good man.
Someday I shall be quite famous.
Someday my brother will be famous.
Someday, young Jenner, you will be famous too.
Don't bridle, it is my prophecy. Guaranteed.

Dark now, dark thoughts, battlefield-dark.
I was an army surgeon in the field.
The flares and flashes, smoke and crack and shrick,
Long agonies for some, dismemberment,
Waiting for anything science could do
To stop the pain, the pain – to have been there,
And kept the head, and helped, and stanched and patched,
Brought me where medicine pours into reality
Its desperately hopeful salve.
I specialized in gunshot wounds.
I made some finds. I went my rounds
As you must do, young man, with patience
For enemies and for friends.

# Sheena Blackhall

## The Doo o Peace
### 11th September 2001

As I cam ower the Brig o Dee,
The drum o hate wis beatin.
In ilkie lug aroon the warld,
Americay wis greetin.

As I cam ower the Brig o Dee,
The Sun wis reid's a weal,
As fae the aisse o birsslin brods,
Daith fulled his grisly creel.

As I cam ower the Brig o Dee,
Fae Crocanition's mools
The Bride o Lamentation raise,
Wi skulls insteid o jewels.

As I cam ower the Brig o Dee,
The pulse o War wis strang.
Thon tide o bluid wis like tae feed
On Skaith, wi sodjers thrang.

As I cam ower the Brig o Dee,
The cloods war grey's a kist.
The saft, curmurin doo o peace
Wis nocht bit mizzlin mist

## Druid

Wirds war framed tae strikk a spark,
Tae licht man's thochts alang the dark,
Gods war ferlies fowk cud see:
Sun, and meen and fish and tree.

Roon the cercle o a flame
Early hunters tied a name
Tae the speerits steerin by
Wid an watter, stane an sky.

In the dyew the ocean saw
Heiven in a watergaw.
Shaddas raxx fae evil deen,
Like the drappin o a steen,
Deep inbye a lochan's pot
Ooto sicht, bit nae forgot.

In the mantra o the hairt,
Dreams an desolations stert,
Een an tongue an lug are gates,
Here pass mervels, myths an hates,
Ken them fur the stuff o play,
Masks an mummers fur a day.
*Spittin wild cat, douce blue-bell*
*Fellow-traivellers like yersel*

## Crystal Sea

*Inspired by the John Bellany exhibition, Duff House*

The skipper o the Crystal Sea lost twa crewmen tae smack
A third man's tendin fields o dulse far nane cam birlin back
Black is his boatie, black his weird, his catch is storm an tyauve …
The psalm that thunners in his lug's the skirlin o the myav.

## Skreichin Gull (1)

The myav is skirlin.
His beak's a yalla V
A wedge o raw sea-soun.
The myav is skirlin
King o the fish-gut kingdom
Challengin sea, wave, quey.
The myav is birlin
Sky-boat wi twa fite oars
Paiddlin ben the lift.

## Skreichin Gull (2)

The diva o the dulse
Winnerfu myav
Singin his paean o joy!

## Sentinel

The bairn that sooks at the sea-wife's breist
Drinks in the soor satt bree
Its faither's rowed in the greetin haar
Tae the left o Eternity

Sae bang the tambourine an sing at the gate o sea an san
Far the fishers' God stauns guaird tae coont
The dreepin Saved, like cran.

## Cod Ee'd Kate

*Inspired by the John Bellany exhibition, Duff House*

Cod ee'd Kate. A physog like a skate
A neb as reid as a labster's heid.
Hair like towe on a sanny powe
Cauld as a clam, like a door ye'd slam
On yer wye oot. She's a door auld troot
Wi a grippit moo nae a smile wins through.

Cod ee'd Kate, grim as fish-gut bait
Stauns bi the tide like a partan's bride
Bi the ocean brine, she's a sherp-tongued quine
A physog like a skate on a cheap chippt plate
An she's far frae blate is cod ee'd Kate!

## Highland Village

*This poem is written in the form of a pantoun, a type of poem found in 18th Century Malaysia. The four verses follow a set pattern: 1234 2546 5678 7183*

Tourists ask the way in phrase book speak,
Gaelic words creek peeling on a gate,
A young deaf woman walks the world in silence,
Two sheets hang dead. Loud insects swim the heat.

Gaelic words creek peeling on a gate,
A throaty stream is gargling over stones,
Two sheets hang dead. Loud insects swim the heat,
Bus convoys crawl up roadways built for goats.

A throaty stream is gargling over stones,
In breezy corries bluebells almost tinkle
Bus convoys crawl up roadways built for goats
Foraging ducks quack hungrily for food.

In breezy corries bluebells almost tinkle,
Tourists ask the way in phrase book speak,
Foraging ducks quack hungrily for food,
A young deaf woman walks the world in silence.

## Ticking Clock

*This poem is written in the form of a kyrielle*

The evening paper's by the chair,
Grey rain runs down the window's face,
A single plate drips in the sink,
The clock is ticking in its case.

The turgid sea turns to the land,
The breathless breakers shoreward race,
Sated, it ebbs and spurns the strand,
The clock is ticking in its case.

The moon's wax seal in every pool
Lights candles in the forest's space,
Life's flickering film reels from its spool
The clock is ticking in its case.

The train rocks in its iron groove,
The spider pleats its noose of lace,
Sandpaper handshakes move, remove,
The clock is ticking in its case.

A falcon climbs, a falcon falls,
Bird-claw, mouse-fur, the ancient chase,
Low in the earth the grave-worm calls,
The clock is ticking in its case.

Through stands of wheat, winds sheer and shift.
The scythe-man keeps a steady pace,
Tall grain and straw are slashed apart,
The clock is ticking in its case.

## *Affirmation*

I will spikk in ma first-born leid,
*Foonert ferfochan fey.*
It is safe and kent,
The lowe is ayewis lichtit in the hearth.
*Drookit, dowie, dreich.*
I will spikk in ma first-born leid,
Far short socks hing on the line,
Far the meen an the eirde,
Are roon an fixed an hale.
*Sleekit, slystery, stoory stammygaster.*

I will spikk in ma first-born leid,
*Glaury, glysterie, gomeril,*
Afore the buik cam,
An the buckled skweelbag,
An the pen that aywis blots,
Afore I learned that silence wis ma frien.

## *Keekin Glaiss*

The loch's a keekin glaiss.
The Ben teets ower it
Jigglin frostit tits.

# Haud Me Fast and Fear Me Not

## *Tom Bryan*

If being foolishly in love is a sin, then forgive me Father,
for I have sinned all my life – *Lizzie Fairbairn*

He said it was *love at first sight* but maybe that night he was either blind or blootered or just sitting too far away from the stage at The Stookie Club to see me properly: a woman nearly fifty, twice divorced, lank grey hair, an erosion of craw's feet running down my cheeks, thin legs like cromachs. *Love at first sight?* See *men?* Anyway, I was the support act that night for the Frankie Devlin Band and the first half went the usual way:

Hank McCutcheon, the Glasgow cowpoke, spliff as long as a stogie, spitting into the mike:

"Oh, I was screwed, chewed and tattooed, til my spliff saved my tail,
  Just a hard-tokin cowboy on the Old Jimson Trail."

Hank fades back into the corner in a smoky haze. Next on is Rattlesnake Jessie with her battered Fender guitar. Could be Little Feat, Steely Dan, even Cream. Jessie older than me by half, looks a real casualty of the sixties poured into jeans and a mingin pair of rig boots; Jessie, voice like a chainsaw cutting through corrugated roofing tin:

"They call it Stormy Monday, baby, but Tuesday's just as bad,
  Wednesday's even worse, and Thursday is oh so sad."

Jessie has them rockin and I always hate following her but that honour goes to a new band in town, something 'Wind'. Ay, 'Wolfwind'. Five of them, nervous, twitching-blues harp, African drums, two guitars. Raw, energetic, working hard, getting there, maybe more enthusiasm than ability but definitely getting there. Then an interval for booze, raffle and final sound check for me and my temperamental guitar. *Love at first sight?* OK, maybe for *him* but never for *me*. He was back in the corner, alone, smoking a roll-up, jeans, green t-shirt, black denim jacket, curly auburn hair. Needed a shave. Not a bad-looking bloke but never one to inspire love at first sight. Couldn't tell his age either, maybe older than me but he had a feyness about him, a kind of childlike thing that didn't go with his denim image somehow. I hadn't seen his generosity then, a generosity his friends and family said was legendary but troublesome.

"Feckless, aye been." His gran, Bridget.

"Shite, Tam? Ah'm surprised he's no naked maist o thi time. Saw him gie a wee lassie this embroidered shirt he bought oot in New Mexico. Cost him thirty quid and he only wore it yince." Cousin, Sean.

"Skint, aye skint, glaikit, man. An easy touch." Friend, Shuggie.

"Och, whit can I say? Tam's jist Tam." Co-worker, Maggie.

Generous lover too, it turned out, if a bit slow on the uptake. A few months after first seeing him at the Stookie Club I was dressed in green just for him. (Had heard green was his favourite colour) Green boots, skirt, blouse, bra, slip, tights, knickers. *All* green. Sat in the corner of my living room. Wasn't sure if he would stay or no. I yawned, then yawned again. Said I was off to bed. *See you sometime* I said. He looked to the door. I waited. I sat back on the sofa. He sat down next to me, lifted my hair, and kissed the soft hairs on the back of my neck. He kissed me more that night and we became lovers not long after. I asked him to move in with me as a partner. He is a good and thoughtful man. He still goes out to work with his shoelaces untied, and if this *is* true love then we both hold Tam Lin responsible.

## The Ballad of Tam Lin

My Tam may be a real Tam, but I'm not the fair Janet of the song, just plain Lizzie Fairbairn. I used to sing 'Tam Lin' for the tourists but never really thought about the words. Tam evidently thought about those words a lot, sitting by himself in the corner. So alone in the dark the only beacon was his roll-up tip glowing through the barroom funk.

In a nutshell, fair Janet wants to claim her property back but it is squatted on by young Tam Lin who also happens to be in thrall to the Fairy Mafioso. Tam gets Janet pregnant but promises to make good by her if she'll break the spell, which she does courageously. I assume they live happily ever after with all their bairns at Carterhaugh.

"Naw, naw," said Tam over a spliff one night. "It's about how much love you can give someone who can't return it for some reason and how much you have to shelter them and protect them until they *can* return it. Janet hangs on to him through all his changes, knowing he'll come right in the end. He'd do the same for her if he had to. It's too easy to love someone who doesn't demand anything from you."

And he said that looking somewhere other than into my green-flecked eyes. I sang the song differently from then on.

## But haud me fast, and fear me not:

Believe me, we're not talking here about fair Janet's hairstyle, or gaining or losing weight, or debating about a size ten or twelve! The green-kirtled Janet had to hold Tam as an adder, a bear, a lion, a red het gaud (rod) of airn (iron) and finally, a burning gleed (hot ember) which she douses with well water! She covers him up with her green mantle and he turns into her naked Tam again. A month later that song was a lyric I could have written myself, even though I'm no the fairest o them aa and my Tam is definitely no Elfen knight.

\* \* \*

Tam loved the fishing and in Spring was all over the place for trout. He was coming back one night from the Yarrow when a carload of drunks ploughed into his car, killing the three of them outright and knocking Tam into the river where a police diver managed to cut him out of his car just before it was swept away in the Spring floods. Oddly, nothing was broken and he was out of hospital in a week and soon back at work making guitars, but by god, he was *among us but not of us*. The Fairy Queen may as well have had him because I didn't. He never slept for a start. I was aware of him lying on his back, staring at the ceiling for hours, pretending to sleep if he noticed me looking. He stopped making love and wasn't interested in me (or anyone else). I could feel his body sweat and tense up when I touched him or came near. Then the ballad became my own, with a vengeance, and I hung onto:

## An ask or adder:

All the Scots dictionaries list an ask as a newt or eft, a wee amphibian. I don't know about newts but I respect adders. My gran's collie got bit by an adder one February day in a Sutherland barn. The adder was enjoying a wee spot of warmth in winter when the dog sniffed him and was bitten. The dog's face was swollen like a rugby ball but she eventually recovered. Adders only bite when they're cornered or angry. I'd have welcomed some fight or bite from Tam but he had become more like a wee slithery newt. I didn't know he was even there, just heard the quiet thud of a wee heart just ticking over; oh to have seen him turn and hiss in anger, fear or fight. But now in winter torpor, his blood had become too cold to even move his own tongue or prise open his eyes to the coming Spring.

## Bear sae grim

The last bear was killed in Scotland before Willie Wallace was a callant and oh my Tam, my kind good man, you are anything but a bear sae grim, sleeping there in your armchair, thick hair falling over the eyes, a quiet sleep on you, like a tired bairn. I think the last time I saw you laugh was when you said the blues harmonica player Lazy Lester once protested in his old age that "folks all my life have called me lazy but I'm here to tell you I ain't *lazy*, man, just *tired*, plain *tired!*"

Bear sae grim? This whole thing is bluidy grim. What goes on in that head of yours quiet troubled man? I can't tell you of the tears I weep for you. That's more grim than any fucking mediaeval bear and I will try to hold on to you but I don't know for how much longer …

## A lion bold

Another exaggeration. Lions in Scotland? Maybe a wildcat. Evidently male lions sleep a lot and let the females do all the hunting and killing but take more than their share of the game in order to keep their strength up for sexual pairing. Tam, lion bold, I would hunt for you and kill for you and rip animals wide open for you if you would just enter me again and let me feel the warm African breezes and the slow muddy rivers of you; the cracking desert lightning of you and the sultry monsoons of you – my lion bold stretching, sleeping in the winter sun but this lioness too is old and feels the hot breath of the younger felines, the slender killing ones, and wonders if Spring will bring back the quickening blood and swollen life; wondering if lions die of worry and care like humans do. And we *are*

*llustration by Colin Dunbar*

dying Tam, you and I. I'm so worried my love. I would easily hold the lion in you but there is now something worse, far worse, and something I fear to hold because it has no shape or name.

## A red het gaud of airn

Ay, right, pull the other one. A red hot gaud (bar) of iron? How much symbolism do you need? Those ballad singers were right on, hip to mens' and womens' needs. Lay it on me big Tammas, your red hot poker, your big hot bar, your hunk of burning love … yet you … you snore quietly in the corner. You will rise to breakfast toast and three-minute eggs and will get in your car and go to work and come home to your chair and smile wanly and God knows what dreams and nightmares you had in that car in the river, knowing your life would wash away. You died that day, although you're still here. Whatever guilt or fear traps you, it makes you a soft and pliant plaything of that cruelty. A red het gaud of iron is what I need to spark me, light me, kindle me and do all of those things for you too. Janet held it, stroked it until the very touch of it made her scream out for pleasure or burning pain and the Elf Queen knew she had met her match but the Elf Queen has *you* my poor wee lamb, my poor rodless man, she is going to take you down. You are more then half way there already …

## The burning gleed

The burning ember, a coal so hot she must throw it into the well to cool it down. Ember November remember December ember death of the year, dying member, flickering ember. Hot ember? When? When last? Your accident in trout season, late Spring, the burns and rivers in full spate and it's nearly Christmas and Tam still works, still sits, still talks but little, and still lives in his little space which doesn't include me or anyone else and calls me 'love' and pats me like an invalid and says *no darlin you go out I'll be fine* and I come home frustrated, needing more than a dying ember. I just yearn to be held or comforted or even noticed. Tam goes to counselling and the counsellor told me privately that he thinks some major organic bit of Tam's brain did go missing; "short-circuited" he said – but might come back in time. He advised me to be patient, that perhaps something might spark it off, put it back. I go to The Stookie Club alone now and sing, but it's not the same with him not there in the corner with his beacon light of cigarette, not the same at all and I could no more sing 'Tam Lin' than I could rip out my tongue with a pair of hot pliers.

And I was in mourning, deeply in mourning for the death of my decent man, my generous man who somehow survived, daily, did what was required; who dressed and shaved and ate breakfast and went to work in his car, mentally still drowning in that river. Sometimes he stared at me, his face puzzled, as if trying to remember who I was.

I slept in a different bed in a different room and he never much noticed but I did it not for him but for me so he would not hear me cry myself to sleep and so he would not see my red eyes in the morning. Musicians sing songs about "I woke up this mornin'" but we usually play at night so don't often wake up until early afternoon. Sometimes I was asleep when Tam came home from work and he would bring me a cup of tea in bed. "Tam," I would begin "we must talk about us" but he would look so puzzled and pained that I just didn't know what to say. Then I realised that he would *never* understand, would *never* come around and that unlike Tam Lin, I could hold my Tam and hold him and hold him but he would never change back into himself. Instead, he had become everything that wicked kingdom controlling him could want. I, not he, would suffer most because the kingdom had *him* already. He was held fast and that Fairy Queen bitch would laugh at me until I joined her as well. Well, Lizzie Fairbairn would haud no more.

## Gloomy, gloomy was the night

I had all my things packed. I would wait until Tam came back from his business meeting that night. One thing sure, Tam would not miss me, he who hadn't noticed me for months. I would kiss him once on the cheek then I would go. Walk down the stairs, out the door, into the car and drive into the night. I would stay with my friend Shona until Tam had time to move out, and for that, I would give him as much time as he needed.

The night was frosty and clear. Jupiter and Saturn were flirting with the moon and Orion hung over my neighbour's chimney pot. I stood there a long time trying to remember all the Christmases of my past when I often looked to the skies – each expectant Christmas of a skinny girl who had became this tired thin woman. This woman who had failed in love all her life and had failed again because her arms could hold no more. I pressed my nose to the pane of glass, to Orion's chest and cried and sobbed like a bairn. It seemed like hours.

Then, I heard the car drive up and the front door opening. I heard some noise in the kitchen and Tam going to his room. I straightened, wiping my eyes with my jumper sleeve. I could not think of facing him directly so I kept my vision fixed on Saturn and Jupiter, so bright, so close together, the Star of Wonder, of Bethlehem, just two planets too close and too bright, thus creating only an illusion of one very bright and special star. But I'd had enough illusion. I had heard Tam come in to my room, come towards me. I turned to face my man for the last time.

Tam was standing next to me. He was naked. His face, lit by the stars and brightness from outside, was calm and healed. He held his hands out to me, palms up. He was smiling the way he used to. He took each of my wrists gently in his hands and rubbed them between his finger and thumb. He knelt down, kissing my hands. He was shivering. I covered him with my coat.

# Helen Lamb

## Little Death Spell

Little death, let me go
Where the stone rivers flow

Where silence sings
Where darkness shimmers
When the moment is
A circle

Kill me now, little death
Kiss me, kill me

Kiss me.

## Root

soon after she learned to walk
she toddled out into the garden

she'd only stopped just for
a fraction of a second when
a root sprang from the ground
wound around her broad bare foot

it squeezed

then where she wobbled
pale petals grew
and hid her broken toes
a golden dew wept
from the bloom and rot
perfumed the air

only the fierce pull of the root
could support her now

the root clung fast

## Where Sea Meets Land

she waits where sea meets land
the white gull hones
his razor welcome

waits on a grey bridge
in uncertain light
between the north-
and south-bound platforms

she's too soon by far
born out of the pressing
impatient haar –

while your train is just
three years or so late
as it snails round
the headland ...

## Getting There

*No guarantee I'll get you there.*
*It's at your own risk*
*if you step on this bus.*

The driver giggles.

His engine shudders
and we plough our furrow past
snow-shrouded and abandoned cars.

The driver giggles.

His brakes are shrill.
The screeching brae
skids to the river.

And I am seated on the edge
as we hang above
the hump-backed bridge ...

The driver giggles.

Then his big wheels get
a grip as the white hill
rises up to meet us.

He says – *if we get over this ...*

And when he drops me
on the High Street
I declare he is my hero.

The driver giggles.

## Crow Spell

The crow's foot tracks
Our human past

He smells our future
The slow rot of tomorrow

When skies are heavy
He flies the straight way

Murder in the wind behind
The birth of rain ahead

The savour of the vital worm
Lives in his iron beak.

## Cooking Spell

Go to her now

And let me get on
I have tears to drain

And boil up in this pan
These raw reminders

To scorch and seal
Your last kiss to roast

On the rotating spit
Of desire and deceit

Don't think I intend to
Let it all go to waste

That I can't find some use
For this mess of pain

I am cooking again
Tender slivers of heartmeat

Salty crisp words
To arrange on this plate.

# Herbert Wilson

## Who Enters Dream?

Not knowing who you are
who strays into my dream;

your body seeks no age
with sullen allure of charm
and timid courage awakes.

So why enter dream,
sensual wet lips open,
gives no welcome or reproof?
You melt into the night.

# Richard Burns

## *Four Codas to* The Manager
### (To wish *Chapman* another hundred)

### *I*

We walked around the hill brow, and stumbled upon a temple. Tucked
　　into a rock-fold and perched on its own outcrop on the far side of the
　　valley. Down we stumbled, then climbed narrow steps, and paused,

Muscles aching, panting before its portals. It seemed half-built or a part-
　　abandoned ruin. The sky tumbled in, etching clean-edged shadows.
　　Dwarfed by lion-topped pillars in the broad, half-roofed arena,

Squatted an old man, white-bearded and barefoot, wearing no more than
　　a loincloth. Poised on the patterned floor like a lizard under the sun,
　　statuesque in the late afternoon silence, self-absorbed as a child,

With mallet and chisel he played, and pegs and a line of hemp. And
　　surrounded by piles of stone-chips, painstakingly he sorted the blue
　　and the green and the red, the opaque and semi-transparent,

The rainbow and spotted and speckled, the glossy and the polished, the
　　rough edged and the pitted, the sparkling and iridescent, and the dull,
　　that glowed, concave, as if swallowing light,

And those that held echoes or promises, gleaming or resplendent. And
　　those that held depths, like eyes. Or mirrored skies, like wells. And
　　those textured like parchment. Or tree-bark. Or flesh. Or leaves.

And my companion approached. And I followed and stood behind her, a
　　little off to her right. And she asked the old master, *When will this
　　mosaic be finished?* And he took, from a pouch at his waist,

An alabaster egg. And gestured to her to kneel, next to him, on his right.
　　And closed her two hands over it, and closed his own over hers. And
　　answered a single word, *Never.*

### *II*

A string of fountains down the hillside. Rilled terraces and tended vines of
　　pearly muscatel. Carved in the slope like steps. Built up as layered
　　soilbeds

And protected from weather's ravages by ancient drystone walls. Trimmed
　　neat and bright as children's beds – as if by a friendly giant from a fable.

And below it, on the valley's far side, as I zigzag down, a hamlet whose
　　wines are headier than any grown in my own country. I long to roll
　　their flavours on my tongue.

This is a place where the air itself is sweet. It collects in greater densities,
　　absorbs more freshnesses, even rushes out to greet me, as I approach
　　the fountains.

Here I have come to ask for peace. To plead for it, with myself alone. I
shall stay tonight at the village inn and in the morning go walk the Hill
of the Fountains.

## III

Hello Hello again. My voice is now approximately eighteen inches from
yours. Give or take a bit. To account for your poor sight and hearing.
Although I am ash in an urn

In Hoop Lane Crematorium. And you not knowing or caring even where
Hoop Lane is. Or was. Not that this matters a dot a zero a windpuff or
dustspeck. But I call that somehow nothing

Short of sheer miracle. And you saying all along you didn't believe in
angels. Or talking to the dead. Or ghosts. Are you still really there.
Haven't you rung off. Hello. Hello.

## IV

If you're still there, my angel. If you have not rung off. Brother. Sister. It's
you I'm talking to.

And you, Mr. Beachcomber on the shore of the world against time. The
label on the package

'To Whom It May Concern' means you. It was meant specially for you,
being the one who found it.

This voice, no longer mine, is yours now. Take it. Use it. Give it your own,
far finer sound.

In hearing these words, rewrite yourself. Having no back cover, now the
Book is yours to complete

For who or what might an angel be, other than you. As for me, nil
desperandum. I've a fair way to go

And am still growing strong. Cheerio for now. Sierra Romeo Bravo
Uniform November. Over and out.

# Three Villanelles on Themes
# Prompted by Jacques Derrida

## Gauge and engage the challenge of your courage
### For Lara, Gully, Jelena and Arijana

Gauge and engage the challenge of your courage.
Throw down the glove at darkness and dance light
On paths unworn by guru or by mage.

Grant nothing is for granted. Get your wage
Only from getting right all that you might.

Gauge and engage the challenge of your courage.

All precedents are clamour in a cage,
Priorities, mere prattle, crass and trite,
On paths unworn by guru or by mage.

If you must cast authorities in a rage,
Cast them, yet with some humour and foresight
Gauge and engage the challenge of your courage.

And if you cannot stay as sound or sage
As saints would, only bind your dreams on tight
On paths unworn by guru or by mage.

You run the gauntlet history. The gage
You have accepted chooses you to fight.
Gauge and engage the challenge of your courage
On paths unworn by guru or by mage.

*One must engage oneself in this thinking, commit oneself to it, give it
tokens of faith [gages]. And with one's person, risk entering into the
destructive circle. One must promise and swear ... Know still what giving
wants to say, know how to give, know what you want and want to say
when you give, know what you intend to give, know how the gift annuls
itself, commit yourself [engage-toi] even if commitment is the destruction
of the gift, give economy its chance.*

Jacques Derrida, *Donner Temps*, p 30

## *Good is the Gift That's Given Right Away*

### *for D M*

Good is the gift that's given right away
And glad the heart its absences have donned
To blow forgotten on the passing day.

Donate, the cause is just – people will say.
Yet *contract, measure, cancel* – you've been conned.
Good is the gift that's given right away.

This thing is not a *thing*, to stretch or weigh,
Receive, catch, keep. Fleeing, it will abscond
To blow forgotten on the passing day.

What good can come of goods? What's here to stay?
Who can soar free barred by a double bond?
Good is the gift that's given right away.

Go, flow like wind on water. Throw a ray
Of sun in prison. Sow spores from a frond
To blow forgotten on the passing day.

Such treasures measured out must tear and fray.
Time is our beggar, life our vagabond.
Good is the gift that's given right away
To blow forgotten on the passing day.

*Let us go to the limit: The truth of the gift (its being or its appearing such,
is as such insofar as it guides the intentional signification of the
meaning-to-say) suffices to annul the gift. This proposition obviously
defies common sense. That is why it is caught in the impossible of a very
singular double bind, the bond without bond of a bind and a non-bind.
On the one hand, Mauss reminds us that there is no gift without bond,
without bind, without obligation or ligature; but on the other hand, there
is no gift that does not have to untie itself from obligation, from debt,
contract, exchange, and thus from the bind.*

*Donner Temps*, pp.26-36; cf p.27

## *Mysterious Voices Chattering in the Wires*

### *For John Matthias*

Mysterious voices chattering in the wires
– Or is it trees, or airs, or in the head? –
Torment us with unanswerable desires.

Mendicant *sanyasin*, travelling friars
Lay garbled claims to have interpreted
Mysterious voices chattering in the wires –

Then call these somethings godhead! Cheats and liars!
Their somethings vanish no sooner than said,
Torment us with unanswerable desires,

Press prisons thick upon us, launch vain spires
To trap their ghosts which have already fled,
Mysterious voices chattering in the wires,

Plungers and soarers, veritable choirs
– Mere nuisance noise, or spirits of the dead? –
Torment us with unanswerable desires.

Oh migrant tenants of blue hearted fires,
You stateless borderers, have we been misled?
Mysterious voices chattering in the wires
Torment us with unanswerable desires.

*Language gives one to think but it also steals, spirits away from us,
whispers to us [elle nous souffle], and withdraws the responsibility that it
seems to inaugurate; it carries off the property of our own thoughts even
before we have appropriated them.*

*Donner Temps*, p.80

# Anthony Rudolf – Translations

## *Yves Bonnefoy*

### Children's Theatre

He was taking a walk in the woods when he heard sounds of laughter, exclamations, merriment. What else therefore could he do but stand still, his heart thumping, and listen to the voices of children through the curtain of branches, then venture towards them, towards their world? He pushed aside boughs blocking his path, leaves lightly catching his face, and advanced in the direction of the children. Actæon too had pushed boughs aside, but it was not gentle laughter that summoned the huntsman, rather a pit from which smoke rose up, acrid smoke as if a fire had taken hold in the undergrowth, soon to put an end to the world.

A stage had been constructed in a clearing. Very rudimentary, with stakes, askew, supporting half a dozen planks, and three or four poles of different sizes holding up, between stage and sky, a vast washed-out piece of cloth full of holes. Behind, you could still see the trees, their high trunks huddled together, soon dark. The stage was barely three feet from the ground. The children were climbing on it and tumbling off without difficulty, a little girl had just jumped with her feet together but had stumbled, and almost landed full length on the back of a little boy in a red sweater. Laughter. The boy turns round, he makes as if he is punching her, she gives a yell, she pretends she is crying.

Then she places her foot in the hands he has linked together, braces herself, and is once more on stage. She turns towards the audience, if that is what he is. "I am the queen," she exclaims, "and you are the king!" Indeed they were queen and king, the revelation had taken place, the ordeal was over, night could fall that morning, fire cease to coil down its road of death, in the nether region of dead leaves, and stones.

from *Le Théatre des Enfants*, William Blake and Co, éditeur, Bordeaux, 2001

## *Francis Ponge*

### To Dreaming Matter

Probably everything and everyone (ourselves included) are but dreams, unmediated, of divine Matter: textual products of its prodigious imagination. And thus, in one sense, you could say that the whole of Nature, including mankind, is only a form of writing, but writing of a certain genre, a *non-significant writing,* because it does not refer to any system of meaning, owing to the fact that the universe is infinite, *immense* in the proper sense of the word, without limits.

Whereas the world of spoken words is a *finite* universe. But, owing to the fact that it is composed of these very particular and particularly moving objects:, the *significant sounds* of which we are capable, which serve *simultaneously to* name the objects of the world for us and to

express our intimate feelings,

Doubtless it is enough to *name* anything whatever – in a certain way –in order to *express* everything of man and, at the same time, glorify matter, the model for our speech and the saviour of our spirit.

'A la Rêveuse Matière' (1963) in *Oeuvres Complètes*, Gallimard Pléiade 1999.

## Claude Vigée
### Almond Tree Beneath the Frost

In every achieved poem, what is important is the secret beat concealed there even as it reveals itself. Thus I summon up the image of the almond tree in Jerusalem, flowering in winter, from the end of January. As it fades beneath the snow, one cannot make it out distinctly. It's a snow tree. Disguised beneath a heavy cloak of frost, the presence of a robin can still be divined. It is almost always winter in our difficult lives. At the very depth of winter, if one knows how to listen even for a brief moment, robin redbreast, perched among the white flowers, sings in the invisible almond tree. He sings alone for the great dumb night, which swallows him up beneath the alien sky.

from *Le Passage du Vivant*, Parole et Silence, Paris 2001

*Illustration by Colin Dunbar*

# Anne MacLeod

## *All About Eve*

### Birth of Eve

When Eve was born, the earth moved:
our shell-packed heroine
sprang full-formed from her father's thigh;
grew, tender as the dawn
in the earth-mother's spittle
on a fresh rose-leaf;
rose from ribless Adam, left him
sleeping in garden dust
took up zoology.

There was always a thorn
or a Barbie in the tale. Eve
knew all the stories, believed them;
studied serpents, learned
to speak in double-tongue,
bit (only when cornered,)
gained a reputation
for sensuous homicide.
Hunted, learned to hide
to glide and sashay, slither
like the slut they thought her,
lived inside her own head
in mixed mythologies

I am daughter of the dawn
  I am Eve, the light-bringer
Eve, the spring's earliest bud
  Eve, the owl singer
Eve, the river's source, the flood
  Eve, the ocean's radiance
Eve, the eternal ammonite
  Eve, the rock stack crumbling
Eve, the soured earth's foolish dance
  Eve, the child's praying
Eve, the spider's subtle bite
  Eve, the rose decaying
Eve, the new moon's hesitance
  Eve, the year's wheedling
Eve, the cities' spoiling light
  Eve, the gulls crying
Eve, the feathers of regret
  Eve, the heart's lurching

Eve, the sharp remembered scent
  Eve, the bat's griping
Eve, the rage of innocence,
  Eve, the shore's burning
Eve, the first wavering of blood
  Eve, the eye widening.

I am all of these, and more.
You will not escape me.
You live in *my* words, in *my* light.
Do not under-rate me.
I am life, love …

*Eve*

The world listened, smiled.
There's one born every moment

# *Trilogy*

### i. best-seller

and then
       the order came for war
Eve said *Please don't go*
but he went anyway –
after fucking –
and she sat hunched over a dirty pillow
weeping
      and then
the barracks were suddenly full
of new soldiers so she
dried her eyes
put on a clean dress, and went
out walking, past the new boy-
soldiers on parade
her hair was golden
nearly clean
the sentry saw her
would remember her
the sergeant saw her too
he remembered her
      and then
she smiled at the sentry
his forward stare
his slate blue eyes
as he stood to attention, stared
took him to her bed
another to lose sleep over
another to whisper

*We're for the front*
    and then
  the sergeant
    that sergeant
Eve remembered him
his slate blue eyes
as he stood to attention
    and then

*ii. crow-steps*

It seemed as if Adam had always lain there
slumped on the sofa, snoring; or
watching world-class football
the roaring television crowd
tidemarking house and street and cloud
slapping over cliff-high gable.
Washed-up
on the highest crow-step
Eve knew she might no longer
delay her jump. Moved in air

The merest wrinkle of a breeze
seemed to rise
from nowhere. Eve found herself
sailing *away* from ground, drifting
higher, higher still. Wilting
in bleak atmosphere
the ground too far away for health
the sun too near
she lost her nerve
screaming for help, *Adam! Love!*

A golden goal inhibited
interpretation. *What?*
*Turn it off? Allez les blues!*
*Fuck you!*
Battered controls
were used, to huge effect.
Eve had not brought the mobile

on her suicide attempt.
he'd not have heard it, pithily
rapt in post-match commentary

Eve wafted endless
opening skies:
Adam waited for
that crate of beer
he'd sent her for

*iii. through the looking glass*

through the looking glass
she saw a world as unlike hers
as sea to land

> *sure as winter cloud*
> *lacing a sky bluer than green*

reliable as one breath
in a lifetime of spilled air

tall lavender, crushed
by a young nun's fingers
on an English path;

a tide of castles, deeply-dug in sand
crusted with broken shells;

a striving for clear movement
perfect grace;

a longing for frills
for greater height
for richer tones
ability with word
with line...

an endless striving, unachieved
unsatisfied, not
what she had
hoped

the mirror did not paint
any of that
            hung
blind and mute
Eve knew
the signs

passive resistance

broke it

## *warm-down*

Each time the yoga teacher talked them through the warm-down
Eve considered in her bones the possibility and truth of it

*Relax. Feel your skin slipping, falling from your forehead*
*falling away ... you're opening, skin on your body, on your chest*
*is slipping, slipping sideways ... ribs are falling open*
*falling away, melting into earth*

Eve imagined opening like buttercups in sun

or like a long-dead seal her dog had rolled in on the beach;
stench unbearable, car and dog defiled
beyond the scourge of soap and water
the day she found the body

She had always wondered about death:
would you feel it?
Would you face the anguish of chemical decay
peach-like bruising, still flesh
putrefying in fire, the cold slow flames of chemical
restructuring, without hormonal steerage
without the body's fluence?
And was it necessary?
If flesh did not decay
remained inviolate, like Bernadette's, like all those other
desiccated saints, was life, was death, then incomplete
a dance of molecules impaled, obstructed?

*your ribs are falling open, skin slipping, rolling down*

Sometimes she lay at night, afraid to sleep; sometimes
she woke too early, stretched her hand towards her mouth
to verify her silent expiration; or
held a mirror closely to her lips, her nose, measuring
its more objective clouding.
Other nights she screamed
focussed on the echoes dying, subsequently timing
preset recordings

*ribs falling, slipping, sliding*

She had never dreamed death would feel so cold, the skin
chill so quickly, so completely; summer's white nights
seemed divorced from death, though the veil
wore thin in sleepless dawn
            As if she might slip under and away, as if
clear morning mist might harvest her and fade
Eve took to walking in a neighbouring wood where blackbird
thrush and cuckoo reigned in fettled song

The joy of those bright mornings! Eve slid from pine to spruce
spring-fresh, bursting life; green larch seduced her, softer
more open than the sheets she'd thrown off, waking:
quiet violets mourned uneven moss. The body tripped her
twisting at an awkward angle, half across the path
face-down

            this pose was not repose, not child pose
not the pose of death, but some
half-remembered stiffening

skin so cold, blood-pooled, livid

Eve shuddered at the coat, blue like her own, marinading;
the hair mud-thickened, the extending trail of ants
She stooped as if to soothe an outstretched hand, drew back
spreading chill defeating her in distance

                                                she fled
the wood, the bright hill, sobbed in bed, her white sheet
tight around her withering

                                        dreamed
of a decomposing swan beached beyond the lighthouse
stubborn feathers tougher than the heart

*ribs slipping, falling*

*illustration by Johanna Gordon*

# Alasdair Gray

*Self Portrait,* Alasdair Gray

Alasdair Gray by Gerry Mangan

## Inge, May 2000

She seems to like me, now there's no denying,
whose contempt used to give me dreadful pain.
Will death undo the burden of her dying?

Nine married years ended in rage and lying;
thirty tears later we're in bed again.
She seems to like me now, there's no denying,

yet rules once more by reckless defying
the courses I consider the most sane.
Will death undo the burden of her dying?

She never thought it false to be relying
on people she regarded with disdain
but seems to like me now, there's no denying.

Defiant reckless is purifying?
Her desperation is a deadly strain.
Will death undo the burden of her dying?

Is it my strength or weakness that's supplying
the company she needs to ease her pain?
She seems to like me now, there's no denying.
Will death undo the burden of her dying?

## Morag, April 2002

"Be up. Be out. Be off," I to me cry
so softly there seems no need to reply.
Warm smoothness is a property of you:
enjoying it undoes the need to do.
Warm smoothness is a property of we
I lie enjoying, almost content to be.

# The *Chapman* **Office**

*Joy Hendry, Editor*

*Ann-Sophie Klemp,*
*Volunteer/ Administrator*

*Ian Montgomery,*
Chapman *Factotum*

*Edmund O'Connor,*
*Assistant Editor*

*Rosemary Whelan,*
*Volunteer/ Administrator*

All drawings by Alasdair Gray

# In the Beginning

## George Hardie

Thinking back to 1970 I find it difficult to recall how *The Chapman,* as it was then, came about. Certainly the reasons given in our first editorial were probably a fairly accurate description of the situation as we saw it at the time. There was a dearth of outlets for the publication of the work of new poets particularly, from my own point of view, for those who were interested in writing in Scots. Also running through our thoughts was the understanding that, in Scottish literary circles, there was a pervading 'political' element. One essential ingredient seemed to be that you should drink in certain pubs in Rose Street, Edinburgh and, as we drank in The Silver Tassie in Almada Street, Hamilton, Lanarkshire, we were definitely on the outside looking in.

There was, of course, the added bonus that we would be able to publish our own work as we chose. I suppose there always is a little bit of an ego trip involved in these situations. So, I suppose, it was to our credit that we resisted the temptation in our first issue. Our contributors in that September issue were, in order of appearance Alastair R. Thompson, Duncan Glen, Giles Gordon, Donald Campbell, Menzies McKillop, David Morrison and Robin Fulton. We also had a page of short reviews. These pieces of incisive criticism appeared above the names of Patrick MacCrimmon and John Clydesdale, and here the modesty has to stop, those being the alter egos of the joint editors. Just why Walter chose 'MacCrimmon' I cannot recall. In my own case it was a name that was immediately identifiable with Lanarkshire – again the East/ West divide. As to why I chose to use a pseudonym at all I think there was an element of cowardice stemming from a lack of confidence in my own judgement. Not the best recommendation for a would-be magazine editor – but there it is.

As was to be expected the appearance of our first issue was not greeted by a fanfare of trumpets by the literary world. In fact it was pretty much ignored. As were the remaining four issues with which I was associated. The only comment I can recall appeared in *Catalyst* where the writer regretted the fact the none of the contents were as dramatic as the tree which dominated our original cover. This I took as something of a compliment as it was a print of a watercolour sketch which I had done some years previously. Unfortunately the original has long since disappeared.

That the magazine should reach one hundred issues or that it should reach its present stature were dreams beyond my wildest imaginings. The fact that these have been achieved is due entirely to the hard work of others and I congratulate them wholeheartedly. My own personal satisfaction comes from the knowledge that I sowed some of the seeds.

# Paying the Piper, Listening to the Tune
## Some Notes towards a Memoir
### Trevor Royle

Almost a quarter of a century has passed since I left the employment of the Scottish Arts Council; I still meet younger writers who know nothing of my incarnation as its first Literature Director and why should they? When I was in my mid-twenties in the early 1970s it would have been as if I had been asked to look back to the end of the Second World War, a lifetime ago. In the time since my departure much has changed. Fixed stars (for so they seemed) in the literary firmament have done the disappearing trick: Hugh MacDiarmid (Neal Ascherson got it right when he compared him to some strange satellite which could only be tracked), Norman MacCaig, Sydney Goodsir Smith, the two Scotts (Tom and Alex), Robert Garioch, Sorley MacLean, Iain Crichton Smith, George Mackay Brown, Naomi Mitchison, Eric Linklater, J K Annand, Alan Bold, a sad litany.

In that time too Scotland itself has changed, the lost dreams of 1978 being revived with the return of the Scottish Parliament and the Scottish Arts Council has been transformed into a sizeable employer with its own independence and its budget increased with added loot from the lottery tax. No longer a medium-sized organisation run by amateurs it is the province of the professional arts administrator and seems big and amorphous. Even its chairman gets paid a salary. It would be easy to criticise the changes – which patron has not attracted scorn and disgust in equal measure, even from those it patronises? – but just as serving soldiers dislike armchair generals who emerge to complain about things being done differently in their day, my own peace has been held as far as SAC is concerned.

And yet we would not be human if we did not want to revisit the past and compare it with today. One mild example will suffice. After Alan Bold's death in 1999 I found myself looking after his literary affairs, amongst which is his unfinished biography of Robert Burns, much of it still in note form but still eminently finishable. It would make a great project for a young postgraduate with literary ambitions but, of course he or she would have to be paid. Perhaps SAC could help? An official from the Literature Department was sympathetic but firm: no funds or policy existed for such an enterprise and therefore there could be no application.

That seemed to say a lot. Writing is not such an organised business that it can be compartmentalised by rules and regulations. Why could they not be broken and an exception found? I could have said, well, in my day we decided to make special awards to the publisher Callum Macdonald, to Duncan Glen, editor of *Akros* and the poet Sorley MacLean as well as to J K Annand and Robin Jenkins to recognise their contribution to Scottish literature. There was no separate fund and no precedent but at the time it seemed the right thing to do and so we did just that.

Except, of course, I said no such thing and Bold's book is unlikely ever to be completed. Curiously, he was one of the first people I met in my role at the Scottish Arts Council, over a beer or three in Milne's Bar.

*1971*
On 1 February I joined the Scottish Arts Council, then in its modest head-quarters in Rothesay Terrace, Edinburgh. Two days later I took my first committee meeting. Never having done such a thing before, far less compose an agenda or minutes, it was a nerve-racking business but it was made easy for me by a small and sympathetic committee – Professor Tommy Dunn of Stirling University, wise-cracking Cliff Hanley and Neil Paterson, a prince among chairmen. Having made his money in Holly-wood, winning an Oscar for the screenplay of Room at the Top, and having secured his literary reputation with novels such as The China Run, he had no bones to grind and was completely without side – a rare achievement in literary circles. Later, in 1977, he was replaced by another disinterested and equally enthusiastic chairman in A N 'Derry' Jeffares, the Yeats expert and a writer with astonishing international connections. From the outset the philosophy was surprisingly clear and it underpinned every decision: if the writing is good reward it, if it is promising encourage it.

That year the budget was a modest £23,000; the main recipient being the magazine *Scottish International Review*, founded three years earlier and edited by the gifted poet and critic Bob Tait; eight years later the budget shot up to £340,000 but SIR foundered in 1973-1974 (that saga is a sorry story in itself and awaits telling) but each year had its own flavour, its high points and its low points.

*1972*
Minutes of Literature Committee Meeting, 6 March 1972: "It was agreed to recommend a grant of £100 towards the establishment and operating costs of *The Chapman*. The Convenor asked that it be made clear to the editor that this was an establishment grant and not the start of an annual grant."

*Chapman* got its first grant at the tail-end of that first financial year and Neil Paterson's remarks notwithstanding it became the recipient of an annual operating grant for three issues per year. I met Walter Perrie and Joy Hendry in early summer 1971 and was immediately impressed with their ambitious plans for the magazine and for their own writing. Joy was and is an enthusiastic promoter of *Chapman* and literary magazines in general and was to be a leading light in the later creation of a co-operative sales and distribution scheme. Walter Perrie was and is an exceptionally fine poet and became a close friend. His high spirits and optimism added to the fun.

But all the magazines were bedevilled by high production costs and low sales, and expenditure on them was not popular with other SAC commit-tees. *Scottish International* was constantly in hot water: when it became a monthly publication and increased its political coverage not a few coun-cillors were unamused and wanted to have its grant stopped. At one stage I received a dressing down after Bob Tait published a piece by the novelist Archie Hind on the Upper Clyde sit-in. Eventually that conflict of interests was to seal the magazine's fate: economics might have been the reason for its demise but it was also scuppered by a widespread dislike of subsidising what was seen to be political writing. Some critics also complained about the presence on the board of Father Anthony Ross, the Edinburgh University Catholic chaplain being regarded as a baleful influence. (The anti-Catholic sentiments came as a surprise and not a pleasant one.)

One of the biggest critics of the magazine was the poet Tom Scott who wrote to the Tory arts minister Lord Eccles to complain "without prejudice" about my stewardship of public funds in Scotland. He ended his letter by saying that when the last trump sounded he would be found like Horatius (with, as I remember, Hamish Henderson), repelling the barbarians at the bridge. That same year Tom was awarded a bursary of £1000 along with Robin Fulton, Alastair Mair and Sydney Goodsir Smith. It had nothing to do with his letter but everything to do with his abilities. Hamish Henderson also fell out with me over an SAC decision not to fund Helen Cruickshanks's' autobiography and challenged me to fight after a meeting of the Heretics in the New Town Hotel. (The incident is recalled by John Herdman in his elegant literary memoir, Poets, Pubs and Pillar Boxes.) Next year I had to struggle to convince the committee to fund the reprint of Hamish's *Elegies for the Dead in Cyrenaica*. As the SAC director Sandy Dunbar (a great man) always told his officials: we had to put service and responsibility above personal feelings – no easy task in Scottish literary circles.

### 1973

Extract from SAC's first report on Bursaries to Writers: "Since 1966, the Scottish Arts Council has spent a total of £22,375 on direct grants to thirty-six writers by way of bursaries. The amounts have ranged from £100 to £1000. In the same period (prior to 1971) the Scottish Arts Council spent £93,000 on literature activities through the Drama Department which means that an average of 23% has been spent on direct aid to writers. This excludes monies spent on prizes, publication awards, fellowships and readings which are the other main channels through which the Council gives money direct to writers."

The award of bursaries always raised temperatures and led to angry exchanges. It was never easy rejecting applications which were based on evidence of work in progress and financial need but fortunately the adjudicating committee was always well served by its members, a roll-call which included, amongst others, Stewart Conn, William McIlvanney and James Allan Ford. It was no better in Wales. Meic Stephens, my opposite number at the Welsh Arts Council became a firm friend and I remember being with him in Cardiff after their bursaries had been announced. In a bar that evening Meic came under fire and stomped out angrily. Being his guest I had no option but to follow, as did a member of the literature committee, the poet Harri Webb who called on Meic to come back. "If you're not for me, Harri," came the reply, "then you're against me."

It could have been The Abbotsford bar in Edinburgh's Rose Street, still a poets' pub in that it was frequented by MacCaig, Bold and others. On a Friday evening it could be quite entertaining. Alan Bold-by-name-and-bold-by-nature was never behind-hand in challenging literary enemies to fight – Alex Scott being a particular bête-noire.

### 1974

Grants to magazines: *Akros* £1995, *Chapman* £1400, *Gairm* £1750, *Lines review* £1750, *New Edinburgh Review* £1600, *Scotia Review* £750, *Tocher* £400. An additional £4000 awarded to the Scottish Association of Magazine Publishers (SCAMP) to enable them to employ a joint sale representative.

Extract from SAC annual report: "Magazine publishers are already befitting from increased sales. It is now possible to see these magazines on sale and selling in most of the larger Scottish bookshops."

No comment is necessary other than to ask why there is no similar organisation in 2002. Even its successor, ALMS, has been the victim of SAC cuts.

### 1975

Extract from SAC annual report: "One of the Council's major initiatives during the year was to set up a special enquiry into publishing and bookselling in Scotland. With members representing various national interests in publishing, bookselling, libraries and education, the working party's terms of reference are: To advise the Scottish Arts Council on its future polices for literature activities, and in particular:

1. To examine ways in which SAC in conjunction with other interested parties can most effectively assist in the development of writers and writing in Scotland and improve its service to writers, publishers, booksellers, libraries and schools throughout Scotland.

2. How best the Council can encourage booksellers, libraries and education authorities to encourage and support literature in Scotland.

Already several trends in the research are discernible:

a. Commitment to give literature a more prominent place in Scottish life.

b. Increased support for publishing in Scotland.

c. increased availability of books; and more promotion of writers and their work."

Due to a variety of factors, not least the nervous breakdown of the researcher, the report was never published and was quietly shelved. It did not help that there was friction between the working party's chairman Ronald Johnstone and Neil Paterson – both successful novelists. It was a lost opportunity. With funds increasing annually and a commitment to the principles mentioned above, the report could have forced SAC to make a bigger contribution to literature in Scotland.

### 1976

Writers bursaries awarded to; Alistair Mackie £3000, John Herdman £2500, John MacPhail Law £2500, Walter Perrie £2500, Jeremy Bruce-Watt £2500, Peter Chaloner £1500, Patrick McVeigh £1500, Christine Meek £1500, Alistair Campsie £1500. These were the first substantial bursaries – £3000 was about 75% of an arts administrator's salary and represented a break-through in SAC thinking. Whereas a bursary had been seen earlier almost as a reward or a prize the larger amounts meant that writers could plan work over six months to a year. Together with writers' fellowships – first at universities and then in libraries – they offered, for the first time, the promise of some financial security.

### 1977

Grants to magazines: *Akros* £4350, *Chapman* £2400, *Gairm* £5100, *Lines Review* £2400, *New Edinburgh Review* £1500, *Scottish Review* £4000, *Tocher* £1200, *Lallans* £350, *Scottish Literary Journal* £1000, *Leopard* £2850, *Words* £500 Total literature funds – £208,000

Minutes of Literature Committee Meeting 24 June 1977: "It was generally agreed that although there were severe financial problems facing most of the magazines, SAC had a responsibility to asses their literary merits and form a judgement on a qualitative basis. Doubts were expressed about two of the magazines, *Chapman* and *Scotia Review*, and it was agreed to rec-ommend that grants to both of these should be discontinued in 1978-79."

This is where memory can play false or be highly selective. For reasons which remain unclear the stooshie over *Chapman* and David Morrison's *Scotia Review* has been blotted out and would have been forgotten but for the contemporary evidence. Several committee members deeply disliked both magazines. Not surprisingly the announcement kicked up a storm of protest, notably in the letters page of *The Scotsman*.

### 1978

Extract from Policy Discussion Weekend - Discussion Paper: "Devolution looms: what will be the special needs of Scotland in the 1980s? Scotland's culture is primarily a literary one: should we stress that fact to the political parties and make them privy to the problems and our suggested solutions? Naturally the Council would want to do this as a whole, but should we not ensure that the 'literature' discussion is not omitted? Too many people think that the book world is safe because John Menzies have several thou-sand paperbacks on display not only in the Glasgow and Edinburgh super-stores but also every retail outlet in Scotland from Langholm to Wick."

No comment required.

### 1979

The questions raised during that weekend remained unanswered, other than that Menzies was replaced by Waterstones in the following decade but by then I had come to regard the task as Sisyphean, it was time to hand over to someone else – a former committee member Walter Cairns became the second Literature Director and a skilful and much liked one at that. Leaving SAC was surprisingly easy, on a warm early summer day in May; it was like throwing away crutches at Lourdes. But two good things were done: individual major bursaries were increased to £3500 and on 15 March 1979 *Chapman* was reprieved with a grant of £2100 for three issues.

# Reflections from the Upper-Palaeolithic

## *Walter Perrie*

If it is the defining characteristic of the past that it cannot change, never-theless, our perception of it, chameleon-like, always takes on the colours of our present concerns. It is thirty-two years since, with George Hardie, we issued, from Hamilton, the first number of *The Chapman* in September 1970, though our preparations had begun that Spring. Certainly, since 1968 we had been attending monthly meetings, at the Carlton Hotel in Edin-burgh, of a discussion group of about a dozen, mainly young, Scottish writ-ers, going under the banner of *Schiltron*, and including in its membership Stephen Mulrine, Liz Lochhead, Eric Gold and Alastair Mackie.

It was another world; one in which MacDiarmid was a local presence. His reputation, thanks in no small measure to the labours of Duncan Glen, had come into public view again after a period of obscurity during which, disgracefully, the only available edition of his poems was an American one. Sorley MacLean had not yet been accorded the recognition which was soon to be his. Neil Gunn was still writing. The more-or-less estab-lished included Sydney Goodsir Smith, Robert Garioch and Norman Mac-Caig. Edwin Morgan was still a 'young' writer. *Akros* was in its heyday, *Lines Review* was going strong and *Scottish International* was the new boy. Trevor Royle was about to become literature director of the SAC and in the process transform literary funding in Scotland.

Politically, Scotland was undergoing a sea-change. The last of the def-erential North British era was fading away with Macmillan and Douglas-Home and the sixties saw a recrudescence of that sentiment which from the foundation of the National Party in the late twenties, through the National Covenant of the early fifties, had made Scotland's identity a live issue again and culminated, momentarily, in Mrs Ewing's sensational Ham-ilton bye-election victory of 1967, where, three years later, *The Chapman* was founded. George Hardie was, in fact, a left-wing burgh councillor for the SNP. So some element of political awareness must have lain behind the founding of *The Chapman*. In that same month, however, September 1970, I quit Hamilton for Edinburgh to read Philosophy at the University.

The attraction of magazine publishing for me – inasmuch as I ever felt it, for I was at best a reluctant convert – lay in its simplicity. It provided, in the eyes of naïve youth, an apparently easy means of doing *something* literary, perhaps of being someone. That it was also quite removed from that necessarily isolating confrontation with the forever more exacting demands of poetry could not then have been a conscious consideration.

Such projects, if allowed to, acquire their own momentum, develop an appetite for our lives, a taste for our time and passion. For some, such self-consuming may have all the dazzle and glitter, the adventure and energy of a youthful self-making. For others, who are perhaps less lucky or less knowing, it may be a burgeoning and malignant mis-direction. Fortunate those then, who, Proust-like, aided by labour and luck, should discover or invent out of such misdirection a *temps retrouvé*.

My immediate background – a very middle-class and academic Hamilton Academy and a very working-class mining village with strong communal and radical traditions – was sufficiently confused as to make any initiatives on my part likely to pull in several simultaneous directions. My only fixed star was that I wanted to write poetry. And whatever measure of fantasy, romanticism or confusion may have been embedded in that fixity does nothing to lessen its reality. The backward glance to a time of such energetic naïveté reveals a countryside of lowering precipice, mist and clotted woodland, a neo-Gothic landscape, imaged perhaps by Caspar Friedrich, but cosy too in the communal self-assurance of its incivilities and appetites. Enthusiasm for such projects is a gift – or affliction – of the young and the young rarely operate alone.

Left to my own devices I should probably not have spent a decade editing magazines; first *Chapman* – which title it acquired in May of 1972 – or, later, *Margin*. I had no appetite for such practical difficulties as distribution and funding. My interest was selfishly confined to content and presentation. I have always so abhorred the notion of selling anything, and especially poetry, as to be incapable of so doing. Others, therefore, and, in particular, Joy, were saddled with that, to me, odious task. In the case of *Margin* it could be delegated to distribution companies.

After thirty two years, what would it mean to remember a day; a twenty-four hours, all those 1,440 minutes? The very numbers make the absurdity at once apparent – a Joycean nightmare. Remembering; a calling up, a present activity, willed or not, of images, ideas, complexes of feeling which we identify as referring to past experiences, as though these 'same' experiences were somehow evoked, which is absurd, since their sole claim upon existence is precisely their being remembered. So what does happen when we remember? What are called up are not 'the same' images, ideas, feelings, but are similar in the way that two occurrences of a word are 'the same' i.e., because of structural similarities we agree *to count them as* the same. Our whole interest lies in identifying them as the same, not in highlighting differences. They are paths retrodden, and sufficiently often to become more accessible than other bramble and nettle- infested ways. Above all, the names we give those patterns [memories of this or that] stay he same. What I remember of thirty-two years ago does not transform what happened. But it does transform my interpretation of it, my feelings about it. Memories above all, even if they are neurological themes, are also how we go on – *they are the shapes of my present understanding*.

It now seems beyond serious doubt that perception itself is penetrated by feeling and therefore by value. We do not perceive 'objective' patches or bundles of sensoria uninflected by feeling, for part of the perceiving process includes a continuous self-monitoring of internal physiological states – those states which we interpret and label, eventually, as feelings. As should perhaps be obvious enough, it is the whole organism and not

the brain which perceives and so any act of perception includes compo-
nents of self-assessment of the *internal* landscape from which the notion
of an *external* landscape cannot be separated. This is what I mean when
I suggest that perception is value-laden. Memory, then: a re-activation of
complex neurological structures: the landscapes of metabolism are impli-
cated in all perception. The links between such patterns of perception and
the linguistic categories with which we habitually associate them has
hardly begun to be explored – except of course by poets.

The point of this 'digression' is that what one remembers is not separable
from how one felt about it, at the time or subsequently. What I remember,
not just of *Chapman*, but of my whole attitude through my teens and early
twenties, is a low-level resentment at having to wade through anything
which did not interest me: like a spoilt child unable to continue to the end
with any dull or disagreeable task. Fields, hills and woods, indeed, any
conceivable adventure were more urgent than textbooks. They still are. So
unless I somehow 'cracked the code' of arousing my own interest in some
topic or project, I simply declined to do anything about it – and what I
absolutely had to do was grudged and reluctant. Much of my time was
squandered on avoidance when I might have been learning – but that
'might have been' is Minerva's fantasy of retrospective omniscience.

I am reminded of Lionel Trilling's fine essay, 'Sincerity and Authenticity':
in it he points out that bumbling, garrulous old Polonius – who is, after
all, rashly murdered by the unreasoning Prince – is not wholly a fool. In
his famous and admirable advice to Laertes he ends with:

> – "This above all: to thine own self be true,
> And it must follow, as the night the day,
> Thou canst not then be false to any man."

But to which Self?: the lazy, whimsical one or the ambitious, energetic
one? Unlike formal logic, they can be mutually exclusive and yet simultaneously present. Or is the temporally present Self the only one to which
we can intelligibly be true? But he-it is, above all, a remembering Self.

Which brings me to what might seem a surprising element in my backward glance at my involvement with *Chapman*; and that is the degree to
which it embedded concerns which have proved abiding across several
decades. It is often observed that the best way to inform yourself of a topic
is to write a book about it – or edit a magazine. My interest in literature
has always been internationalist and European as much as Scottish – and
that interest was reflected in issues of *Chapman* devoted to east European
poetry, to Dutch and Flemish writing to Chinese arts and to R M Rilke. That
internationalism arose not just from having fallen so early under the spell
of MacDiarmid, but from the fact that his influence only strengthened one
already deeply felt as a result of my time at Hamilton Academy and, in particular, under the tutelage of A W S Dubber. It was certainly in part that
very Scottish impulse to self-education which led to *Chapman* and to Edinburgh but which later led also to membership of the CPGB and to involvement in *Margin*, which was as much a North American as a British journal.

I ceased actively to edit *Chapman* in 1975, although my name continued to appear on it until 1976. It seemed to me by that time to have less and less to do with what truly concerned me and it is no coincidence that 1975 was also the year in which I began work on the first book of poetry which I can regard as anything other than juvenilia – *A Lamentation for the Children* – the writing of which was also a step towards an explicit politics. Of that summer of *Lamentation* I could perhaps reconstruct much but what I actually remember, freed from the exigent pains of cramming for philosophy finals, are a handful of sunlit afternoons of Lowenbrau and dictionaries and other curtain-drawn days of mad, bedridden, black depression. Or so I see it now; all highlight and shadow.

I do not doubt that *Chapman* over the past thirty years has provided a point of entry for many aspiring writers. Such outlets are a pre-requisite of any healthy literature. It is perhaps inevitable that publishing now – and I am thinking above all of poetry publishing in Scotland, if that is not already an oxymoron – should increasingly have fallen victim to commerce, to the academy and, disastrously, to fashion.

One can only deplore the lack of any independent intelligence in literary publishing in Scotland now. Three and four decades ago it was still represented by Callum Macdonald, Duncan Glen and, in his day, Willie Maclellan.

I was recently sent a copy of *South-West Review*. Perfect bound on good quality paper and beautifully if conventionally designed, it runs to 458 pages of text, costs $12 and is published quarterly. It is not unrepresentative. There is nothing like it in the UK, far less in Scotland.

The lack of large-scale funding which restricts Scotland's literary magazines cannot, however, be wholly deplored, for prolonged and extensive state sponsorship can lead to laziness, cliquery and worse. However, Scotland, to state an obvious fact of geopolitcs, lies somewhere between eastern Europe and the US. It is better if magazines have only a limited element of public sponsorship for production and distribution costs – perhaps up to 25%. But, with complete editorial discretion, the burden of paying contributors at a standard and reasonable rate could easily be borne by public funds. At present the magazines pay little or nothing, which is no less disgraceful for being understandable. At least that way money would get to the primary producers.

For myself, what has endured from those early forays into literature is perhaps no more than a structure; the spine of a ridge, unbroached summits. The early morning haar and over-lush undergrowth, with its confusion of feeling and strangeness, sense, ambition and desire, has given way to a necessarily harsher light. What has endured, above all, however, is something I gained from my early mentors and which *Chapman* in its way sought to represent; a sense of the objective worth of literature both to the individual who produces it and to the society which receives it and, most especially, in its highest, most-demanding form – poetry. Of course, such objectivity is purely human but the Kantian dilemma of Things Without Us no longer troubles my dreams.

# A Little Century Firework

*or, Decline and Fall into Birdwatching*

## Robert R Calder

One could wish that Aristotle had read a few novels (W P Ker). A text:
> If history has taught us nothing else, it's that we constantly need resistance
> and vigilance. So, where are we going wrong? Well, let me count the ways.
> We have allowed the literary and critical establishment to classify fiction,
> ever more strongly, as autobiography: not pure, but very simple. Feel free
> to assume that this is a personal bugbear, that when I'm asked for the eight
> hundredth time "Well, yes, I know it's fiction, but who are the real people
> it's based on, the real events – which part of reality did it you steal it from?"
> I want, at the very least to scream… what is far more important is the
> essential denial of imagination in this approach to fiction –
>
> If fiction is reprocessed fact and nothing more, then imagination is unnec-
> essary, the contract with the reader is that they should accept the cast-offs
> from another life which is closed to them – fiction becomes a puzzle which
> is only truly opened by intermediaries – the critic and the academic. No inti-
> macy, no mind-to-mind collaboration, no uninterrupted communication,
> no faith, no dreams. This is a theft we accept on an almost daily basis –
> please, when you're protesting against false imprisonment, torture, murder,
> the more urgent, larger crimes – protest against this smaller one too,
> because it prepares us (however unwittingly) for all the dehumanising steps
> that lead us to those urgent, larger crimes.

A L Kennedy, PEN Lecture, Edinburgh Book Festival 2001.
Ms Kennedy's reference to those 'urgent, larger crimes' isn't excessive,
witness the full text of her lecture, easily available online. Think through
the implications of dehumanisation as a working principle.

Kennedy is talking about what I call the *ornithologising* approach to
poetry, whose application to the writing of fiction has troubled more than
the one Scottish writer. Ask anybody who knew Jessie Kesson. Intensive
use of material close to her own biography rendered her a sitting and
unprotected *rara avis* (hardly *duck!*) for too many who liked that narrow
kind of view from within a thick hide. It's all a matter of treating literary
works alike with the cries, calls or song of birds. Nothing to do with the
affectionate phrase 'a nest of singing birds' for a few mutually connected
lyric poets, this is a patronising dehumanising refusal of important considerations relative to the what and why of all manner of literary activity.

A corncrake, a thrush, a budgie, each has its range of possible vocal
sounds, produced in respective response to, for a few instances, the prox-
imity of a cat, a potential mate, birdseed, fish. Perhaps someday there will
be a *Scribes of Scotland* handbook with references to the plumage and
habitat, dimensions, genus (lyric poet, short story writer, etc.) and if not
exactly 'breeding habits' a category which would overlap with that, for
every Scottish author the compiler has cared to include?

Novelists of course produce texts, in words and phrases and stories and
characterisations. I am suggesting something like ornithologisers are actu-

ally trying to get rid of – not so much the words – certainly some aspects and implications of the words: screening, airbrushing, soft-focusing, veiling. An excursus into the delusions of 'reception theory', according to which the work you read is independently constructed by each brain's associational patterns (though this does seem to happen in some press reviewers) wouldn't be out of place here if there was room. The errors underlying that theory were scotched in the 19th century and have enjoyed a recrudescence only because the overambitious academic has such a nose for trendy silliness that 'with his nails he'll dig it up again'. The climber's thrill of nothing but air below, in the pseudo-heroic age of literary theory.

Merely from modesty some writers can seem, consciously or not, to acquiesce in equating their works with the *cuckoos* of cuckoos, since they eschew pretentious claims for their work. Maybe they'd be embarrassed producing a string of references to considerations called variously humanistic or spiritual or imaginative, being dragged down into dealing with notions often betrayed by silly inflation. It can be hard to detach one side of a clear argument unequivocally from the continuous internal argument you sustain. Both having something to say and a way of saying it matter. Not being able to put things otherwise is not that relevant. Poor performances in interview don't signal a lack of anything to say.

Nor do interviews dominated by an ornithologiser's habitual persistence in posing the wrong questions. Some ornithologisers are trainee journalists, some were trainee journalists prior to the atrophy (incomplete? reversible?) of a certain capacity to learn: a specific capacity to learn which has been no barrier to several academic careers. Witness some third-rate teachers in senior posts, professors philistine and pharisaic, good at passing on mechanically the almost entirely rules of thumb which got them to the top, perpetuating the underlying ignorance. The best teacher communicates the ability to learn things for oneself, like the best poets and philosophers and the sort of 'fiction' Kennedy has in mind to extol.

Techniques can be taught, students be led to appreciate this or that author's ability to persuade. There's still always the question of why the novelist is neither con artist nor camera, whereas the ornithologiser seeks to defeat the beginnings of a better judgment, and have a two-dimensional image taken for the real thing. Obviously enough description, suggestion or evocation of sheer physical settings, habitat, sense-impressions, atmosphere or 'magic', aren't irrelevant aspects of literary works. Some authors equate themselves defensively with cameras, poets talk of tricks or sleights, or echoed Dante's *bello mensogno* phrase, calling the work of fiction a 'beautiful lie'. All this really means is that no Bovary listed in any 19th century professional directory of French pharmacists had a wife called Emma and otherwise fitted the description of his namesake in Flaubert's great novel. There have even been novelists who talked about money, some in direct proportion to their gifts and inverse proportion to their profitability.

Kennedy's reference to one-to-one communication rightly makes nothing of the 'lie' business. Plainly she has in mind something like conversation. Michael Oakeshott's 'The Voice of Poetry in the Conversation of Mankind'? Oakeshott's image of an informing interaction throughout history between different interests and specialisations and ways of looking at aspects of reality, that conversation may be conducted well or badly; or hardly at all. Ker's little aside may say more about novels than about Aristotle, but as the greatest of all Scottish literary scholars he wasn't conspicuously agin either. He believed they should both be in the conversation.

Some books called novels are monologues quite outside any 'conversation of mankind', as ephemera and saying nothing. They are not at issue here, unlike for instance a sort of too exclusively literary preoccupation which distracts from that conversation, neutralises reading, compartmentalises and obscures by conducting a sort of sub-conversation R D S Jack has been known to complain about (in his book on J M Barrie) and likewise, vehemently, Doris Lessing.

The 19th Century Scottish thinker John McLeod Campbell articulated an differently focused idea and ideal of conversation (which continued in John Macmurray's work a century later). McLeod Campbell discussed and carried on conversation as a potential mode of often incidental discovery, 'one-to-one'. The discoveries might never find their way into words which could be set in print as clear and distinct statements, but can be definite and plain enough to participants whose understanding the conversation extends and deepens. The participant minds stimulate each other because both know what they are both talking about, and saying, with resources of expression, gesture and intonation and reference. Reading of MacDiarmid's feelings at the loss of his first wife, Peggy, one can see why he thought the best line in Burns, 'Ye arena Mary Morrison'. What would that line mean without some common context and basis in common feelings and common language? Is Burns calling Ms Morrison a stadium?

Conversation brings references, connections, associations to mind, even beyond what could be made explicit for any non-participant. This is not collusion but co-operation, critical not carping or point-scoring, and person to person. What can a consistent ornithologiser have for conversations, given a preoccupation with the language of printed classification. Some folk do talk like pre-recordings, not like Stephen Hawking through his machine but the machine through the human body; or field things said in the drilled tones of the sheerly verbally catechised. Some chields to start conversations unaware how like formal interviewers they sound: above all fluency rather than any risk of a stutter or falter. It's not hard to regress to a sort of linguistic imitativeness, collage of phrases picked up here and there (for insight into much modern literary theory dipping into Piaget's *Language and Thought of the Child* can be immensely suggestive).

The jargon of an earlier generation of proto-ornithologisers prompted the wonderful Malcolm Cowley to contrast the linguistic sensitivity crucial to awareness of literature, with the steelware and wiring jargon of what used to be called New Criticism. Given the effect on Cowley of reading the metallic prose, what did writing it do to the souls who wrote it? What sacrifice precedes fluency in a slick journalese?

In face of superficial or theoretical impressions perhaps the uninformed journalist and reconditely technical academic varieties of ornithologiser aren't that different inside. They may well impose identical stereotypes, conform to stereotypes much the same. All catechisms of avoidance have a lot in common: initial puzzlement at the unexpected reply, a moment's blank look, then childhood rules of thumb leap out: *'there are strange other people in the world,'* or (the colonial pioneer's wariness of the incomprehensible aborigine) 'this might be a *dangerous person'*. There is the imperiousness of the theoretician in the India office: a step back and shake of the head, a pitying look. One mustn't forget competitive resentment at the author's ability to influence friends or even make people. Jessie Kesson was oppressed by the implicit *What are you trying to hide from my inevitable and always legitimate inquiry?* Where on personal grounds she had every right to scorn prying, far from wishing to conceal she wanted to reveal the purport of her novel. She might have been banging her head against a brick wall, and some questioners might just as well have been goggling at EEG printouts and brain scans.

Apparently Kennedy's PEN lecture was a protest against authors tarting up mere disguised autobiography as fiction or novels. Plainly she wasn't! There are explanations (masquerading as advocacies) of some literary works as *tours-de-force* of literary technique working over sheer autobiographical detail. To parody what was said of the pointless waste at Balaclava: *peut-être* c'est *à clef, mais ce n'est pas un roman serieux,* for all that any 'intermediary' her well-chosen word) tries to say. It isn't the way in which some novelist distorts, or turns some alleged actuality which is of proper interest, what matters are the implications of the novel, but what price characterisation which serves only odd looks at 'strange people'?

The ultimate dogma of ornithologising biographism (why should the Devil have all the ungainliest phrases!) is its giving priority not to 'life' so much as muddled biography: not to 'life' or human life, but a kind of 'life without art (or metaphysics or religion etc., including imagination)' as commonly contrasted with at the very least 'art'. The contrast is very much a contemporary one, made nowadays and made about nowadays, often as if contemporary circumstances and *mores* represented states, conditions and situations somehow permanent – a kind of setting up house on the summit of Mont Blanc, on the moon or Mars. Looking at various real improvements in practical management, technology, medicine, it has seemed to too many that things have only got better; and that some 'we' are on a plateau from which it is possible to look down.

The magnificent Viennese Jewish exile Hans Keller, musician and writer on psychoanalytic themes, football, British literary parochialism and more, one of the past glories of BBC radio, had something to say in talking about 'taste'. He didn't mean by 'taste' some magical intuitive faculty at home in a classical era, but something nearer one snooty aristocrat's reference to Mozart's music as 'this German swinishness', *questa porcheria tedesca.*

The Mozart didn't belong to her *present*, and what Keller was talking about was limitation of responsiveness and potential comprehension (very much themes of Kennedy's lecture). There is a problem when comprehension is confined by narrow categories of the already existing, of things liable already to be known in nearly enough all of their wider respects. The novelty which would not have narked the stuck-up dispraiser of Mozart would have been new but of an old quickly recognised kind, to be accepted without an effort of attention she never presumably thought of making. She didn't ask herself what this music was.

It is this sort of *'present'* I think Kennedy has in mind in making her case for 'fiction'. The ornithologiser's response is not of 'taste', just call it a response. It occurs these days at no period of transformation (claims of increased productivity notwithstanding) in some supposed course of advance of the art with which it's concerned. It might be a kind of natural product, by no means *necessarily*, therefore good, of the way in which the half-heard and part-read sift quickly into widespread uninformed presuppositions of the day. Conversation involves listening, unlike a garble which grossly misunderstands the place and nature of science, and religion, and associates 'fiction' with time off in a compartmentalised life. Whatever the word 'pleasure' is supposed to mean in translations from Aristotle (I'm sure neither I nor Ms Kennedy would advocate books *dull, but good for you*) it becomes a silly word when it confuses (Alasdair MacIntyre's cited examples) experiences of bottles of Guinness or (Lord Denning's term, says MacIntyre) of 'popsies', with what is at the very least a different experience.

In an ornithologising Gradgrindia or Hedonia, notions of reality as mysterious, complex, involving changes not comprehended in daily dealings with the more or less familiar – the old line about more things in Heaven and earth than are dreamt of in your theory – are literally alien. The common public idea that Darwin's enormous discoveries imply a general progress in everything, and that there is a law 'adapt or die', is nonsense. There is change and what is made of it by what (or who) is there. The individual creature (it/she/he) undergoes a succession of changes without any passing on of these except by example, experience, precept. Its behaviour is however adapted to or by its environment, in relation (Ms Kennedy is saying) to perspectives and views, understanding and feelings and awareness of possibilities; and not merely to habit, or implicit rules of thumb which seem thus far to have served.

A famous literary case of ornithologising is of course Joseph Conrad, who never quite got out of his head the handbook of how to minimise possible bother with non-Europeans you've no experience of. His political incorrectnesses have been ornithologised extensively without enough thought of their practical rule-of-thumb origins. How aware anyone is of the full range and operation of his or her own habits, good or bad or indifferent, is a question whose enormous importance gives Ms Kennedy's profession a stronger kinship to that of the research scientist than most journalists and theoreticians on their way from one museum to another.

"Fiction is always about people other than the reader," says Kennedy.

In isn't absolutely "always". Some people do recognise themselves (and feel the fact needs kept secret) in characters in novels whose authors could never hear of them. Both cases are an operation at the depth of response Ms Kennedy does crucially and correctly indicate. It is at this level that "by agreeing to read [fiction]," at least some people "agree to collaborate with the minds and the voices of the authors, to let them put their words into [their] mouths, [their] minds – one of the most intimate intrusions possible". At this level too, intense fruitful questions start to stir.

There are however readers whom reading novels supplies fulfilment of a liking juggling or conjuring tricks (which is all that a great deal of published fiction could fulfil except for a specialised study), or a kind of music for the deaf. As a student in the 1930s Thomas Merton read what the 'smart' aunt and uncle he lived with in England read, took the 'advanced ideas' as a model for living and made a horrible mess of things. He had had no idea his aunt and uncle read these daring books to be diverted by the alterity of the characters and their conduct (like being amused watching dumb animals and other folks' children). "In the case of the novel," Kennedy continues, "we may sustain this intrusion for days, if not weeks … because we tacitly acknowledge that [the authors'] thoughts can be as important as our own and because they address us, uniquely, with the "uncritical respect that you give to friends and relatives".

The serious novelist, it is implied, is not the player of tricks some academic reviewers suggest. There are moral considerations even where there is no moralising, but not in every case. That this is by no means according to the (what gets called post-modern) current post-evangel goes without saying. That Ms Kennedy's speech according to that theory, and to the ornithologiser, is *impossibly naïve*, does not go without saying. Untruths are frequent, common as that fear of getting caught, of being exposed, implied by a great deal of current literary theory and practice. A browse around Ms Kennedy's website will demonstrate that for all her disclaimer of being a retailer of processed gossip and the oddness (given what I've read) of supposing her to be one, she still believes the novelist exposed by the novels she publishes. This observation can't be accused of superficiality.

Kennedy wants serious fiction taken seriously, not a critical establishment ornithologising, but critical discussion, thinking and feeling, conversation, and within the reader. The one aspect of what she described as fiction, and McLeod Campbell's 'conversation' is that it (horror of horror for the ornithologiser!) affords no escape to an external standard. What *are* these characters, and *who?* When and where can what is happening happen, and to whom? Not to Mummy, surely? Little sister Molly? Millions?

God bless uncertainty where wondering can be a wonder.

Ignorance alone makes knowledge possible.

Even a little knowingness is a nasty business.

Aristotle probably wouldn't have understood a novel, but his is a better excuse than most. He's not entirely dead, but not entirely dead in ways quite different from the ornithologiser.

# Sebastian Barker

## *Athenagoras*

Deep in the midnight of my Christmas heart,
    Athenagoras came, a whole world apart.
He taught me what the reindeer know,
    who sniff the interglacial snow.
He taught me what the termites feel
    incessant in their hopeful hill.
He taught me what the rivers say,
    which slice through continents of clay.
Like phosphorescent fish that burn,
    he taught me what the martyrs learn.
*We know the truth. We know the lie.*
    *We do not live until we cannot die.*

The megabucks, the superstars,
    the mobile phones in mobile cars,
The perky poet, the lucid don,
    the Valley of the Silicon,
Lace our language, chip the head,
    eclipse the unremembered dead.
The junk hawk drills his thinning skin
    to pump the lethal liquid in.
Like children surfing on the net,
    he taught me what the wise forget.
*We know the truth. We know the lie.*
    *We do not live until we cannot die.*

Get up, my darling, shake the sheets.
    No blissy wipe-out bed competes.
The ruddy rocks are red with blood
    insurgent in our saviour's head.
What made us makes us what we are
    when he becomes the evening star
And like the planet rolls away
    the giant circumference of day
And leaves us in his rocklike hands
    Athenagoras understands.
*We know the truth. We know the lie.*
    *We do not live until we cannot die.*

## The Virgin Muse

Look on her once and know, the kneeling knee
Proud to submit to the known to be holy,
Toned in the azure of a loving mind
Commanding respect, respect of humankind.

Look on her once and speak, the encountering tongue
Reacting in a language no English poet has sung.
Look on her once and speak. The Virgin Muse.
To few souls ever popular. Whom none abuse.

The tabletop is teak. Sunlight slants the room
To a low-roofed triangle of pre-Euclidean light.
The murmur of the wood-doves consecrates the gloom.
The wind disrupts the trees. Down comes the night.

Look on her once and know, the kneeling knee
Proud to submit to the known to be holy.

## The Venus Virgin

Sphinx to reason, sacred as the day
When the great Parmenides sat down to write,
I see the wheels of what I have to say
Break on the beauty which you command tonight.

Two ways there are, so the great man taught,
To live on earth. One is to enquire
To know the truth. The other to be bought,
Bullied, bound, and butchered by desire.

He did not teach desire on its own
Misled, but desire coupled to opinion.
Desire to enquire to know the truth was known
By his pupil Plato to reach the true union.

The Greeks were right. Desire to look on you
Was never more necessary, never more true.

## On the Anvil of the Tongue

Terror conscience struck me down.
    The bad old days had come,
Conscience sunken, fit to drown,
    An anvil round its tongue.

Terror conscience struck me hard.
    The beatings had begun,
Beatings fit to break the word
    On the anvil of the tongue.

Terror conscience took my sex,
    Sprayed it with a gun,
Sprayed it fit to break yours next
    On the anvil of the tongue.

Terror conscience knows no bounds,
    No circle to its aims.
The head of states, the diamond hoards,
    Attract its wicked ends.

Terror conscience guards the words
    To offset these laws
Crouched at home with fourteen leopards
    In its iron claws

## *Father Alban*

No fairer Father has a living man
    than he who makes it to a stranger's door
To find a fierce Franciscan beaming smiles
    fit to lift God knows how many
Centuries of grief. I walked beneath
    conscious of that strange phenomenon
The weightlessness of being. We wandered on
    down corridors and stairs

To what encounter in his tiny cell
    crammed with books and courtesy so sharp
We cut a friendship on the common air?
    And did we meet as I remember it?
"You have made me a happy man."
    "Then you have made me a happier man," he said.

Spinning with delight, my gyroscope of brain
    tried every angle in its new career.
All were steady. None could over-rock
    my patient progress down the River Thames
Along the long Embankment to a shop
    To buy a book his knowledge of my state
Knew how to name. In steep initiation
    I opened it at home and there I saw
The *Catechism of the Catholic Church*
    tunnelling time, edited by those
Who'd scrubbed that subway clean and studded it
    with jewelled mosaics. I took the book to bits
And found it made of human flesh and blood
    in which no fairer Father found his feet.
        In its iron claws.

# Between Editorials

## Hayden Murphy

I first encountered *Chapman* in late March 1972 when Trevor Royle introduced me to its co-founder and editor, that fine poet Walter Perrie. Royle was then the first Literary Director of the Scottish Arts Council and co-ordinator of the emerging annual exchange visits between Irish/Scottish poets and musicians. Perrie had founded the magazine with George Hardie in 1969. It was then titled *The Chapman*. It became *Chapman* in 1971. He was joined by Joy M Hendry as co-editor in 1973. In 1976 she became Editor.

Since 1967, from Dublin and elsewhere, I had been editing a literary broadsheet containing poetry, prose and graphics. It survived for thirty issues until the Summer of 1978. Subsequently, *Broadsheet* was subject of a retrospective exhibition in the National Library of Scotland (1983).

I had been coming to Edinburgh for Festival since 1966. Usually in the audiences. Though, in 1971 I directed/produced and performed in a Yeats inspired show; 'The Foul Rag and Bone Shop of The Heart' (with Robert Somerset). A close encounter with a sole spectator, beneath the tilting stage in the front row, ended my thespian career. And my ambitions. Well; on stage anyway.

I was to meet Joy during the Festival of 1972 at a poetry reading in the New Town Hotel. There were to be many similar social collisions. In 1976 she suggested an Irish contribution to *Chapman*. This became *Chapman 19* which appeared in February 1977, featuring Irish poetry, a lengthy editorial and new work from fifteen Irish poets. There was also an extended review section where, among others, I welcomed *Secrets,* a first collection of short stories by the then comparatively unknown Bernard MacLaverty. "The virtue lies in the timing, themes are drawn taut and then (released as) breath lines," I wrote. How our purple prose returns to haunt us.

For the curious bibliophile, MacLaverty was the featured fiction writer in the next Irish Issue, *Chapman 92,* which appeared 21 years later in Winter 1999. Those who appeared in both Irish issues are Desmond O' Grady, Hugh Maxton, Brendan Kennelly and this writer.

In the years between 1977 and 1999 many things happened. Not all literately related. I moved from Dublin to live in Edinburgh full-time in Autumn 1979. *Chapman* became a quarterly and it was a privilege to contribute to it over the following decades. In 1997, again at the instigation of Joy Hendry, I began planning another Irish issue which, I hoped, would record the optimism generated by the Peace Talks in Ireland and the reality of a devolved Scotland. Timing was on my side.

Following the Good Friday Agreement, Daniel Mulhall was appointed first Consul General of Ireland to Scotland. He was to write a generous and perceptive preface to the Irish issue. He emphasised the "nurturing cultural connections between Ireland and Scotland".

John Behan (AHRIA) provided not only a dramatic cover graphic but also an evocative frontpiece. 'McGinty's Goat'– symbol of a shared Gaelic pagan pleasure in hedonism.

The *Dedalus Press* founder/editor, poet John F Deane, in his poem 'The Dead and the Undead of St Michan's' inspired both a thematic core and a title. His poetic personae were "like martyrs, for centuries … stood like sand-shapes/ abandoned by the tides, their language courtesy/ and silence … till – with a communal sigh – they yielded/ to the flames. Farewell, our old familiars, / our seafarers, our progenitors, our clowns". Those images, redolent but resolutely independent of Yeats, provided the emotional heat that emanated from the 'Flames of History' issue that ensued. For me it was comparatively easy after that. The poets wrote, forty in all, ranging from Nobel laureate Seamus Heaney to newcomer Nancy Doyle.

Repeating the '77 format I monopolised the review section announcing new poetry, drama and prose. My first editorial in 1977 had discussed the placement of Irish literature within an Irish/Scottish context *(Where? Why? Whither?)*. My final one, in deference to Ireland's first woman president, and other important and overdue cultural changes, read *"Thank You Mrs Robinson for Putting Our Writers on Your Stage"*.

At the end of my first farewell I feared I might become a "Claqueur of Comment". Editors do. So finally, as a retrospective glance to celebrate this centenary issue of *Chapman*, may I address an Editor who has not yet retired to gossip and ask that a tune be given to the toast *"Thank You Joy for the Pleasure of These Dances Upon Your Pages."*

*Hayden Murphy, editor,* Broadsheet, *c.1973 (by Edward Maguire) from NLS Catalogue cover (1993)*

# Grains of Barley

## *George Gunn*

The new century barely two and *Chapman* venerable? Or is it? How did this rickety enterprise ever get so old? *Chapman* has always been about debate, questions, the floweriness, false starts, disappointments and genesis of new writing and writers. The more the magazine progresses and develops the more the constraints put upon it increase. The more new poets the imprint produces the more the glaring hole which is Scottish publishing becomes apparent. Each new book acts as an indictment as to the paucity of vision and resources available to contemporary Scottish poetry. If one was objective and looked closely at what passes for a publishing industry in Scotland you would see an activity which is no more than a hobby for some and no better than a side-line for others. Individual energy and Lottery assisted three year phenomena do not for vitality make. The rather gruesome chairman of the banking group which owns the Cup-die-sac Bank proclaimed in April 2002 that Scotland has been in recession for over 200 years. Perhaps it takes an outsider to see the truth? For all that the other art forms such as theatre, music and dance seem to be flourishing (if you believe the spin) then why is it that publishing seems to be the missing link, the poor cousin, the "kink in the dialectic" as Morris Ploughman put it? All this when Scottish writing has never enjoyed such a high profile in U.K. and internationally since the time of James Metaphors's *Asian*, Burns and Alter Scott. Is it the hard truth that publishing, like broadcasting, is a reserved matter for the Westminster Government, or is it that within Scotland we do not have the wherewithal to sustain a publishing industry above the level of a cottage industry?

Why does the story about the grain of barley the size of a hen egg come to mind? This fable has found its most popular expression through Leo Tolstoy in his collection of stories, *Divine and Human*. In it a young boy is out in the fields and he finds a grain of barley the size of a hen's egg. Astonished he takes it back to his father and asks him what it is. The father tells him it is a grain of barley but that he has never seen one that size before. The father takes it to the King. The King is very impressed and consults his wise men. "It is a grain of barley the size of a hen egg", they tell him. "I know that", replies the King, "But where did it come from?" None of the wise men know, so they send for a very old farmer.

The farmer duly arrives at the court. He is old, his skin is green and he walks with the aid of two crutches. He is almost blind. "Do you know where this grain of barley the size of an egg comes from?" asks the King.

The farmer looks at it. "No", he replies, "I have never seen anything like it before. But my father may be able to help you." So the King sends for his father. An old farmer arrives. He looks younger than the previous one, although he walks with the aid of a crutch. He has the sight of only one eye. "Could you tell me where this grain the size of a hen egg originates?

We have never seen its like before," says the King. "Neither have I," replied the old farmer with the one crutch, "but my father will be able to help you."

Much perplexed the King sends for the old farmer's father. In walks an upright man of indeterminate age. His skin is fresh and his eye is clear and bright. "Could you tell me," asks the King, "where this grain of barley the size of a hen egg came from?"

"Yes," replied the clear sighted farmer, as quick as flash, "we would find them in the fields I worked as a boy, but you do not see them anymore."

The King looked at the man for a moment. "I have two questions for you," said the King. "Firstly, why are there no more grains of barley the size of hen eggs? Also, why is it you appear younger than your father who himself appears younger than his father, your grandfather?"

The farmer, who was holding the grain of barley the size of a hen egg in his hand, replied. "The answer to both questions is the same. You have enclosed our lands and broken the ancient bond with the ground we work. You have made us compete with ourselves so that our sense of co-operation and mutuality has gone and in its place greed and mistrust. What you have taken you do not put back so we are the results of your actions." With that he set the grain the size of a hen egg down before the King and left.

Until the literary stock which is drained from Scotland is reinvested the development of our literature will not be sustainable. Even now the latest crop of 'bright new things' looks ever thinner, less bright and ever more desperate. Until Scottish writing stops being treated as a marketing phenomenon it will never meet the needs of the society which produces it in educational or moral grounds. Every writer is an existentialist outsider; but publishing, books generally and magazines in particular, has a specific role to play in the intellectual and political development of a society. A society where that activity is Americanised is a society which will constantly be at odds with itself and will not develop the confidence to see itself in world terms, but only in opposition to its nearest, largest neighbour.

In this the Scottish Arts Council has a crucial role to play. The funding level Scottish literary magazines are at only ensures that they expend their energies in survival rather than in planning debates, forums, special issues, celebrations, as well as the vital activity of introducing readers to new writers and to introduce new readers to writers. In this, again, the Scottish Arts Council, through the direction of the Scottish Executive, must take the lead.

With the 100th issue of *Chapman* it should be obvious that whatever criteria for a more secure future has been defined *Chapman* has met it. This is a critical moment. The sheer volume of achievement in reaching this issue demands that this forum be maintained, re-vitalised and continue to be a service to the imagination of the country. It is poetry which flexes the imagination and it is in imagination where the future is born. Scotland is forming in the minds of the next generation. If there is no place for them to debate and think in public Scotland will be less the nation as a result.

Either that or we end up like the blind old farmer with green skin, on crutches unable to recognise the thing in front on them.

# Atoms of Delight and Despair

## David Morrison

*The Atom of Delight* by Neil Gunn had a profound impact on me, hence the the title of this piece. Despair is inbred in me because of my Presbyterian upbringing. Joy and meaning in life is hard to find. However I wish to dwell on small magazine publishing, as requested by Joy, with special reference to my magazine *Scotia Review*. I really applaud *Chapman* as it now reaches its 100th issue. Long may it continue, and in fact it started roughly at the same time as *Scotia Review,* but the magazines have gone along different tracks, probably because my energy and finance ran out, but has been renewed again and Joy has made a professional business of *Chapman*.

An editor of a Scottish literary magazine is usually the vision of an individual being spurred on by the influence of literary mentors. And the editor knows nothing about distribution, finance, in fact he or she tends to be an idealistic dreamer. That is why many small magazines don't last long. *Scotia Review* lasted for 20 issues in its magazine format, then came the duplicated *Scotia Rampant* and in the last few years, when some energy came back, 100-page, duplicated issues, No 21 in honour of Tom Scott, No 22. 'Scotland the Where?', No 23 'Tribute to Alan Bold and Iain Crichton Smith', No 24, the William Neill issue. You may well ask why I just don't give up. Today *Scotia Review* has £1.67 in its account and I feel fine about that. The inspiration for the original folded broadsheet was *Rocket,* edited by Alan Bold. Very short lived, basically because Alan couldn't be bothered selling. I first met Alan in Milne's Bar along with John Bellany and Sandy Moffat, the self-styled Big Three of later years. Then I was a librarian in Edinburgh College of Art, and frequented that great pub. There I met so many poets and writers, Sydney Goodsir Smith, Norman MacCaig, John L. Broom, Robert Garioch, ay, many more. These were glorious, glorious days.

In 1965 I moved to Caithness and immediately started to publish *Scotia*. I did not feel that living in the far north was a disadvantage. I already had writers who would write for me. Between 1970 and 1978 much was done. In 1978 I was pretty exhausted and gave up the magazine to concentrate my efforts on the Wick Folk Club and the Wick Festival of Poetry Folk and Jazz. This was at the height of a new public enthusiasm for folk music and poetry readings. It was also the period of the Hamilton by-election whereby Winnie Ewing got into parliament, and the SNP were driving forth. The 'heady days' as John Herdman has described them. This was also the days of *Catalyst* the magazine for the 1320 Club and from 1968-1974 the days of what I regard as the worst over subsidised, Scottish Arts Council funded, magazine Scottish International. In those days *Scotia Review* got only about £150-200 per issue, and I'm sure it was the same with *Chapman*, but *Scottish International* got thousands and the editor was full-time paid. Try as a small magazine to fight against that little lot!

It's all to do with grants, accountancy, distribution, advertising, accountability with sponsors and especially the necessity to make sure you don't 'rock the boat'. It can be sheer hell to edit a small magazine. Is it any wonder that many last only a short time. It was interesting to read the editorial by Gerry Cambridge in the last issue of his fine magazine, *Dark Horse*, whereby he complained about the fact that the Scottish Arts Council had offered him money to pay a certain rate to contributors while he, almost full-time edited for the love of it. Many times editors despair and give up.

But, at the end of the day, there have been more than a few atoms of delight in editing. The meeting, and being close friends with so many writers, who basically wrote for me for a few beers, but believed in my editorial policy. Though when I stayed with Alan Bold often in Gayfield Square, sleeping on his stone kitchen floor, for quite a while he was on Guinness and Drambuies. But Alan, Tom Scott, Francis Thompson, Stanley Roger Green, Iain Crichton Smith, John L Broom, George Mackay Brown, to name just a few were always willing to contribute to *Scotia Review.*

I remember with great fondness the years, once a month, I had to travel to SCAMP the Scottish Association of Magazine Publishers. I left Wick at 8 pm, after work to travel to Edinburgh in all weathers. I arrived in Edinburgh in the wee smaa oors. Slept awhile, went shopping, mainly to Mothercare for the family before meeting up with the editors of other magazines. Meeting, 2.30-5 pm, then lounge bar for drinks till, roughly 7.

Next port of call the Abbotsford, to meet writers along with Alan. Party in the evening, me, naturally buying the cairry-oot; leave at 8.a.m, to head north to Wick, totally shattered I would arrive home in the evening, lying though my teeth, that, 'Yes, love, I've had a quiet, inspiring weekend'.

How the body stood that time I'll never know.

In the past there have been fine meetings, both in the cities and in Wick, but there have also been hellish meetings. To this day a few of the older generation of poets hate my guts. And the reason is simple. It was through my editorial policy. I knew what I wanted to do and solicited work from the best of writers. Any editor must have a toughness about them which I found extremely hard at times.

At the end of the day *Scotia Review* survives in a small way: limited runs, duplicated, but hopefully visually appealing. I am now out of quite a debt, I am beholden to no-one, and just publish as I please. *Scotia Review* and other little publications have their place just as many other little magazines do, but I would advise anyone proposing to produce a magazine to think long and hard. There must be a determination and a focus coupled with a business sense. *Chapman* obviously has these qualities in abundance and I applaud Joy and her staff. It is nice to think that one of my early poems, 'Lilt tae Me', appeared in either the first or second very slim pamphlet of *The Chapman*. Along the way Joy I know has had many atoms of delight and despair. Joy, I raise my glass of a double Old Pulteney malt tae ye.

Mair pouer tae yer elbuck, lass.

# An Amazing Weekend

## *William and Patricia Oxley*

Small circulation literary magazines are the most democratic, freethinking and serious cultural organs available in the Western world. Their samizdat character provides the sole defence we have against the tyranny of Establishment conformism in poetry. In 1972 I started my first such magazine, *Littack*. How this came to pass, what form the magazine took, etc, is fully described in my autobiography, *No Accounting for Paradise*, (Rockingham Press, 1999). It was a highly combative magazine based on the neo-romantic notion of being 'agin everything'. *Littack* was so sweeping in its 'attack' as to include my fellow poets as well as just about everything else, so I lost even the vote of my most natural allies. Today, thirty years on, I am not welcome in certain establishment quarters because of *Littack*. However, from the start, some poets were interested in what I was trying to do: Tom Scott and Peter Russell gave it the warmest welcome; Hugh MacDiarmid, Kathleen Raine and Robert Graves later on. But among those figures just starting out on their literary careers who seemed interested in *Littack*, were Walter Perrie and Joy Hendry. So interested, in fact, that Walter, shortly after the publication of the second issue, turned up at the Oxley household in Epping, Essex – quite a distance from his home base of Edinburgh.

*(I remember Walter arriving; a shock of hair and a blinkered obsession with talking about poetry. I felt he didn't remember that I fed and watered him and he exhausted me with his concentrated talk. I also remember being impressed that he got A's for his essays at university. – P )*

Walter was a student of philosophy and a poet; and had right-wing sympathies which, not long after he met Hugh MacDiarmid, appeared to swing the opposite way. *Littack's* politics – insofar as it could be said to have any – were perceived to be 'right-wing and reactionary'; but that is always the mistake made by people who cannot believe that anyone is anti-political, which I still am at heart. *Littack's* political, philosophical and poetic outlook seemed to chime in with Walter Perrie's. And it is certainly true that both Perrie and I – and I think Joy Hendry too at that time – wanted "a new aesthetic for poetry": a phrase that occurred in *Littack* and I seem to recall was often on the lips of Perrie. During that visit to Epping, Perrie also told me of his plans for *Chapman*, which he and his wife had just started: a special 'Blast Issue', as a homage to Wyndham Lewis's Vorticist journal of that name which had created a stir around World War I; a special Chinese poetry issue; a Dutch issue; and a double issue devoted to Rilke's work.

All of these plans came to fruition, but probably not in the way envisaged at the time – autumn 1972 through to January 1973. Shortly after, Perrie came to England again, this time with Joy, and I met them for an animated colloquy in the buffet bar at Liverpool Street Station. They were on their way to Cambridge to meet Richard Burns and Anthony Rudolf of the Menard Press, with whom I had put them in touch.

In January 1973, Patricia and I accepted an invitation to visit Joy and Walter at their flat in Edinburgh. The weekend was intended to be a kind of working holiday with a pooling of our joint magazine experiences, so to speak. Also, the address of this flat, situated in one of those tall, grey, very stone buildings which characterise Edinburgh, was 10 Spottiswoode Road. I know this because, additionally, our visit had to do with the fact that, very early on in our relationship, Perrie had asked me to join the advisory boards for both *Chapman* magazine and Chapman Printing.

I agreed to this. The idea was to run a printing business from the Perries' flat, which, it was hoped, would make enough money for them to live off and run the magazine. A Gestetner printing press had been transported up two flights of stairs and was now sitting like a metal gorilla in their spare bedroom. Fortunately, Edinburgh tenements are so solid, such a monstrous machine could be run there without inconveniencing neighbours.

*(One of my strongest memories of the weekend is of how Joy and I cooked roast chicken for one meal and shared the preparation of haggis, neaps and tatties for another. Then drinking red wine and sitting on the floor listening to the bagpipes playing pibroch: haunting melodies which induced tears in a wine-heightened sensibility. On Sunday, we were taken to Crawford's in Princes Street: a famous tea-room which has now disappeared – P)*

One afternoon was given over to the two board meetings, both chaired by Perrie: all the other members of the board, myself excepted, were either Perrie or Hendry family members who appeared altogether bemused about it all. The minutes of the meeting not only tell us that the projected total printing costs of six issues of the magazine was expected to be £2,500, but also had this to say about *Littack* under the heading of 'Publicity':

> The sum of £250 is included for joint adverts and personal adverts in various newspapers. The co-operation on publicity with Littack is based on their similar and complementary aims and will allow coverage in both Scotland and the South of England, as well as encouraging, cross-subscriptions from readers of both magazines.

Everything was well thought out, judging from the copies of minutes and constitutional standing orders which I still have. The clear driving force at that time was Perrie: a small dynamic figure of great eloquence, despite a noticeable speech impediment. His words to me, as he greeted us off the train, were a gleeful, "Be prepared to have your psyche broken this weekend!" Although my psyche wasn't broken and I returned home in euphoric mood, it was shattered two days later by a telephone call from the wife of my best friend saying he had taken his life – but that's another matter. The principal impression I gained of Perrie was of a man with sound ideas, much enthusiasm, but someone in danger of burning himself out too soon.

Joy Hendry – then Joy Perrie – was a tall, strong-boned Highland lass to my Sassenach eye. She impressed me as someone of strength, temporarily overborne by a stronger force. The openness of her gaze matched the openness of her heart: she spoke her mind, as many northerners do, and it was a mind worth speaking. But I cannot say that I perceived the future course of *Chapman* lay in her hands rather than in her husband's. Much more evident was the fact that theirs was a partnership that was unlikely to endure. Which proved to be the case.

During that weekend, much of what was perceived of as joint magazine business was discussed. Also, there was a great deal of talk of the perennial topic of poetry itself. I was introduced by Joy and Walter to the work of the German poet Rainer Maria Rilke, even taken to a bookshop on The Meadows where I purchased an edition of the Leishman-Spender translations. Then, I acquired a volume of *The Duino Elegies*. So, quite apart from what I learned of this new phenomenon in Scottish letters called *Chapman*, I had one of the most important introductions to a modern European poet I have ever had. Yeats and Rilke – both of whom figured largely in that weekend's talk – remain two of the most important poets to me.

For several years I kept in correspondence with Walter Perrie, and I saw the gradual emergence of those early *Chapman*s which he had predicted during that amazing weekend. A weekend which also inspired my long poem 'Grey Cities' which I dedicated to Joy Hendry and Walter Perrie in its first part, and which was published in my *Collected Longer Poems* (University of Salzburg Press, 1994). But I only ever met Perrie once after that, and it was some eight years later. Like some others of the early 'Littackers', Perrie became disenchanted with what I was doing. Also, in 1976 I abandoned a lucrative career to follow the Muse, which meant that I could no longer afford to subsidize a substantial literary journal. Though I did run a reduced service, as they say, in the form of a newsletter-style supplement called *The Littack Supplement*, which I finally terminated in 1980.

I can't remember when I became aware that Walter and Joy were no longer living together; nor indeed when Joy took over *Chapman*. But from the mid 1970s onwards it became clear she was the new, and now sole, driving force behind the magazine and the periodical was becoming a more catholic and broader mirror of the arts, while still reflecting its first love, poetry. More even than *Acumen* – another female-edited literary journal – *Chapman* was very broadly based in artistic terms: theatre, music, poetry, short stories, artwork, plus a degree of social awareness and political discourse. In short, *Chapman* became both a major force in Scottish letters, as well as an established feature on the literary/ artistic landscape. This it did through Joy Hendry's undoubted flair for choosing good material and her ability to get each issue out regularly. I gave up editing magazines in 1980. But in 1984/5 the other member of that Edinburgh quadrivium of 1973, suddenly informed me she was going to start a magazine.

*(I planned and began* Acumen *by calling on much I had learned listening to the Edinburgh discussions and also helping William on a number of publications in the 1970's – most importantly – Littack. But I wanted* Acumen *to be different in being edited by a reader not a writer of poetry. – P)*

There can also be little doubt, and Patricia would be the first to admit it, that Joy Hendry's development of *Chapman* proved at least a partial inspiration for *Acumen*. And when I witnessed the two editors, stood side by side, in the English Bookshop in Vienna talking about their magazines,

I was definitely impressed by a mutual symbiosis of artistic development, as well as seeing a fine example of the results of that "cross-fertilisation of ideas" of which Matthew Arnold spoke.

*(But even to that day, Joy was a more dynamic personality. I often envied her out-spokenness, and her ability to talk fluently in public. By comparison with* Chapman, Acumen *is a quieter journal, with no political edge. But one thing we do have in common is a desire to try and publish the best poetry being written. – P.)*

## Strangeness of Wind

Today is a good wind, a clean wind, a wind without travail.
It somersaults the headland and prods the dragon swell
of a smoke-grey bay. A good wind, a clean wind
that courses down from moor to sea and mind.

It finds its way into words, singing
through invisible grasses, whispering little shells of meaning
that litter the human shore. A wind of wit,
an irony pulling at leaves and dust that

insists we see and feel things lost or never there.
But like bellows it also blows up fair,
with hidden mouth, yesterday's embers that give
fresh form to dawn and what in the world it warms to love.

Wind that shapes and haunts and never leaves this coast –
a western wind, a flying force, a kiss, a ghost
that plays around the rocky edge of bitterness
in strange ambiguities of happiness.

## Numinous

The glass weeps in this window near Waterloo Station
and coldly hisses on rails
that loop away to Surbiton

or elsewhere. Nowhere so ugly as
in rain, bedraggled bushes of town,
buildings leaking and looking
their age, skies that are down-

cast. But there is something numinous too,
shiningly implicatory
in the out-there of roofs and streets.
Like the mad whisper of history

it floats out and up from shapes
even of shops: edging along walls like a cat
its creeping luminosity of
how and why and what.

# Semi-detached Sentences
# on *Chapman*

### *Peter Cudmore*

If poets are the unacknowledged legislators of the world, then the literary magazines are their unacknowledged Hansard. (Individual's collections might be regarded as election addresses, and such platforms as Edinburgh's Shore Poets their Parliament – deserving to be recognised with proper respect as such by the funding bodies.)

Some years ago, in the currents surrounding the '92 election, Artists for Independence and all that, someone – Joy, as it happens – asked why I, as a recently-arrived Englishman, seemed so committed to the cause. I didn't have an answer.

Some weeks ago, listening to a lecture on the French philosopher Deleuze, the speaker asked the assembly if there was anyone in the room who had not seen Star Wars. (He wanted to draw an analogy with the helmet Jedi knights apparently wear in training.) Along with one other – Ron Turnbull, presently Managing Editor of the *Edinburgh Review*, as it happens – I raised my hand. Relating this episode subsequently, when the 'why' question arose I had an answer: it's about resistance. Not anti-Americanism, but resistance against the creeping homogenisation of corporate culture, a homogenisation in relentless pursuit of the lowest common denominator, a homogenisation that sees in the English language, for example, not beauty and richness but mere convenience.

I owe that epiphany to the time I spent at *Chapman*.

(Academic note: I use the word corporate in its original, neutral sense of a group of people acting as one. But you knew that.)

I believe passionately that the creative individual's fundamental right of self-expression is indivisible, yet articulating that self-expression is intimately bound to a sense of identity that can only be defined in social terms. Man is born free, and is everywhere bound in social links.

Being born and raised in Gloucestershire, and having continued living there well into adulthood, I am nevertheless conscious of not being *of* Gloucestershire. My parents, born in London with roots in South Devon, Lincolnshire, the Welsh borders and Ireland, had been ground by the metropolitan mincer into some kind of British sausage of indeterminate identity. Coming to Scotland I found a refreshingly different and inclusive welcome. A place that values roots, certainly, but in doing so one that understands the value of nourishing soil for its natural and adopted children alike. Working in the literary magazine world is bad for one's financial health. It warms my heart that SAC has now focused its attention on the editors' plight. Is Hansard expected to show a profit?

In that respect, *Chapman*'s ideological commitment to access for all, irrespective of the fortunes of birth, is entirely in accord with my own.

# A Personal Response to Chapman 100

## *Paul Scott*

After working abroad for about 40 years I came back to live in Scotland in November 1980, not the happiest and most confident moment in our history. A century of effort to recover a Scottish Parliament had been frustrated by the fraudulent conduct of a referendum, the 40% rule and Alec Douglas-Home's promise that a Conservative government would introduce a bill with stronger powers. Margaret Thatcher, who had just become Prime Minister, clearly had no such intention. The then Secretary of State for Scotland, George Younger, said that the whole idea of a Scottish Parliament was now a dead duck. For decades the cultural vitality of Scotland and the hope of political autonomy had advanced together. Had they now suffered a fatal setback?

I was among the optimists. I was so confident of the case for autonomy, and the strength of the cultural identity on which it rested, that I thought that they were bound to prevail. Most of my friends in Edinburgh thought the same and very few were prepared to accept defeat. You might well ask what did I know about it and who were these friends, If I had been away for 40 years? The truth is that I never lost touch with Scotland. Wherever I went in the world I took with me Scottish books, pictures and recordings of music. Nearly every year I came back, if only for a few days, and usually during the Edinburgh Festival. I always went round the bookshops and looked for the new books. Newspapers and magazines were sent to me. One of them was *Chapman* and I have been a subscriber to it for about 20 years. It is a good barometer of the cultural health of Scotland and it was apparent from it in the early 80s that the referendum of 1979 had not strangled our cultural self-confidence. On the contrary, it probably made it more determined.

And, of course, I met Joy Hendry as anyone with an interest in these matters was bound to sooner or later. She was not an editor content to sit in an office and let the magazine sell itself. She went round the pubs, meetings, conferences and seminars with copies and made sure that everyone knew about it. Also, it was not the magazine alone; Joy is a great organiser of events to celebrate poets such as MacDiarmid, MacLean, MacCaig and Iain Crichton Smith, not only in special issues but in public gatherings.

Also Joy is a determined campaigner for important causes. Part of this was through AdCAS, the Advisory Council for the Arts in Scotland. This was a think tank, launched by the Saltire Society, representing some 80 cultural bodies of all kinds in Scotland which from 1981 to 1999 produced ideas to stimulate the cultural life of the country. It campaigned successfully for such things as paperback reprints of important Scottish books (which Canongate Classics now do admirably), a greater Scottish content in the Edinburgh Festival, the defence of the Portrait Gallery against closure and the achievement of a National Theatre. Joy contributed, not only through ACAS, but through the pages of Chapman as well. The final phase of the campaign for a National Theatre, which is now on the verge of success, was launched at a conference held by AdCAS in May 1987. Joy prepared the way for this by publishing articles in *Chapman* before the conference and a full report after the conference itself.

One of Joy's more recent activities has been as one of the four (with Colin Donati, James Robertson and myself) which has produced a document in Scots about the Scots language and what should be done about it on behalf of a cross-party group of the Scottish Parliament. This will be launched this summer and it should lead to a major enhancement of the role of the language in the life of the country. It is after all the vehicle of much of our best literature.

So-called 'small' magazines play a vital part in the life of Scotland. They may be small in circulation, but not in influence nor in developing our self-awareness. They give a platform to new writers who might otherwise not be heard. They allow the expression of ideas which cannot find a place in commercial journalism. It is against these commercial pressures that they have to survive. Under modern conditions, it is a formidable feat for an editor to lead such a magazine for more than 20 years and to reach the hundredth issue. Scotland owes a great debt to her.

# Tessa Ransford

## Stoic

*to Callum Macdonald for St Valentine's day 14th February 1999 when he was in hospital prior to his death on 24th February 1999*

My dearest love's a stoic
who will endure his pain
his deepest grief, believing
nothing is in vain.

Stricken, he will ask no help;
in silence he keeps his fears:
he will suffer, nor seek relief
in anger, talk or tears.

To others he'll give counsel
wise and closely thought:
the individual, universal
entirely interwrought.

His feelings do not interfere
with judgement and good measure
for generosity runs clear
in humour, love and pleasure.

In all that's beautiful and true
of good report and pure
a stoic gives to worth its due
and love that will endure.

## Kashmir

You speak with me in dream – eastern ascetic man
Commune with me whatever we seem to say
   When I ask you where you come from
      Turning you look at me telling "Kashmir".

High land of sapphires, walnut and mulberry
Whose lakes reflect the hills in their violet depths
   Glaciers melt to crystal rivers
      Kingfishers skim amid water lilies.

The Fisher King may dwell in the Shalimar
And we catch fire – to selve and to bear the light
   Whose the face we each reflect?
      Jesus the one and the thousand thousand.

Kashmir afar I love and remember you
Fine wool, fine rice, fine silk such as dreamers find
   Once in life and ever long for
      Now I must rest in the bluebird's promise.

*Callum Macdonald,*
*photograph Tessa Ransford*

Lines Review's *40th anniversary party at the Cafe Royal on*
*Callum's 80th birthday, 4th May 1992, photograph Roddy Simpson*

# Death in the Forest

### by Bertold Brecht

A  man died in Hathoury Wood
where the Mississippi torrents;
he died like an animal, clawing at roots,
gazed up high at the tops of the trees
where a storm howled without remit
for days over the forest.

Two or three stood around
and to shut him up they said:
"Come on, we'll be taking you home now, mate!"
But he butted them and spat at them, cried
"Where? where?" Because he had
neither home nor country.

"How many teeth are left in your jaw?
And how is the rest of your body, let's see!
Die a bit more quietly, can't you,
And not so disgustingly?
Last night we cooked and ate your nag
so why don't you wish yourself in hell?"

Then the forest bellowed around them all;
they observed his clutching at a tree
and they heard how he screamed at them.
They stood and smoked in Hathoury Wood
and watched as he gradually froze to death,
infuriated that he was human like them.

"You've the manners of a shaggy bear!
Be a gentleman, no complaining!
What on earth is the matter with you?"
But he stared at them, weak and desperate:
"I want to live, eat, rest, breathe deep,
and ride away with the wind, like you!"

Not one of his friends could understand.
Three times they shouted "Gentleman please".
Three times he gave a hollow laugh
while soil matted his scratched hands
and he lay rotting in the black pines.

When Hathoury Wood had consumed him
they buried him there, drenched in dew.
Still full of disgust, cold with hate
they buried him in the early morning
in dark undergrowth and weeping branches.

Then they rode away from the dense forest;
looking back once more towards that tree –
the very tree where they had buried the man
who had not desired his ghastly death –
and the tree was crowned with fire.
They crossed themselves hastily, baby-faced,
and galloped like hell for the prairie.

## Translations from Rainer Maria Rilke
### I Love the Dark Hours of my Being

I love the dark hours of my being
wherein my senses drown;
for there my daily life's already done
as in old letters found again
or, like a far-off legend, overcome.

Within the darkness I discover scope
for a wide eternal second life.
I'm like a ripe and rustling tree that leans
above the grave of my own inner child
and warms him with my roots, enfolding him,
unfolding for him that unspoken dream:
the one he lost in elegiac song.

### Magic

From transformation such amazing shapes
appear. Oh do but feel and trust!
To ashes often turn our flaming hopes
yet art can set on fire our very dust.

Magic is here. In the enchanted world
the ordinary word appears translated
but sounds as real as if the ringdove called
to seek its mate, invisible, awaited.

### Nightsky and Falling Star

The sky is vast and full of hidden wonders,
a great storehouse of overflowing planet;
its beginning just too distant from our borders
its end too near for us to contemplate.

A falling star – we glimpse and make our wish,
a sudden shocking glorious connection.
What has begun and how much do we miss?
What is our guilt and what can be forgiven?

### Grant me, Oh Earth

Grant me, Oh Earth, a pure
clay for my pitcher of tears;
let my whole being outpour
all its imprisoned fears.

To fill this earthen vessel
let what I'm containing be freed.
Nothingness is what's evil
for all that has Being is good.

## I Live my Life in Widening Rings

I live my life in widening rings
that work their way through this world of things.
The final one I may not complete
but not because I accept defeat.

I encircle god and the ancient tower
a thousand years in outspreading gyre;
am I falcon or am I storm
or some unending song?

### Now it Should be Time

Now it should be time for the gods
to emerge out of the everyday ...
so as to rifle my house, page upon page.
A new page. Only the wind,
tossing some leaf in a spiral, reaches in here,
turns air over air like shovelling turf:
a new breathing field. Ye god, ye gods,
you, oh who visit again and again,
you who sleep within things,
who rise up in joy, whom we imagine
rinsing your wings at fountains
and who lightly bestow your tranquillity
on what seems full, our busy lives.
Let it be morning for you once more, ye gods.
We are copies. You alone are archetypes.
The world rises with you and that power
of renewal gleams
through our every fracture and failure.

# George Hardie

## Drunk in the Park

No for the first time I saw him
sprauchlan, disjyntit
on the binch, his latest bottle
on the fuitpath haundy.

His een screwed ticht, in pain or juist
ti haud the warl at bay.

Ae flailin airm fechts aff tormentin deils
while obscenities spew frae his slevrin mou.

His fanklt hair lik midden strae
clings roon a face reid as fire,
scabbit and scaured
bi fists or feet or faas.

Wha kens his name, whit his airt
or, hoo he cam ti this?
Aiblins there's some but,
the feck o fowk 'll nevir speir ti ken
but turn awa content
ti let the deivil tak 'm.
As, nae doot, he will
as suin as he is ready.

## Set the Bottle Haundy

Set the bottle haundy
the gless and joug alsweil.
Pour oot a guid gaen meisur
wi water, no ower much
but juist eneuch ti tak the edge.

Noo, again, and yet aince mair.
See hoo the licht
strikes gowden fire frae oot the hairt.
Feel hoo the lowe
gars aa the senses stairt.

Noo's the nicht and noo's the hour
ti scrieve the muckle sang's
been soundan in my heid sae lang.
Thonder she cums, the taislan jaud,
a daunsan reid gowd flame
as hard ti claucht as reek.
See hoo she lichts the ruim,
gars ilka schadaw flee,

while wi her oorie sang
she sair bewitches me.

But aye she daunces,
oot o reach, lauchan aa the while
at this puir drucken fule
wha staichers roon
on fanklt feet.

## Stieve the Keel
### (I M George Mackay Brown)

Stieve the keel and
strang the timmers
gied ti ilka sleek hulled poem
its substance and its shape.

Its buirds o words
weil saisoned i the wund's saut souch
syne, wrocht ti fit
sae perfit its gien space.

The ootraik duin,
ilk ane was launchit furth
upo the boustrous sea
and noo, at ilka compass pynt,
they chairt their coorse
ootower the warld's horizons.

## Approaching Seivinty

In my mind's ear I fancy I can hear
the grey wolf sea howl and snarl.
Syne, faintly see ahint its faemin veil
the shairp fanged skerry wait.

Sall the daurk angels
wha bide on constant watch
abune thon place o wrecks
grant passage thru?

Sall I be gien leave
ti chairt a new laid coorse
ootower a peacefu sea
ti ground at last
on sum faur distant shore?

Or, sall I hear the selkie sing
and pree the savour
o her saut glisked mou
syne hear the deid bell ring?

# Mario Relich

## *John Grierson*

Remember the zealous filmmaker
Whose scorn lay in his glance
So beware of looking askance
At the postman's round
And the miner's sweat
Flickers of film in Grierson's eyes.

His focal vision aimed for truth
Not the sadistic *Schadenfreude*
Others call a slice-of-life.

Hear the lyric energy of booming shipyards
Hammering away in documentary montage
Remote from the labyrinths of personal lives
Men at work, not play, or domestic routines.

He recorded a world now vanished
Collectively inspired, individually hard
Life for many in Britain, at least when in work
Still worse for the workless
Before Big Brother, Stalin being too remote
And Hitler then only ranting
Yet in the twilight of his life
He came to admire Leni Riefenstahl
Overwhelmed by *Triumph of the Will*
That Führer-mad fantasy, a crooked lie
In the shape of a swastika

Declaring it sublime,
Its politics irrelevant.

For Grierson nearing death
Documenting truth
Lost its urgency, but *Drifters*
Still records sea-sprayed risk
If blind to the gathering storm.

## *Saint Francis*

ditch mobile
kill walkman

I see a blackbird
build her nest
another, on patrol

oh yes, freedom
in your head
not in trainers

you jog
if you want
I won't

## Sunglint

The trout
knows nothing
about water

An osprey
nothing at all
about air

Yet its claws
glinting death
tear trout
into prey

## On a Bust of T S Eliot by Jacob Epstein

not even
the ancient busts
of countless Roman proconsuls

quite match

the piercing dignity
and aquiline stare
of the Old World poet

from Missouri

the sculptor
was undoubtedly gripped
by a predatory vision

perhaps a newspaper
at the breakfast table

headlining a rigidly neat
whiteclad figure

handsome
with furrowed face

ageing as well
as the best wine
just as gracefully
and just as exclusively

the frontpage text

quoting
his worried concern
at the instability
of recent events

this boyishly
silver haired man

hardly a Lowell
yet not an Eliot
but a Lodge

the bloody proscriber

of an equally bloody
Vietnamese procurator

quotes Tennyson
in his dispatches
as a substitute
for washing his hands
before Kennedy

like the refined poet
this accomplished diplomat
had slid
from the darkness
of the womb

into the light
of the New World

but they are both
Patrician
and
however worldly
Christian

one
emerged like ore

the other
submerged like scrap
in the transient slagheaps
of the sculptor's mind.

# The Incalculable

## *John Herdman*

It's a right nice early Edinburgh evening near the beginning of July. The temperature's soaring towards the mid-sixties Fahrenheit, there's a pleasant touch of humidity in the air, and though the sky is partially overcast and there are dark, ominous thunderclouds building up over in the south-west, still the sun keeks through from time to time and quite often remains visible for up to ten consecutive minutes. As I stroll relaxedly down Meadowbank, headed for the Anthracite Bar, I think to myself – not for the first time: "What a beautiful people the Scots are!" For they are on display this evening, the Scots, in all their multifarious near-nakedness, taking advantage of the glorious weather, pretending they are in Lanzarote, the men stripped to the waist, the women in bikini tops and shorts, lounging around on the pavements drinking and smoking on every kind of bizarre makeshift seat, on steps at the mouth of stairs, outside pubs, in shop doorways. The Scottish people. A people moving towards freedom. Not yet free, in fact everywhere in chains, yet moving towards freedom, and with what extraordinary grace. Wonderful. I feel like delivering myself of a paean of joy.

I wish I could stay outdoors myself, actually. In a minute or two I will enter the hell of the Anthracite Bar, the smoke, the heat, the noise, the juke box, the one-armed bandit, the discarded crisp bags, the overflowing ashtrays, the beer bellies, the smelly tee-shirts. Why am I not water-skiing on Lake Maggiore? Wind-surfing in the Bahamas? Tending the organic courgette patch in Harpenden? Mere fantasy, my friends. Fate calls and I must obey. Why? I have to meet the boys. The lads. Every Thursday evening for the past seven years or so we have met, give or take a few. (All right, take, you can't add to every.) And for many years now it has been in the Anthracite Bar. At one time we used to meet in the Goth, but people were always getting confused and ending up instead in the Vandal, the Lombard, the Visigoth or even the Pechaneg.

I enter with a sigh and there they all are, over in the usual corner. I'm uncharacteristically the last to arrive. Alec, Erchie, Dougie, and Wee Cookie fae Gorebridge. The boys. A typical macho Scottish Thursday night. Not a woman in sight, I regret to say, and I can't put one in, not even for the sake of political correctness. As I go over to the bar to get my pint Erchie shouts at me, "Hey, Boab, ye're late! Thought ye'd went tae the Artichoke!", and he carries on like this when I join them at the table.

"Mind o the time we wis meetin in the Goth," he says, "an you endit up in the fuckin Pechaneg?"

I blush lightly at the memory of my foolishness.

"No blamin ye, mind," he adds with a conciliatory gesture, "easy done. One lot o barbarians is much like another."

"The Goth's got naething tae dae wi Goths," puts in Dougie with his usual irrelevance. "It's a system of pubs that was stertit in Gothenburg,

*Illustration by Simon Kidd*

Sweden. That's why it's ca'd the Goth. There's a lot of folk don't know that."

This naturally enrages Alec. "Whit dae ye mean, naethin tae dae wi Goths? Gothenburg – fortress of the Goths! That's the meaning o the name!"

"Ay, well, in a manner o speakin …" Dougie's a wee bit disconcerted.

"Fuckin right!"

An awkward silence follows Alec's outburst. Dougie sits looking sulky and crestfallen. Nobody can think what to say. Not even 'The nights are fair drawing in', for that phenomenon is as yet barely perceptible. Too early in the season, too, for "Stags'll be roaring the night". Anyway, this is Edinburgh, not Altnaharra. So in an attempt to restore social harmony I draw from my pocket a leaflet advertising some literary prize inviting us to write almost anything vaguely related to the theme 'Scotland into the New Era'. This really gets them going. The Millennium, so-called, is in the air, after all.

"Scotland *intae* the New Era'?" asks Wee Cookie. "Ah dinnae understand that. Why no 'in'?"

"Too old-fashioned and descriptive," I surmise. "They're looking for something more thrusting and dynamic – something more in tune with the New Era."

"Who says there's going to be a New Era? Nostradamus says the world's going tae end tomorrow. Ay, the morn. 'The great king of terror will come from the sky.' That's whit the boy says."

"That'll be Shug fartin on the flight tae Lanzarote," says Erchie. It is this kind of delicious, demotic wit which, captured and enshrined in literary texts of a shimmering, breath-captivating stylistic beauty which defies rational analysis, has resulted in a recrudescence of Scottish culture in the eyes of the world unpar," says Dougie, regaining his confidence. "'Scotland intae the New Era' disnae make any sense withoot a verb. Am I right or am I wrang?"

When Dougie uses this last phrase he does not do so neutrally. It is like the Latin *nonne* which expects the answer "yes" or *num* which expects the answer "no" (or is it the other way round? – it's all so long ago). Dougie expects the answer "right".

"You're right," I say obligingly, "but there it is."

"Dae nane o ye's care aboot Nostradamus?" yells Cookie. (He's a persistent wee bugger.) "'The war that's prepared in the West' – that's Kosovo. Cannae be anything else. An see Big Slobo – ah reckon he's the Beast 666!"

"That was Aleister Crowley, ya wanker!"

Oh yes, I reflect with delight, this is just what it must have been like in the Enlightenment!

"Ah ken whit they're eftir here," says Alec, tapping the leaflet with the back of his fingers in an authoritative way. "Consensus politics. That's whit they're eftir."

"Cannae have consensus politics withoot a consensus," observes Cookie reasonably. And here Auld Andy, who's sitting at the next table eavesdropping on every word, sees that it's his moment to butt in. (His name's really Andy Auld, but everyone calls him Auld Andy.) Andy is one of those fine old fellows who are still sometimes to be found in Scottish pubs on Thursday evenings, sitting drinking his pint slowly with his kep on, a mildly amused look on his fine old features, his stick planted solidly between his thighs and his hands clasped comfortably over the handle. One time he had nearly got to ask a question on a radio phone-in programme.

"Good afternoon, Christine, good afternoon panel. How are you today? Well, I hope. I am as well as can be expected, thank you. Feeling the cold a bit, but I suppose that's to be expected in one of my advanced years. Now, the point that I would like to make is this. I am seventy-four years of age, and consequently I have been in receipt of the Old Age Pension for some nine years at present. Now, the point that I wish to put to you, Christine, and to the good members of your panel, is this ..." And then, just as he was getting to the point, Auld Andy was suddenly and inexplicably cut off! ("Are you there, Andy? Can you hear me? Andy? ... Oh dear, we seem to have lost Andy. Oh well, never mind. Maybe we'll come back to that later." Or maybe not.) So the world never did get to know what point it was that Auld Andy Auld was so anxious to make. But it is more than probable that it was the identical point to the one he makes now.

"See thae politicians? A' the same. They're aa fu o promises, then wance they get electit that's the end o it. Forget the lot. Juist gaes on the verra same as before. Disnae matter which pairty, they're aa the same."

"If they're aa equally dishonest like Andy here says, 'spose ye could caa that a consensus, eh?"

"Ye've got a point there right enough, Erchie," says Dougie sagely, "ye've got a point there."

Wee Cookie fae Gore's been rather quiet for a bit, but now he pipes up. "Say the warld disnae end the morn like Nostradamus says it will – I'm no sayin he's wrang, mind, but juist for the sake of argument, like – juist say it disnae end eftir aa ... what's this New Era they're on about, what's it aa about?"

"Age of Aquarius, I'd say," Alec opines.

"New Age, like?"

"Ay, somethin like that."

"No the New Era for Scotland, like? Self-determination, demands for greater autonomy, independence in Europe – is that no whit they're talkin about?"

"Naw, I'd say mair tae dae wi the precession o the equinoxes, an in particular wi the spring-point moving fae the sign o the Fishes tae that o the Water Carrier."

Well, at that all hell's let loose in the Anthracite Bar. The boys really get tore in. By the second pint we're discussing naive apocalypticism, numerology, synchronicity, the Antichrist, the Woman Clothed with the Sun, the Knight Faithful and True, and knowledge of astronomy among the astrologers of classical antiquity. By the third we've broached paradigms of the *eschaton* and the way in which prophecy can be disconfirmed without being discredited, and this leads naturally on to a probing and searching debate on recurring myths of empire, decadence and renewal. Then some-one – I expect it's Wee Cookie – brings up the name of Joachim of Fiore! That turns out to be a right can of worms! Was the "New Era" the Age of Aquarius at all – might it not rather be Joachim's Third Age, the Age of the Holy Spirit? Was the Franciscan friar Gerard of Borge San Donnino maybe some seven hundred years out in his calculations, and were we only now about to witness the advent of the 'everlasting gospel' which would replace the gospel of Jesus Christ? Or did it after all have to be understood in this heretical way – could it not be seen as fulfilment rather than supersession? The possibilities are heady and limitless. But I'm afraid that by this time we've lost all sense of time, proportion and human decency: tea-time has come and gone and nobody cares or even gives it a thought. It's wonderful, all the same. Just like it must have been in the Enlightenment.

"Haud on a minute, though," says Dougie suddenly. "Where dae we fit Shcotland intae aa this?"

"It's like MacDiarmid said," says Wee Cookie, sticking his chest out like a pouter pigeon. "'Nothing that can be foreseen and guided is worth a curse; Scotland needs a great upwelling of the incalculable.'"

That stops us in our tracks and no mistake.

"No a lot ye can say about the incalculable," says Erchie with a sigh.

A short silence, then Wee Cookie comes up with another of his quotes.

"'That whereof one cannot speak, thereof one must remain silent.' Wittgenstein."

Thank you, Wittgenstein. Thank you, Cookie.

An entirely beautiful people, the Scots.

# Stanley Roger Green

## *The Short-Cut*

Once a sportive route home from school,
an Indian-file path between tangled woods
and a holly hedge, an urban no-man's land.

Two generations on, now an interlaced
tunnel of greenery flecked with gloom,
a diminished light at either end.

When my grandson has reached manhood
this lane may be a trackless jungle;
he will need a panga or flame-thrower.

A gap in the hedge survives: from here
we stared over a wall at white cricketers
enacting patient summertime rituals.

In Spring archers plied archaic skills;
the soft *thump* as arrows struck targets
resembling insignia on Spitfire's wings.

As woods advance and playing-fields shrink,
more boundaries or bull's-eyes will be hit –
till nature stops play, reclaims its own;

then no more refreshments at the pavilion,
no aloof gull perched on the rusted vane,
when ash and willow split open the roofs
and red tiles clatter on deserted verandahs.

## *Spider in my Bath*

Forgive me, spider, for killing you,
though I doubt if you'll resent it;
in your place I would welcome death
or make no effort to prevent it,
if the only sports you find appealing,
your best means of obtaining delight
are by falling off my bathroom ceiling
or crawling up drains at dead of night.

Too bad I couldn't bear to touch you
and used a sponge for your quietus;
but soon you could be reincarnated,
transmuted to a loftier status,
and given time plus judicial karma
you may elevate to the human drama

So don't despair as I pull the plug,
flush you back to the drains of town;
just pin your hopes on times to come
when you are up and I'm cast down,
you, like a god in the judgement seat,
myself an insect, trembling at your feet!

## *Pendulum Dowsing*

Today, dabbling with the unknown,
I tried dowsing with a pendulum
made from twine and a leather button.

I held it over an official document:
it twitched like a bored clerk
wishing it was five o' clock,
then it fell limp
like a corpse on a scaffold.

I dangled it over a geologist's report:
there were impatient oscillations
as if the facts were already known
and I was wasting its time.

Next I let it read my latest poem,
of bay horses charging over snow-fields.
The button pranced around so wildly
I had to keep a tight rein!

Suddenly I thought of an old flame,
whose image lives on in a sketch
I keep hidden in my attic,
among other things.

Yet I'm loth to apply the pendulum
lest it spins and lets fly like a bolas
entangling the heart a second time.

I began to dread this puppeteer
who manipulates my nerves
with such weird art.
Am I no longer to have a free hand?

If we're now to work in tandem,
who will be blamed for mistakes?
Not the invisible culprit, you can be sure,
who hides in my basement
among unknown things.

## *What Fun it Was*

What fun we had then, setting up house,
scouring junk-shops for cheap curios
and *objets-d'art*, gathered as Australian
bower-birds do, to decorate a unique nest,
making it sparkle to astonish friends
and prove how we shared the same tastes.

A pot-bellied carboy found in Leith Docks,
with a hessian shade it became a lamp
to cast a glow on our prize exhibit,
a blue-glaze, lion-clawed fake Ming vase.

A painted Chinese ginger jar for fifty-pee;
the armadillo carapace formed as a basket,
eyes shut and jaws clamped on a scaly tail,
like a mythical serpent devouring itself.

A clay death-mask of Beethoven for a fiver,
we hung from the bathroom's toilet cistern
to shock guests when they put on the light!
It never failed to amuse; what fun it was.

No one's laughing now – now removal vans
are at the door, the spoils of old forays
divided hastily, packed and borne away,
except for relics whose appeal had worn.

As vehicles move off I stuff remnants
of shared tastes in bin-bags.In a cupboard
Beethoven, cradled by an armadillo, glares
at the intruder like a disturbed hermit crab.

## *Love Song*

Without you by my side
the Islands of the Blest
would seem as inviting
as mudflats at low tide,
the Gardens of the Hesperides
a post-industrial landscape,
the golden orchard a wind-farm.

Without you there beside me,
the Petit Trianon or Taj Mahal
in their heyday, would seem
as luxurious as army Nissen huts
in Essex, in midwinter.

Compared with the memory
of your slightest touch,
zephyrs from Mount Helicon
would abrade my epidermis
like eczema or emery-cloth.

Without your voice's echo
in the mind's ear, melodies
of nightingales would rasp
like rooks with laryngitis,
the warble of heavenly choirs
seem like maudlin songsters
in downtown Yankee barber shops.

End this suspense, come back
and I'll speak plain as pikestaffs,
no bush in danger of a beating,
with no hyperbole or bathos
to mislead you,
for as you know I deplore exaggeration.

## *To a House Mouse*

Most nights, arriving late, my kitchen
is the scene of a long-running farce,
when a sleek brown well-fed shadow
dodges on tiptoe between toaster
and blender, hoovering up crumbs
*en route* to a skirting bolthole.

If I block it up, another will appear,
for that's part of our routine, like
his side-stepping my hamfisted efforts
to zap him among worktop gadgets.
He even hams up his casual stage exit.

From traps I set he snaffles cheese
with the delicacy of a safecracker, so
only my knuckles are caught. Inventors
of hi-tech devices have toiled in vain,
but don't ask me to empty cat-litters.

Sometimes doing the rounds, eyes meet,
and in that flash of contact, he sneers;
my performance insults his bravado,
for this leader of mice needs action,
a craftier opponent, a domestic Nimrod.

I can't compete – not only is youth
on his side, he hears genetic voices,
of nocturnal mammals in fern forests,
by dawn or twilight adept at dodging
pterodactyls' beaks, the feet of dinosaurs.

Giants ruled the roost in those days,
lords of creation; while his ancestors
lurked in the wings, biding their time,
and ours, hardly a blip on the horizon,
before the walk-on part as a stunted ape.

## It Seemed only a House

As we were introduced it seemed to say,
looking down its long Georgian nose,
"I wonder if you are quite our sort?"

We were both beggars of a kind,
neither could afford to be choosy.
It hadn't seen a lick of paint
for years, an overhaul in a century.
Nor did I care for the expression
on its smug but cracked façade.
Subsidence might have explained
its status of a listed building.

"You had better come in," it said,
reading my mind; "but wipe your feet!"
I did both, and a deal was struck.
The house would allow eccentric guests,
impromptu parties, domestic squabbles,
and the clatter of a grand piano
pursuing Bach's well-tempered fugues.

In return I'd paint walls and ceilings,
burnish ornamental brass escutcheons,
make pine floors gleam like chestnuts,
repair the Adamesque décor and ignore
the possibility of ill-tempered ghosts.

Then my own facade was riven by faults
no paint could hide nor builder mend...
Shutting the front door for the last time
was less like severing a partnership
than turning my back on an old friend.

# Gerry Stewart

## *Epiphany*

At the gunshot's echo, crows lift from the stubbled field, an old woman's shawl sweeping across the sky. She waits to hear the sparkling shower of glass from the church's empty well, but hears only wind in feathers.

The church stands on the hilltop surrounded by willow trees, their long branches fluttering against the weathered boards like an old maid's hair ribbons. Her oversized boots drag as she walks, gathering dust in the upturned cuffs of her sister's jeans.

A small boy jumps from long grass edging the field, spooking a grazing colt. It runs to the fence's border, ears thrown back along its neck, snorting its panic. As quickly it stops to stare at the boy.

He is the colour of sepia photographs, golden rust on the edges of his hair, elbows and hands, pale grayed jeans and eyes. Along his arms droop bat-like wings made from an ancient lace-up corset. He jumps and flaps his wings; swinging out into the wheat rows in a dance of the sky. She rushes to the church. He follows, zig-zagging around, stepping on her heels like a puppy. The nave brightens with sunlight as he pushes open the door.

The glass remains dark on the floor, sopped in blood. She catches the boy by the shoulder to keep him from running onto the shards. She doesn't want to hear the dry, dead crunching beneath his sneakers. They walk up the aisle side by side to the altar.

She crosses herself but he stills her hand. The sun fades behind the gray rack of clouds. He turns on the light in the vestibule.

A single uncovered bulb brings the room to life, saints and angels fallen to their knees among the willow leaves. The boy runs into their midst and tosses up handfuls of coloured glass. They drift out the windows, butterflies caught on the breeze.

## *Dispossessed by the Rain*

She lets the rain fill the space he abandoned. It draws a long finger along the part in her hair, runs down her nose across faded summer freckles. She could forget her accent, her anger in the water's delicate brush.

She wants to sink into the flat tombstones and clean-edged grass of the Cathedral and remain in this stillness. The mound of the Necropolis rises above her, its gnarled fists and fingers of monuments over-run by greenery. She is unbowed by Knox's flat stare and admonishing arm.

She stands on the slick black stone in the square's centre, grounding herself. She is restrained by stained glass held in place with blackened cages. Puddles varnish stones into broken mirrors, casting her glare back.

She walks down the tilted street beneath the sky set up like an orange-green screen. The wind catches a crushed flower from her jacket. It tumbles under the wheels of a bus, a lemon-green Chinese paper umbrella, its matchstick arms and toothpick handle splintered, bent. It bleeds into the rain-slicked road.

## Control

The cat rolls onto its back and bakes itself golden brown on the radiator shelf. It squints at the new red Buddha beside him who wishes he could untangle from his perpetual lotus position to join him in a sprawl.

She moves into Toe Balance yoga asana and pushes her breathing along her diaphragm. She doesn't trust her own balance and falls forward. She needs to go back to the beginning positions, to regain focus.

The house holds his memory like a breath. Simple conversations remain curled in the Roman blind, elaborate ruined dinners settle amongst the pictures on the mantelpiece.

The cat jumps down and wraps itself around her ankles, tail to nose. Another ten minutes of her workout before she will feel she has brought her body into the new day properly. The brown cat, nudging her with its head, insists it's his time. She sits on the floor for the Side Stretch, reaching out with one hand and rubbing his back with the other.

The cat conspires with him. They play ghostly games of chess, moving one piece through the night's silence. She never touches the board. The cat claims his pillow and in the morning kneads her back with its soft paws.

Her calf muscles feel the stretch, not quite a burn. She notices brown cat hair covers the rug. She has cleared away the clutter and made space for her things. She crawls into a bed where the duvet is in the shape of her body. The cat, bored, washes an ear with a methodical slick and smooth, watching her over its paw.

She tries to pull herself into The Tree. Her book says this asana is used to build a foundation for further positions. Balanced on one foot she can start over, reshape her muscles. This will become part of her new routine.

## Prayer

They walk beneath olive trees towards the white shrine. Coils of snakeskin shade crawl over the bark and their faces. Crossing herself she enters the cool cell.

He remains outside, smoking. His echo moves past her as he talks with children who have followed them from the village like a pack of dogs.

How many generations of monks in stovepipe hats and grimy black clothes kneeled in this darkness, how many old women crossed themselves before this ikon and began their penance by sweeping dirt and refilling candles? They had a focus for their devotion when they stepped through the door.

Hanging candles swing with her whispers, the once reassuring prayer. The thrum within her will not let her words reach the wide-eyed saints.

She longs for his body, washing away the heat in the hotel's tiny shower. The traffic raced below as they lay on the stripped bed, lingering to touch through the wall of humidity. She cannot hold those memories distant here, the rich scent of henna in her hair, strong, iced-coffee on his tongue.

El Greco sought escape for an internal fire unquenched by the stark soil of Greece. In Spain's tossed landscape he rediscovered the ikons of his fathers. The solemn eyes of his figures, their acidic, thin faces drawn up the canvas were freed from the weight of sins, washed with a clear, alien light pushing away the darkness.

She cannot find passion in this empty room. She wants to be supported by his arms and her faith, even among the glaring eyes of these mountains. Use both stone and flesh melded together as a foundation. Words do not hold the strength she needs and she returns to the sharp sunlit heat.

## Foreign Soil

The harbour draws away from an anchored ship and with the force of a proffered kiss pulls it close again. She watches the fluid motion until her breath keeps time. It is like falling into sleep with that sudden jerk back into awareness.

Waiters hourly replace her empty glass with full without a break in rhythm. Retsina catches her throat with an after-thought of pine forests.

A group of local fishermen move to a nearby table, their clothes ripe with brine. A basket handed to the kitchen staff is transformed into a plate of delicately fried fish, smaller than a pinkie. Sliced lemons, salad and bread follow glasses of ouzo.

As the men start eating, a foreign couple stumble to the table behind a large native man. Joking with the men, he half-heartedly translates for the couple. They laugh politely and speak halting Greek. They sit to eat, though the woman only picks at a bit of bread. After a while she falls asleep against her partner's shoulder.

The watcher leaves them floating at the edge of her vision, like swallows under the eaves. She would also have looked out of place if she had been doing anything besides drinking. She could drink anywhere, in any language.

Ulysses once sailed these straits searching for his home. Each island lays claim to his exploits. The local people speak of him as if he landed on their shores only last week.

That is why she loses herself in this ancient land. Her past is no longer carried around like over-stuffed baggage, but is continually taking place around her, in as simple a moment as a woman sleeping beside her lover, the laughter of a communal meal. It will never be forgotten or rewritten. Here she exists with her past in the present tense.

## *Walking Chichen Itza*

i breathe the same air
she once did looking to her gods
in treetop heavens
those faces carved in stone
found still in men and boys
selling water and trinkets
to intruders entering their jungle

i walk down roads dust-red
past the gates of cool hotels
her ancient spirit burns through
as a quetzal's green wings
emerge from her back
she lifts herself above
cameras and tour guides

she circles the unearthed mounds
to reveal the snake they once held
coiled around the trees' silence
a white temple lost in deep growth
roughened by rains reappears
jaguars and warriors form from mist
to bow before her

she throws her soul back
to the darkening night cries

did they toss her fighting
into the sinking cenote
she would float
fingering brown waves
face turned to the sun
laughing as it called for her death

did she speak to her feathered gods
bringing their words of light
back to her people
with a shallow breath

she breathes now
opening the frayed doors
imprinted within her

and i pass through
to the pyramid's heights
the foreign voices falling below
grasping for stones
of the way she once knew

*Chichen Itza* – a Mayan site; *cenote* – a sinkhole used as a well and holy site. Sacrificial victims were thrown in and if they survived they became messengers of the gods.

## In a Stavanger Café

Abandoning the dark cloak of the storm,
she fades into the waiting café.
The candles flicker to a jungle beat.

The white king serves tea,
braiding the ceiling nudes
with the chequered floor.

She has fallen down no rabbit hole,
just the stairs of the tower hanging
over the town, its sleepy eyes closed.

Fairy tale characters come in and out,
laughing and calling. The immortal Caesar,
curled up in his corner niche, smiles
like that English county cat.
Sharp tongues purr fluent language.

She tries to predict her future in a cup
of raspberry tea, but the leaves are blurred.
Voices creep in with the opening
door, fighting the flow of music.

Outside all is swept clean
by the wind. It ushers her out
beneath dull street-lights,
into the city's arms at long last.

## Reflections During a Bassline

He offered to cut out my heart
and pull it from my rib cage through a slit
just above the breast he lay against.

The lights spun around the room like water
in a fishbowl. I was growing too big,
swirling around with rusty scales.
I knew I would soon jump out and travel
past castles not made of plastic.

I wanted to be corrupted before I left.
I tried to lose myself on the edge of his solo,
watching shadow girls dance on the wall.
Heads down, braceleted in silver
they wrapped their uncombed hair
around me in loose knots and pulled me forward.

The bass's throb fell from the air
as if it were bronzed. I stroked it
as it purred around my knees.

I wanted to sleep against the stretch of his back.
Under the string of lights he held only himself.
The music buried me in heavy sand, his face
in my hair, smelling the lace of salt, sex and hash.

I rewrote all the stutters and silences
in the morning as I walked home –
no red carpet laid out for me down the alley.
Didn't he know my heart was already gone
from the place he reached into?

## *Still Holding My Breath*

*Inspired by the painting of Eleanor Reeves*

A moss-grown face
of sad disdain.

She hides behind
the water-bleed curtain of hair.
Leaving her half-finished
amongst coffee stains
with last night still
smeared under her eyes.

The moon rises in her brows.

Mermaid thrown
on sand, tossed with
seaweed and memories.
Broken oars and candles
left to melt away.

A cast-off mist flows
over her turned away,
rain-smoothed chin.

She clouds over,
her lashes smudged
blue moods.

Catch the scent
of the last cigarette lit
in impatience,
waiting for the phone
to ring. She never answers,
leaving it to echo
across the flat.

Drawn curtains
and the scent
of an unopened room.

Still Holding my Breath *by Eleanor Carlingford Reeves*

# The Poet and the Psychopath

## *Hugh McMillan*

Joe McIntyre deserved to be a famous writer. Ever since he'd been a boy, scribbling love poetry to the girl next door, he'd dreamed of literary fame and had always been convinced that one day his name would stand with Seamus Heaney and Philip Larkin as one of the century's greats. To that end, he'd spent years churning out screeds of verse but, by his early 40s, had only achieved a very moderate and local success. He became embittered. "A sometimes underrated writer", the editor of a small magazine had said. Joe did not underrate himself and knew exactly what was wrong. The poetry scene, he thought, was dominated by an élite of self-serving individuals who conspired to keep newcomers out. They had developed a house style with cute intellectual references, meaningless line breaks and little rhyme. Joe wrote more muscular poetry, in the style of Ted Hughes, about natural subjects like ferrets and budgerigars. Joe was convinced that while a coterie remained in charge he would reach old age without achieving his creative ambitions, one of which was to teach creative writing in an all-girls American college. He dreamed of murdering those he saw as the main culprits but lacked the nerve and the practical abilities to carry it out. Besides, Joe knew that there was a second or third rank of equally insipid writers ready to take their place should the first lot be justifiably, or accidentally, wiped out.

Joe wrote a series of long and well argued letters to newspapers and literary publications outlining his position but, like his poems, none of them were published. He'd gone to see the local writer in residence. She'd promised him help but, soon after their meeting, she'd moved out to a small inaccessible croft to work on her forthcoming anthology of menstrual poems. It occurred to Joe that everyone was getting published because they had a gimmick. Because they wrote in some impenetrable dialect, because they were handicapped, or women. Joe struggled to find an angle himself but somehow being one of the school of short-sighted, balding writers of ferret poems was not enough. His iron will was such, however, that he could not give up, and, through the increasingly dark and desperate months, he continued to recycle his pointless little poems, spending the small amount of money he'd inherited from his parents on huge amounts of brown envelopes and broad green acres of second class stamps. Then, one day, he met, or rather re-met, Kevin McCutcheon, a psychopath.

He'd known Kevin from years before when they had both attended a writing class run by a fat man called Justin Everard Duckley, who had since, to Joe's incandescent rage, produced a slim volume of poems short listed for a major book award. Kevin had only been interested in writing lurid crime fiction and had left the course early. Joe assumed that he had abandoned any literary ambitions and so entered into their new found relationship with at least one dangerous misapprehension.

They had met together in the Douglas Arms and, since it had been their only real point of contact, had begun talking about the writing course, a conversation that inevitably led to Joe's agenda of injustices. Kevin was impressed by the other man's passion on the subject for, ironically, in spite of having no apparent talent at all for writing poetry, Joe did have considerable talent in the field of complaining about it.

"Just cos I'm not trendy, just cos I'm not gay, just cos I've not seen caribou galloping across the tundra, just cos I'm not living in a big city crawling up the right people's arseholes doesn't mean I'm no good," he sobbed, over his eighth pint of Guinness.

"You could move," said Kevin. "Or travel and see interesting things."

"It'd be no use," cried Joe, "I'm a man of my environment. A woodland poet. Take me out of trees I'd be useless."

Kevin, having heard Joe's seminal work 'Ferret at Dawn' six times, had concluded that he was useless anyway but, being a highly intelligent and complex man, he listened to Joe's slow disintegration into self-pity with interest, and no small compassion. He wanted to help. He also hated Justin Everard Duckley and had many times thought about killing him.

"Of course," Kevin said at last, "poets usually become famous when they're dead." Joe's pitiable weeping was now attracting the attention of the bar staff but he managed to stutter, "Only if someone takes them up. Decides they're brilliant. None of these wankers are going to take me up, dead or not."

"Or," said Kevin, "become famous by the nature of their death."

Joe wiped his eyes with a grubby handkerchief. "What do you mean?"

"Well, think of it", said Kevin. "Chatterton, Baudelaire. Dissipation, death and poetic fame."

Joe shook his head, but at least had stopped weeping. "They were young, and I couldn't be dissipated where I live. They'd move me to a council house."

After a long pause, Kevin leaned across the table and whispered "I could kill you … In a really, really imaginative and innovative way. It would make all the papers. And it needn't hurt."

Joe stared across at him. "It would make all the papers because it was a gruesome crime." He was speaking slowly, as if addressing an imbecile. "You'd become famous, I wouldn't. I would just be some bloke who keeps writing crap ferret poems who's had his head cut off by a really gifted and clever killer."

Kevin's eyes were unblinking. "But what if," he said with growing excitement, "a manuscript of poetry was found shortly afterwards which seemed to prefigure the death, predict it in every detail, mirror the feelings of a man who knows exactly the imminence and the manner of his death but is powerless to prevent it." Joe shivered. "You could call it," added Kevin quietly, 'Stalked by the Reaper'.

Joe shook his head. "But, how would … ?"

Kevin interrupted, his face flushed with enthusiasm. "Yes. It would work. You finish the manuscript, give it to me, and after the … deed, I'll send it to the papers and publishers, pointing out as a friend and confidant of the deceased how chilling and resonant the poems are and how much of the detail seems to mirror the murder, or at least such detail as has been released by the police and the press!"

Of course the idea was ridiculous. Joe knew it even as he staggered away from the pub. Poetry without forest life was beyond him anyway. The next morning he put the little card with Kevin's phone number at the bottom of a drawer and forgot about it. Two months later, though, months spent in the usual revising of poems, sending them off to, and receiving them back from more and more obscure publications, Joe was informed in a matter-of-fact way by his doctor that he had stomach cancer, and had probably had it for some time. The prognosis was not good, the original centre had spread, surgery was not an option. There followed weeks of debilitating treatment during which he did not lift his pen once. His focus became drips and sheets and drugs and nausea. He seemed to be disappearing from the world, shrinking into himself. In all this misery and darkness, one flame still burned: his desire, his obsession, to be immortal through his writing. Maybe because he was depressed, but more and more in sleepless, sick nights he thought of Kevin McCutcheon and his idea, began to visualise the stark black cover of 'Stalked by the Reaper', could see his own name in gold letters under the title and just above the T S Eliot Award sticker. So, after his second course of treatment, when he had regained a little strength, he phoned Kevin McCutcheon, and arranged for them to meet.

Kevin was sorry to hear about the illness, listened to Joe with real sympathy and interest, hoped that he would be better soon. When Joe brought up the subject of their previous conversation in the pub, he didn't scoff as Joe had feared, or laugh it off as a joke. Instead he cupped his hands under his chin and listened intently. He looked like some kind of bank manager.

"Of course in these matters," he said, "it is the practicalities that count. Everything must be worked out to the last detail and with great care. All must be in place. This is not a murder, after all, rather a business plan."

Joe nodded. Kevin resumed. "You can leave all the logistics to me and when it comes to the actual deed … " he coughed discreetly, "I can promise you'll feel nothing. We'll use drugs. There will be no pain."

Joe agreed. "No pain," he repeated. He'd had enough pain. Kevin stared into Joe's eyes. "You write the poems. Just concentrate on that. You are the artist in that field."

Although he entered into the work with no great optimism, Joe found that the poems came easily. They had a force and urgency completely lacking in his previous work. His time in hospital had added an extra dimension, a new vocabulary, into his poetry which, though dark, was now compelling. He found himself writing a series of poems about his mortality, his feelings of impending death, which far excelled anything he'd ever written before. Into these poems he laced tantalising details as to the place (a remote barn), the time they'd chosen for his death (Halloween), and, as importantly, the manner of it. Kevin had announced this on a day out they'd had to a country pub. It was Autumn, leaves were red and falling, but somehow trees didn't seem to matter to Joe anymore. He was a real poet, and soon his poetry would live forever.

"I thought I'd slice you completely in half," said Kevin, "top to bottom. Don't think it's ever been done before as far as I can see."

At such times Joe had to concentrate on the end goal. After all, he wouldn't feel a thing. "I'll need a chainsaw. Would you buy one? It'll be pretty messy." He shook his head apologetically. "No avoiding it, I'm afraid. All these intestines, brain matter. Not to speak of blood."

Joe shuddered. Well, his intestines hadn't been very good to him anyway. He wondered what they'd look like gleaming on the cobbled floor of the barn. He was already forming the lines of his last poem in his head.

Kevin reminded him of details of their last rendezvous, reassuring him with a measured calm that recalled, for Joe, the doctors in the hospital. They shook hands in a civilised manner and parted. In the two weeks, Joe typed up the collection, tidied it up and bound it between sheets of card. He wrote 'Stalked by the Reaper: Last poems by Joe McIntyre' and sent it, along with a brand new chainsaw he'd bought, to the address supplied by Kevin McCutcheon. All was organised, and for the best.

At 11.20 pm on October 30th Joe got into his car and drove into the country. Kevin had assured him it would take about 30 to 35 minutes. It did. He parked his car by the farm track and, his breath coning, moved towards the isolated farm building. The moon was high and round in the sky. With a few yards to go he paused for just a moment and listened to the wind in the branches, the distant bark of a dog. He would never hear these things again, but it didn't matter. He looked at his watch. It was midnight when he opened the door to the barn.

He must have fainted at the sight of Kevin McCutcheon's dismembered body because, when he came to, the police cars were already blaring along the little country road. The chainsaw, covered of course in Joe's fingerprints, lay among the shining viscera. Kevin's hands, what were left of them, were gloved. It was, after all, very cold. As he was arrested, Joe was wondering, almost with admiration, how a person could inflict so much damage on himself. There was no sign of drugs.

Kevin McCutcheon's book, 'Stalked by the Reaper', was published the following Spring to overwhelming critical acclaim. Seamus Heaney called it "a superhuman vision of life and death almost without parallel in this century, or perhaps in any other." It won fourteen major awards and is currently being made into a movie with Robert de Niro as Kevin McCutcheon.

Joe McIntyre, after his defence was rejected by the judge as a callous and incredible attempt to "manipulate the boundaries of belief and blacken the character of a man with almost limitless artistic potential", was sentenced to life imprisonment. Having had successful treatment for stomach cancer, he is now at Peterhead Special Unit where he has shown no aptitude at all for creative projects.

# Christopher Whyte

## *Air cho òg 's gu bheil thu, air cho guanach*

Air cho òg 's gu bheil thu, air cho guanach,
a dh'aindeoin t' fhèinealachd, t' àrdan, do neo-
sheasmhachd, rinn thu pearsa daonnda dhìom

is cha b' e sin a bh' annam gus an t-àm.
Shoirbhich e leam an còmhnaidh fuireachd air
taobh thall dhe bhalla glainn' a dhealaich mi

bho ghnothaichean is bho oidhirpean chàich,
a b' àbhaist dhomh neulachd a sgaoileadh air
le m' anail thais, gus m' fhalach is mo dhìon.

Cha bhi an tèarmann soirbh sin agam tuilleadh.
'S mi dèiligeadh riut, chaill mi maighdeannas
's motha as fhiach na maighdeannas a' chuirp,

's ath-chosnadh cho do-dhèanta. Ach carson
a b' fheudar seo uile bhith coimhlionta
le cràdh 's le call? Dh'iarrainn do shealbhachadh

air dòigh 's nach b' urrainn dhut bhith 'g èaladh ás.
Ach tha thu mar sheòmar, is mi ga chur
an òrdugh gach oidhche, thèid bun-os-cionn

roimh uair an dùsgaidh, air dòigh 's gu feum mi
gach rud a sgioblachadh uair eile. 'N e
sin freumh an àigh a bheir thu dhomh, gu bheil

thu ri t' ath-shealbhachadh gach latha den domhan?
Mas fìor seo, ciamar a dhèanainn do chall?
Seallaidh mi mum thimcheall air an t-saoghal,

an fhìrinneachd, gach rud ga thairgse dhomh
mar chòrn a dh'fhairtlicheas e orm daonnan
a thraoghadh, dreuchd do-sheachanta mo bheòil.

Tha fadachd air mo bhilean ri do bheul.
Bha mi ro fhad' a' trasgadh dhe do phògan.
Fadachd, trasgadh, iarraidh, togradh, àgh...

*

*For all that you are young,*
*for all that you are fickle,*
*in spite of your selfishness, your arrogance, your in-*

*constancy, you have made me fully human,*
*something I never was until now.*
*I had always managed to keep myself*

*on the far side of a glass wall*
*that separated me from the affairs and the approaches*
*of others, and on which I would spread*

*a mist of my moist breath, to veil and protect me.*
*I will no longer have that facile refuge.*
*In my dealings with you I lost*

*a virginity more valuable by far than the body's,*
*and equally irretrievable. But why*
*had all that to be accomplished by pain and loss?*

*I wanted to possess you*
*so that you could never steal away.*
*But you are like a room which, arranged by me every night,*

*goes tapsalteerie before the morning,*
*forcing me to tidy everything up once more.*
*Is that the root of the joy you give me,*

*that you have to be repossessed every new day that dawns?*
*If this is so, how could I ever lose you?*
*I look around at the world, at reality, at everything*

*being proffered to me like a drinking horn*
*which I will never be done draining,*
*my mouth's ineluctable vocation.*

*My lips long for your mouth.*
*I have fasted too long from your kisses.*
*Longing, fasting, yearning, pleasure, ecstasy …*

translated by Michel Byrne

## *Nan robh thu air bàs fhaotainn*

Nan robh thu air bàs fhaotainn, nan robh 'n ionnsaigh
a rinneadh leat ort fhèin air tighinn gu buil,
nan robh an corp a chunnaic mi 's e sìnte
mach air a' chabhsair lom gun deò da-rìribh,
bhitheadh fad do thuiteim bhon uchd-bhalla
de mheatailt thruim, a bha peant dubh, 's e boillsgeach
a' còmhdachadh gach uile mais' is car dheth,
co-ionann ris an sgarachdainn a th' ann
eadar a' chuid tha beò 's a' chuid tha marbh.
Ach bha do shùilean lainnireach, a rinn mi
an coimeas aon uair ri dearcan a' snàmh
air uachdar aibhne dian-shiùbhlaich, 's an dà
shoilleireachd a' co-fharpais le chèile.
Rinn thu sgreuch, a chuir mi seachad uairean
's làithean a' feuchainn ri a mhìneachadh,
mar sgreuch aig beathach a dh'aithnicheas cràdh

cho geur 's gun tèid e thairis air a shaoilsinn,
ach bha cràdh daonna cuideachd ann, is tu,
's dòcha, a' tuigsinn gun do dh'fhairtlich ort
an t-uallach nach bu deònach a chur dhìot,
do bheatha fhèin. An uair a dh'fhaighnich iad
gu dè an lath' a bh' ann, bha thu gam freagairt,
'nad chànain fhèin, is bha am poileasman
coibhneil, 's na daoine-eiridinn dìcheallach.
Chaidh do thogail air clàr rag, is rinn thu
faite-gàire leis na thuirt iad. Bha
am bàs a' caogadh oirnn, is b' e do làmh
a chuir an cùirtean sin ri taobh car sealain,
ach cha do sheall e dìreach oirnn, is dh'fhan
an dithis againn le 'r cuid bheathannan
fhathast 'nar dùirn, gu ball-chritheach, ach slàn.

*

*If you had died, if the attack*
*you made on yourself had succeeded,*
*if the body I saw stretched out on the bare*
*pavement had really been without breath,*
*the distance you fell from the parapet*
*of wrought iron, with gleaming black paint*
*coating every twist and flourish,*
*would have been equal to the distance that exists*
*between the living and the dead.*
*But your eyes were brilliant, eyes I once compared*
*to berries swimming on the surface*
*of a swift-moving stream,*
*one brilliance competing with the other.*
*You gave a cry which I spent hours*
*and days struggling to interpret,*
*like an animal's cry when it experiences*
*a degree of pain it cannot contemplate;*
*but there was human pain there, too,*
*as if you realised you had not managed*
*to shed the unwilling burden, your own life.*
*When they asked you what day it was,*
*you answered, in your language. The policeman*
*was kind, and the nurses were business-like.*
*They lifted you onto a rigid board. You smiled*
*at what they said to you. Death winked*
*at us, and yours was the hand which put*
*that curtain aside briefly. But he did*
*not look directly at us, and we both*
*were left with our lives trembling on our palms,*
*trembling, but whole.*

translated by the author

# Gael Turnbull

## *from A Zigzag Wake*

Marking, adjusting course
    inscribed by time
against tidal current, vagaries of wind
    each shift, each tack
as furrow that divides
    that calls to us, that signals
what was from what might be
    as image and reflection
glimpsed far astern
    that we reflect upon

or through a window, over shoulder
    as once, yawning awake
not quite yet dawn, coming into Dijon
    rain puddles in the gutters
velvet drizzle, charcoal light
    with passers-by, their feet, each stride
each impact mirrored, shimmering
    and droplets, breaking surfaces
each pulse, a wavering
    as the bus jolts forward, nearing halt
to reach a station, make connection
    in time, on time, through time
by arrival to make welcome
    then depart.

## *Some Assumas for Bluna*

*Je fuis,/ donc, je suis* – Bluna

Seize the occasion
for evasion.

Feet
are for retreat.

Rejoice
to avoid choice.

Don't believe
and you won't grieve.

Decisions
are prisons.

Aim
invites blame.

Distraction
is the best action.

I scram
therefore I am.

## Amorous Greetings in Terms of 'Maturity'

It may improve malt whiskies
even some wines, but not much else
to recommend the inevitable
accumulation of years

except to sharpen the appreciation
of the caress of your lips,
the savour of the assurance
of your arms folding mine.

## Amorous Greetings in Terms of 'The Barefoot Contessa'

Perhaps it was just
that she couldn't find
a comfortable style
or size anywhere
while we can celebrate
the perfect fit.

## Fragment

Smiling, she spoke it
(He, with furrowed brow):
"What is love, poet?"
He kissed her,
"How else can I know it
but with you, here, now?"

## Always

the lure of just
one poem more ...
as if the reshuffled
words might yet
reveal that whatever
It is we're
persisting for?

# Something Rich and Strange
## The Scottish Tradition in Dramatic Writing
### Donald Campbell

Last summer, I placed 22 playscripts in the Scottish Theatre Archive at Glasgow University Library. This deposit, which includes contemporary and historical plays, adaptations, solo plays and musicals, represents the sum total of my work to date. All these have been professionally produced, a number have received awards, one or two have been published and some have even enjoyed the privilege of occasional revival. The main intent of my work for the stage is to celebrate human values in difficult circumstances. To do this, it is important to challenge all kinds of stereotypes and to contest certain received opinions. While I may seek to accomplish this in a variety of ways, I am usually aware of working in a Scottish context.

For some people, however, this concept represents a contradiction in terms. A few years ago, at the Netherbow Arts Centre, I gave a lecture on the history of Scottish dramatic authorship. This covered the work of Allan Ramsay, Archibald Pitcairne, John Home, Archibald MacLaren, William Murray, James Ballantyne, George Reston Malloch, J M Barrie and James Bridie. After my lecture, I was treated to a harangue from a member of the audience, who as good as told me that I had spent the last hour telling lies. This gentleman identified himself as an Associate Director at the Traverse theatre, he thought there were *no* Scottish playwrights? there had *never been* any Scottish playwrights and *there would never be* any Scottish playwrights! Not unnaturally, I felt more than a little insulted by this observation and dealt with him accordingly, but I knew where he was coming from.

Little more than forty years ago, the establishment of the Independent Television Authority drove the last of many nails into the coffin of the private sector of Scottish professional theatre. To all intents and purposes, the theatre ceased to be a popular art form, capable of drawing a mass audience from every section of the community and became what it remains today – a minority interest. Within less than a decade, scarcely a theatre in the land remained in business without being in receipt of some form of grant or subsidy. By the time my writing career began, at the end of the '60s, any idea of a popular audience – if one discounts the pantomime season – simply did not exist. Not only that, but the theatrical forms that the infusion of subsidy had allowed to survive into the television age were not very attractive as far as I was concerned. There were, broadly speaking, two varieties of those; one fairly new and the other surprisingly old.

The first one – the new one – was what I like to call 'amenity theatre', founded on the idea, first mooted in the '20s, that theatre is a kind of social education, making a contribution to the quality of life. The companies of Perth, Dundee, St. Andrews, Pitlochry and, to some extent, the Lyceum in Edinburgh and the Citizens in Glasgow, owe much of their support to the belief that the existence of a theatre company in any given community adds a bit of tone to the place. My chief complaint against this rather worthy approach was, and is, its tendency to encourage artistic timidity, to favour what Terence Rattigan used to call the 'Aunt Edna' audience. As a theatregoer, I have always had a certain degree of affection for such an audience, and, as a playwright, I have had reason to be grateful to not a few of them – but, as a young writer who was just beginning to find his voice, I can't say I had much enthusiasm for Aunt Edna.

I had even less enthusiasm for the second form of theatre that came into its own then. The studio theatre encouraged at places like the Traverse in Edinburgh and the Close in Glasgow liked to think of itself as very new and up-to-the-minute. 'Trendy' was a word that was beginning to gain currency then, but there were other words, too. Words like 'innovative', 'avant garde', 'experimental' and, of course (that great Scottish weasel word) 'international' were bandied about. In fact, what was re-emerging was a very old tradition – the tradition of the private theatre, in which wealthy and learned ladies and gentlemen presented plays for the benefit of their friends and social equals. This kind of theatre has never moved me, except occasionally and a negative way. Sometimes, watching a play on the stage of the Traverse in the late sixties, I would find that I had to restrain myself from jumping up and crying out "the Emperor's got no clothes on!" – and, as it happens, in those days this was often quite literally true.

I am not seeking to argue that productions in Scottish Theatre thirty years ago were in any way second-rate or sub-standard. On the contrary, the infusion of public subsidy led to a great surge in creativity, not to mention a steep rise in production values. (Prince Philip, on a visit to the Royal Lyceum in 1966 to see a performance of Brecht's *The Life of Gallileo,* declared his total amazement that costumes of such quality could have been designed in a Scottish theatre!) What I am saying, however, is that the activities of the Scottish theatre at that time held no appeal for someone like me.

Yet this is not exactly a personal view either, for there are a great many people in Scotland who are, in many respects, exactly like me; people with whom I share a common background, a common set of perceptions, a common imagination, a common inheritance. We're called Scots. In the late 60s, one might easily have been forgiven for believing that the managements of Scottish theatres had a definite policy of alienating Scots.

In those days, it was not at all uncommon to hear the adjective 'Scottish' being used in a pejorative sense. Everything, from the snootiness of front-of-house staff to the arrogance of artistic directors who seemed to believe that the concerns of the local community had no relevance to the work they were doing, seemed calculated to convince people like me that the theatre had nothing to do with us. As a consequence, we tended to leave them alone; if they didn't do us any good, they didn't seem to do us any harm either. In point of fact, they didn't do anything very much for us at all.

Oddly, it was then I wrote my first play. *The Jesuit* simply came out in the form that it did, the way that most plays do, and nothing would have been capable of stopping it. What I can say, however, is that I always knew it was unlikely to receive a production on any Scottish stage without a great deal of difficulty. What I did not know was that even as I was writing the play, in the winter of 1971/72, important changes were taking place. The first hint I had of this was in February 1972, just after I had completed the first draft of *The Jesuit,* when a new play was produced at the Royal Lyceum in Edinburgh; Bill Bryden's *Willie Rough.*

Set during the First World War *Willie Rough* tells the story of a Clydeside riveter and his struggle to come to terms with the times in which he lives. This plot (based, incidentally, on the experiences of Bryden's own grand-father) is appealing enough, but what excited everybody who saw it was the manner of its presentation. Written as if it were a film script – full of short effective scenes that ripple along in perfect harmony with each other – *Willie Rough* is a convincingly accurate recreation of its chosen time and place. There is much more to this, however, than naturalistic dialogue and well-researched set and costume design. The play is clearly in touch, not only with its period, but with *its audience's awareness* of that period – and, as such stands up as a vital expression of a common Scottish experience.

*Willie Rough* was the most impressive Scottish play I had seen since Roddy McMillan's *All in Good Faith,* twenty years earlier. That, however, as the late Alexander Scott might have put it, is a long time between drinks and, much as I admired Bryden's play, I did not think its production sig-nified any kind of real change in the theatrical environment. It wasn't until the following year that I began to realise that I was mistaken, that some-thing new, something rich and change, was about to take place.

The occasion was a conference held in April 1973, in George Square Theatre, Edinburgh. Organised by a group of Edinburgh intellectuals, led by Bob Tait (then Managing Editor of the quarterly *Scottish International),* the purpose of this conference was to ask the question: "What Kind of Scot-land?" At first glance, this seemed to be nothing more or less than a festival of hot air, at which politicians of various parties would make speeches on behalf of their different points of view. The practice of asking questions, however, is often productive of answers and (strange as it may seem to us now) nobody appeared to have asked that particular question before.

It was the kind of occasion in which I would normally have had no more than a passing interest and I might easily have missed it altogether. As it happened, I had a couple of friends among the organisers. Since the event was to take place during the Easter vacation, there was a severe shortage of students to act as stewards, etc and I was asked to lend a hand.

Apart from the speeches and the debates, the organisers had arranged a programme of entertainments, including the first performance of a new play by John McGrath, an English playwright familiar to me for his pow-erful *Events While Watching the Bofors Gun.* Since I admired that earlier play, I was pleased to find myself on duty that evening and was more than a little disappointed when McGrath came on stage to tell the audience that, since rehearsals were not quite complete, a full performance of the piece was not possible. What would be given, we were told, was not much more than a reading, a run-through with actors still having scripts in their hands, and the musical numbers added. I'm glad to say that this most unpromising introduction did nothing to prepare us for what was to follow.

The play, of course, was *The Cheviot, the Stag and the Black, Black Oil*. In all my years of play going, I can truthfully say that I have never, before or since, witnessed scenes of such excited jubilation as took place in the George Square Theatre that night. *The Cheviot* may not have been quite ready for the audience, but the audience was certainly ready for *The Cheviot*. It took us all by storm, creating an effect that would be replicated, over and over again, throughout the length and breadth of Scotland that summer. It wasn't so much a matter of the talent on display – although talent was there in abundance, with such as Elizabeth MacLennan, Bill Paterson, John Bett, Alex Norton and Dolina MacLennan in the cast – but of an idea being expressed at exactly the right time.

That evening in the George Square Theatre marked the beginning of a new movement which lasted for the next decade and which completely transformed the situation as far as Scottish playwrights were concerned. So many new plays and dramatists began to appear in the Scottish Theatre that, often enough, they seemed to be coming out of the very walls.

The most exciting thing of all, however, was not the numbers of playwrights who were active, but their diversity. Unlike other groups of writers, the current crop of Scottish novelists, for instance, it was not simply a matter of a number of talented individuals taking different approaches to more or less similar themes. Although we were all certainly in touch with each other, largely through the activities of the Scottish Society of Playwrights, there is no way that the dramatists of that period could possibly be described as a school. Everybody was doing something different, with the result that an astonishingly wide range of drama was created.

There was, for instance, Hector MacMillan, who I always think of as the standard-bearer of Scottish popular tradition, with plays like *The Sash*, *The Royal Visit* and *Take Your Partners for the Gay Gorbals*. At the other end of the spectrum, there was the witty yet incisively satirical comedy of John Bett, a very sixties writer whose plays always seemed to be named after Rolling Stones songs; *Goodbye Ruby Tuesday*, *Talk About It* and *Street Fighting Man*. There was the highly visual, achingly funny, completely original cartoon theatre of John Byrne; *Writer's Cramp*, *Normal Service* and, of course, *The Slab Boys* trilogy. Complementing this was the more cerebral, more language-based and, usually, more serious work of such as Ian Brown, Eric Macdonald and Stewart Conn. My work at that time tended to adopt classical models, whereas Tom McGrath's fascination with the contemporary world was applied to the style as well as the content of his drama, in plays like *Mr Laurel and Mr Hardy* and *The Hardman*.

Issue-based, political drama we had in plenty, not just from the likes of 7:84 (and later Wildcat) but also from writers like George Byatt, whose work in plays like *The Clyde is Red* and *Kong Lives* sought to stretch the audience theatrically as well as politically. There was a plethora of solo plays, notably from W Gordon Smith – *Jock, Vincent, Xanadu* – but quite a few spectacular productions – I think of McGrath's *Animal,* McMillan's *The Rising* and Tom Wright's new version of *Ane Satyr of the Thrie Estaits.* Most of these writers were men, of course, but with the passing of the years, a number of female voices began to be heard; Marcella Evaristi with *Commedia,* Liz Lochhead with *Blood and Ice,* Sue Glover with *Seal Wife.*

One incident, involving two playwrights and one play, crystallises my feelings about the entire period and had a profound effect on my own career. One wet Tuesday evening in the early months of 1976, I was in the bar of the Traverse theatre, arranging a poetry reading with the artistic director, Chris Parr – a man who was responsible for much of the activity I have been describing – when I suddenly found myself in the vibrant presence of Elizabeth Clark, who wrote her poems and plays under the penname of Joan Ure. Now, Joan Ure was herself one of the most energetic and individual talents of the time and her death in 1978 was a great loss, not only to Scottish writing, but to her many friends and colleagues. Although, like us all, she had her share, perhaps more than her share, of neglect and misunderstanding, the most endearing thing about her was her open, generous, enthusiastic and encouraging attitude to all other writers.

On this occasion, her business with me concerned the play that was currently running at the Traverse. Had I seen it yet, she wanted to know. I replied politely that I intended to see it later in the run and was about to leave when she grabbed my arm and told me that this just would not do.

"Now!" she cried, "Go and get a ticket and come with me to see it now! This man can write – he can *really* write!" The man to whom she was referring was Tom Gallacher, a pivotal figure in those days, not just as a prolific playwright (in the late 70s, barely a month seemed to pass without a new Gallacher play opening somewhere) but as the active and efficient Chairman of the Scottish Society of Playwrights. The play was called The *Sea Change* and it altered my whole attitude to the place of theatre in Scotland.

The effect that *The Sea Change* had was less to do with its quality – it is a very fine play, although not, perhaps, Gallacher's best – than with the initiative it represented. In transposing Shakespeare's *The Tempest* to the oil-rigs of the North Sea, *The Sea Change* brilliantly matches theatrical tradition with contemporary awareness. This is not only what Scottish dramatists should be doing, but is in fact the only real justification for writing for the stage – as opposed to books or broadcasting – and everything I have since achieved in the theatre owes its inspiration to that Tom Gallacher play.

Playwrights, particularly Scottish playwrights, often feel as if they're wasting their time. You spend six months or so working on a play, they rehearse it for three weeks, run it for two, then they trash the set and your work is history. Perhaps the play was a success, perhaps not – except in extraordinary cases, it doesn't seem to make any difference. Occasionally, a play will struggle into print and, even more occasionally, it will be given a second production. It is difficult sometimes to wonder why you bother.

And it is, of course, true that at present – and for the foreseeable future

– dramatists face many difficulties in Scotland. Our theatres are under-funded, restricting the scope of our work; Scottish publishers avoid drama like the plague, consigning many fine plays to oblivion; we have no body of criticism (I don't mean these nice people who are bold enough to display their ignorance in the newspapers, I mean *real* critics, devoting considered essays and books to drama) and, as a result, we are denied the status that is automatically available to poets and novelists. At the end of the day, however, none of these problems – which were all, of course, in place in the seventies – will have any real effect on the future of our theatre.

Tradition is what is important. Every play that's produced, every performance that's given adds another chuckie-stane to the great cairn of tradition. The tidal wave of playwriting that swept over Scotland in the seventies did not happen by accident. It happened because there was a demand coming from the audience to which Scottish playwrights were able to respond. These playwrights have been followed by younger playwrights – John Clifford, Peter Arnott, Chris Hannan, Rona Munro, Lara Jane Bunting, John Binnie, Mike Cullen, Janet Paisley, George Gunn and David Greig – and a genuine tradition has become established. As a result, a permanent and irreversible change has been brought about in our theatrical environment. The tide may have ebbed a little during the eighties and nineties, but that only means that it will inevitably come to flood once more.

This much is certain; the situation that I described truly belongs to the past. The flat calm of the late sixties is no longer an option as far as the Scottish Theatre is concerned.

# Norman Kreitman

## *Conversation at Peebles*

We sat outside the pub by the river. The ale
glinted in his glass, and he laughed
as he talked about our youth. And I smiled too,
recalling those days drunk on girls and Mozart,
the excitement of each new fact, our landscape
of perfect possibilities.

                  A boat sculled by
glass beads dripping from the ends of the blades.
The sun warmed my cheek, and the water
ran sweetly.

              Later I wrote in my journal,
of a douce afternoon. But I wondered about Styx,
those shades, and all whose lives are laid out
on the other side.

## *Ellipse*

    Meeting her after years
I think of planets, how they speed onwards
faster, faster in the exhilarating sweep
    of the greater arc. How then
like the arm of some tenacious lover
gravity gropes out to hold them. Ambiguously
they slow, begin to turn.

    At her temple, surprisingly,
a grey touch soon ceasing to surprise; her smile
still youthful, but with less youth.
    From my perspective
she has raced through the time
since last we met, yet in this turning hour
    is almost still.

    Tilting her Chardonnay
she stands by that window, her shadow
all that now remains of her past
But her gaze curves round,
comes at me from a new direction
into which she will accelerate faster, faster,
    towards old age
and all its open, uncharted spaces.

## *Prosecution Service*

Not a popular job, these days.
Alright once, when you sat at the Gates
listing names in italic script, your plume nodding
over golden parchment.

But now with computers
you have to cross-link the evidence, assemble
everything needed for Judgement. Those upstairs demand
all the moral facts.

That last to arrive, for example.
A worried, petulant man, who with an axe
had bisected his wife. The data-base shows his father
lived on alcohol

abusing neighbours but polite to lampposts,
and drowned one foggy evening. For the mother
there are full details of her taste in stevedores. And then
the grandparents...

Everything must be traced
to the first deflection, but the recorder
has reached only mid-13th century, has scarcely begun.
The Assembly grows impatient

begins a slow handclap. Nervous eczema
is causing his wings to moult unbecomingly.
According to rumour a post will shortly be vacant
in the prosecution service.

## *One Day*

One day I'll wake up, and opening a gummy eye
will prefer, as usual, to close it again –
till the message hits. Then gagging with excitement
I'll leap from the spiral sheets, and tremulous
point. For there, reborn, will be the chair,
the bedside table, the dressing-gown and glass,
and perhaps I'll see our tall silver birch
holding her court by the garden fence.
And still incredulous I'll bestride the landing
to offer my wrists to the bite of hot water
on the day I wake up.

# Magi Gibson

## Grief

You carry it for weeks
like a father carrying a hurt child
through a dark forest.

Lost in darkness
you hear the child whimper
you feel him grip you tight.

But open your eyes!
The child you carry has already healed,
the whimpering is your own.

Let the child go
set him on the forest floor
let him run off.

Then look up through the darkness
you thought was solid as a slab of rock.

Even in the thickest forest
light filters through
when the blackest hour is past.

## Regret

a dull hard stone
it cannot be polished to a sheen

has no beauty – why
do you carry it so long?

cast it into the depths of the past
watch it sink into the dark forgetting

turn and face tomorrow lighter

## Between Snow and Sky

By the ice-bound loch we walked alone,
our feet scrunching virgin snows, casting
echoes in the still pool of the dusk.

A deer, startled by the noise as we drew near
darted off between dark trunks of firs
elusive as a dream.

At last we stopped – just where the old bridge
heaves its stony back over the flow of time.

And there we stood and watched
crazed waters dash in swirls and whorls
with no beginnings and no ends.

We were mesmerised
by the magic of those liquid runes,
the low laugh in the river's throat

and would have stayed all night, all year
but the wind came tugging at our coats
to wake us from that trance.

And then we realised –
there can be no staying here
between the old year and the new.

But still we stood, caught
on the hook of history,
our breath white in the freezing air,
trying to hold that moment, as if
in living cells, in human memory
we could preserve the ending of a century.

A blackness dropped down from the sky.
The hand of time had turned
the mirrors to the wall, had drawn
a blind down on the dying year.

And in the deepest darkness of that death,
carried on the old year's final breath
we heard the newborn's mewling cry.

## *Recovery Room*

light shines through
from the other side

voices murmur, wash to me
in slow waves, almost as if
lovers are meeting there
and I eavesdrop illicitly

the creak of bedsprings
the sound of breathing
a sharp intake
the rustle of sheets ...

somewhere a phone rings
but no-one answers

then the footfall of a doctor
and half-a-conversation floats
vague as smoke, along the corridor

perhaps death will be like this
this otherness, this being/not being
in the world

perhaps the soft hissing
I take to be the radiator's song
is the gentle whispering
of those already gone

## Dead Bird

I find you shrouded in leaves
beneath the sheltering trees

a wizened fledgling
in a cradle of jagged shell
claws curled around emptiness
black nib beak glued shut
unfeathered wings half-formed

and I know that your fate might
so easily have been my own

the thrill of flight unrealised, the song
stillborn on a shrivelled tongue

## Thistledown

I still have the thistledown
that tangled in my hair
that day we lay together
on the high moor.

I combed it out, kept it
in an envelope by my bed.

I combed out kisses too.
I've kept them all this time
in the envelope of my heart.

Why don't you come by soon,
collect what's yours?

## Stone Child

downstairs,
her mother's voice erupts,
flows red and hot as lava
her father roars,
his rage a heaving ocean

upstairs, in her bed
the child lies

foetal-curled
still
as the stone child
in the ruins of Pompeii

## The Hunter

only kills for the table, he says

the table shifts uneasy
on its four stout legs

a shadow drifts across
its polished face

as it wonders
what will be put on it next

## Comprimés

take one at bedtime
with a glass of wine

if affected do not drive
do not use machinery.
do not make love.

store yourself away from children
in a warm, dry place

in the case of overdose
weep copiously
until adverse symptoms cease

## Loneliness

is soured milk in a week-old carton
is opening letters addressed to the householder

is a picked-at chow mein congealed in a tinfoil dish
is keeping the tele-sales woman chatting

is hollowness in the pit of the stomach
that chocolate and crisps and chips can never fill.

is saying hello to the tv show host
and sending the queen a christmas card

is sitting up on hogmanay, house sparkling
shortbread on the plate, whisky glass in hand
hoping that (at least) the phone will ring

loneliness is at its worst
in a world full of people
chattering

# I-chabod

## *Angus Dunn*

*"... and they shall call his name I-chabod, meaning, thy glory is departed.'"*
This is the night. I have been expecting it. A draught blows through the window, and in the wind I can smell the edge of the long knives. There are people out there in the woods and desolate places, people moving secretively. Somewhere a goat bleats, or a lamb. There is something strange tonight about the haze that lies over the sea. The wind does not disperse it. There is something eerie about the suckings and soughings of the sea, licking the nooks and crannies of the shore. The wind too is bitter beyond its combination of temperature and humidity.

I dreamt last night that I was out in the North Sea, fishing. The boat was going down beneath me and I sank deep into the night sea. As the thick water slid over my face, the stars went out – but there was a gleam below me. I drew closer to it, and saw a silver fish swimming, swimming through the black oil. I woke still covered in the slime of it, and I had to shower.

When I went back to bed I could not sleep, though that didn't stop the dreams. Rigs in the desolate sea, no boats, but icy spray stinging the side of my face. A fish nuzzles into my side. And tonight the moon like a sickle disturbs memories that do not belong in this century. It hangs over the barley fields, the stalks heavy with grain, rippling in the slow cold air. The Ancient Band of Horsemen have finished their meeting early and gone to their homes to prepare. All but one, who stands near a bush for shelter, the Guardian of the Temple, his collar up to thwart the weaselling breeze.

Poised above the harbour is the giant crane with its wrecking ball hanging low. There is symbolism in this. Someone arranged it. The last shipyard goes down to debt, and there are the pawnbroker's balls, by implication at least, though two of them are missing.

I was sitting on the bench this morning, in Greig Street. The one that commands a view of the harbour and the Bull Inn. I was thinking about the mysterious bull tokens they found when they were dredging the harbour. Then I was thinking about the fish in the oil. Trying to imagine how its gills would feel, thick with crude oil. I could feel the suffocating cloying presence of the black stuff in my breathing places, I could feel the fin and tail muscles twitching, throttled from oxygen.

I was just slipping from the bench when I saw them coming down the street. I started breathing again and watched them approach. A woman and three children. Everyone else was giving them room, and I wondered why. Two of the children were boys, one of them in a pram, though he was too old for a pram. The girl pressed close to the woman as she walked along, her eyes watching the other boy who was roaming from side to side like a dog being taken a walk. He walked with his head held forward, and you could tell he was disturbed from the look on his face. Everyone felt it. Passers-by moved away as he approached, not letting him get too close.

I sat on the bench being inconspicuous, as I do at such times, and studied them carefully. In addition to their odd behaviour, the children displayed clear physical evidences of urban deformation. The boys both had strange bulging foreheads, not inhuman by any means, but distinctly unsettling. The woman did not exhibit any such obvious traces. Her history was written on her face, and it was a violent story, but the actual structure beneath was sound. She had somehow managed to maintain her bone structure in an environment of terrible pressures and degrading expedients.

The girl, strangely, looked perfectly normal, though her face was pinched thin below to give an effect rather more like a goblin than an elf. Her hair colour was different too. I wondered whether they had found her somewhere, or if perhaps they were borrowing her. They walked past me and as they approached the pedestrian crossing, the woman spoke.

"Take the pram Lindsay take the pram Lindsay take the pram Lindsay before I smash yer face."

There was no emotion in it at all, just a flat chant. Lindsay took the pram. The woman rounded up the boy and they crossed the street.

I watched them down the street. They turned at Cullen Road. I guessed that they must be renting Mrs Leitch's house. There was no point in following them. It is a short road, with no exit.

Everyone is doing their best. Most people are putting a brave face on it. As if that will help. The women in the WRI are preparing their sad document; when it is finished it will be no more than a middle-class plaint against the overwhelming forces of economics. History barely even notices this tiny north-eastern port. Nothing short of the direct manipulation of the arcane energies of economics can save this town now.

This has been obvious to me for some time. When they took the boat I felt that they'd taken something greater than my livelihood. There was a space left inside, and all around me was empty time. I spent much of that time in the library. There, I found one or two neglected books that excited me with the sense of a world outside of this one. There seemed to be people who had names for the longings and needs that I'd always felt, but never talked about. They had names too for the objects of these longings.

I read and read, and discovered that though many people had glimpsed this other world, no-one had grasped the whole picture. Crowley for example, had some notion of what was involved. His books were not on the shelves and the librarian looked at me oddly when I ordered one of his titles. Crowley understood about the importance of symbols, but even he did not see that money itself has become more symbolic than real. Indeed, monetary flow has attained a power that rivals that of Baphomet or Azrael. That is the energy that now confronts us, and must be diverted.

Behind the bush, this evening, the Ancient Horseman is preparing to do just that. He is deluded, as are they all. They think their arcane powers are commensurate with their worldly status. I know the Horsemen, who they are: he is a banker, others are landowners, company directors. All of them compromised already by their collusion with the forces they are hoping

*Illustration by Simon Kidd*

to divert. How inadequate they are to the task, he does not know, nor will he. I rather imagine that he will be swept away in the flood of energies which he is even now beginning to awaken. Throughout the countryside other practitioners are raising other energies.

Foul promises and a diatribe against the non-conformist butcher feature largely in his invocation. The promises – in an attempt to seduce these powers that are greater than any combination of economic units, yet somehow still tied to them. The diatribe – because there is more than a hint of blind fundamentalism about the Horseman's part in the affair, and anything that will hone the edge of his concentration will help him in his attempt. He has a grudge against this particular butcher, and hopes to cause his downfall along with his main task.

Just after nightfall, I walked along to Cullen Road. It was as I suspected. Mrs Leitch had rented them her house. I forced myself to creep across the lawn and look in the living room window. The girl and the older boy were sitting on the sofa apparently watching television – the set was not visible from where I stood, but there was a blue light flickering on the ceiling. I felt queasy looking at them. I was now certain that they were mutants, but they looked almost normal sitting there. It was deeply disturbing.

I watched for some time, and noticed that they were both eating chocolate bars. It proved nothing, of course, but I have noticed that an increased sugar intake often goes with moral laxity. Not that mutants are necessarily immoral: I think that old-fashioned view belongs in the dustbin along with notions of the superiority of the white races. Rather I think they just have a tendency to be immoral.

Having confirmed my suspicions about their mutancy, I was about to go home when the mother appeared in the room, carrying the younger boy. I was immediately alert. She had come out of the corner that the children were watching, where the blue light was coming from. There was only one logical interpretation. That was no television in the corner, that was their matter transmitter. They had established a beach-head in Mrs Leitch's house: once the docks had been demolished, they were going to beam in more of their type. I felt sick. I lay in a heap beneath the window and shivered. What would happen to us then?

I thought about the Horsemen and their Great Horse, and I thought about the Fishermen with their semi-divine strictures and their raw tough Sea-Being. What then would happen to Manannan mac Lir? Then there were the farmers, who mostly still followed the old ways and sustained the Barley Spirit, ragged in his awns, but everlasting in his rejuvenation.

But what of the Bull, whom we had managed to sustain for centuries? The glory of the Bull could not be allowed to depart. We could not allow ourselves to be swamped by these sub-humans. They had to be stopped. They threatened more than our existence as a community. What Crowley did not understand is that we do not worship pre-existing spirits. Any group that is fundamentally distinct from the rest of society and believes itself special, creates around itself a composite being, a spirit created by the harmony and intensity of belief. This results in a psychological robustness in the group, a feeling of commitment and certainty. The strength of this is due to the fact that an actual being, able to act without physical intervention, is created by the rituals, the worship, the shared belief.

Once this being has reached a certain critical size, it is no longer efficient for it to operate purely through physical agencies. Miracles become possible. From the merely improbable coincidence to the wholly impossible event: these occur without a doubt, but are not necessarily noticed. Why don't we notice these strange occurrences? Because there is one enormous being, bigger than any of the others. This living being is sustained by one of the most the widespread of beliefs: the conviction that everything is mechanically explicable. The immense inertia of common sense. Sometimes the odd little parapsychological event will wave tantalisingly from under the basket of physicality, but mostly these events are accompanied by a wash of circumstances that obscure the operation of arcane forces.

The urban environment is almost wholly a product of this mechanistic viewpoint. With an influx of urban viewpoints – associated, of course, with physical bodies – there would be less and less chance of actually seeing the various manifestations of the holy and unholy beings, as their ideas conflicted with ours. Unable to see the actual physical effects of non-physical intervention, our people would have to rely on faith alone to assure them that the rituals were having effect.

The Secret History shows the end of that road. Gods wither to nature spirits, then to archetypal myths. The lucky ones end up shrunken, with only a parasitic life left, existing on the energies of the occasional imaginative thought. In a celestial waiting room, faded ghosts of Gilgamesh and Wayland Smith tell stories to each other, waiting to be called.

They must be stopped. I broke in and stole their matter transmitter later that evening. It had of course been disguised as a television. I had suspected as much: the mutants are cunning in all their ways. I managed to get it out of the window before the police turned up. Before they took me, I threw it onto the pavement and destroyed it. I did not struggle. This cell is as safe as any place tonight. Even through the thick stone walls I can feel the presence of people waiting, out in the woods, for the right moment to begin, each according to their own beliefs and practices. Some of them will undoubtedly be sacrificing lambs or goats. If there is one left who is powerful enough, there may even be a bull slain tonight.

Myself, I cannot stand the sight of blood. Until now, I have tried to help in other ways. But will it all be enough?

I chide myself for my squeamishness. Should all this glory vanish from the world because I am not able to face a little blood?

I have managed to catch a spider. It is scurrying between my hands now. I am waiting for the right moment. It does not have a very big life, but it is the only one it has. Will it be enough?

Lod, the god of the Underworld, only he knows. And he isn't telling.

# Kaiser Haq

## *Spend, Spending, Spent*

How do I spend my days?
Late nights and rising late,
distracted by celestial lights,
meaning sun, moon, stars,
nature's changes of fashion,
overdressed summer, nudist winter,
lingual monotony of fellow creatures,
shrilling kite, shrieking parrot, rasping crow,
lazing till hunger overwhelms, then
eating without relish,
scanning violent headlines
while straining to overcome constipation,
breaking into nervous sweat
as clock hands admonish,
and yet somehow managing
to get clothes on, get through
the day, the murderous decibels
of hucksters, honkers, sloganeers,
and seized with sudden enthusiasm
for health and strength and vigour
once again attack a pair of
rusty dumb-bells –
                    they seem heavier
each time. I no longer spend
my days, they spend me.

## *Monsoon Poem with Prose Postscript*

Even large print blurs
            in draining light.
One could imagine Purgatory –
        a vast shanty town –
set ablaze, smoke
            becoming ink-black clouds,
setting the mood
            for monsoon's advent.

Find yourself a bamboo hut –
            mud floor, tin roof –
and wait as moist air wraps
you like a winding sheet.

It comes:
            a drop

on the tin roof –
        C sharp!

And more,
        beating a tattoo,
pounding dust
        to release earth's bouquet,

then speeding up
        into ceaseless roar;
it seems the ground beneath
        might dissolve
like sugar cubes in tea.

*Buddha says: everything is transient; clutch at nothing – and his disciples' practice was of holing up in monasteries to meditate till the rains let up. But then I have to go to a party where the inane chatter on the monsoon's beauty – unique to our land – and Rabindranath Tagore's divine lyrics on the theme is enough to drive me nuts. My monsoon thoughts are now of noxious gutters swelling into a deluge, carrying away the detritus of all our days.*

## *Truth on the Prowl*

Suddenly filled with spiritual longings
He browses in bed
Through Vedantic verdure,

Reads: "The Truth is one
And indivisible …"
It lulls him to sleep.
He dreams:
Truth is single

And lonely,
On the prowl.
But everyone keeps away.

Truth goes to singles bars
But no one's interested –
Neither men nor women,
Straight, gay or lesbian.

Finally Truth meets Falsity,
Fixes a date –
                and is stood up.

Truth looks into a mirror,
Touches itself –
                nothing happens.

Truth sits alone
Drinking, lugubriously
Watches men and women at their pleasures.

# Kathleen Jamie

## Hame
*(efter Hölderlin)*

Whas tae ken
if whiles Ah dauner
yur back-braes, O Yird
and pou wild berries,
tae slocken ma luve fur ye,
– here whaur jags o roses,
and gean-trees
pit oot thur sweet perfume,
aside the beeches, at noon,

when, in the yella glebe
grouin corn reeshles,
and the ickers nod, like at hairst-time;
– but nou, ablo the aiks' lift,
whaur ah wunner an spier
heivenward, yonner
weel-kent bell jows
– gowden notes,
at the oor the birds wauken
aince mair. An a's weel.

## For When the Grapevine's Sap
*(efter Hölderlin)*

For when the grape-vine's sap
thon canny plant, seeks shadda,
an the grape swells
ablow a caller pend o leaves,
it gies smeddum tae men,
but tae lasses, sweetness
– an bees, steert wi the speerit
o the sun, bedrucken
wi Spring's perfume,
bummle efter it,
but when the sun beeks,
fey-like, they turn hame
                    abune
                        the aik reeshles.

# David Campbell

## *September 11th 2001 – Glenuig Scotland*

Mountain and sea impart perspective
When the great icons fell
                              to fell intent
The twin towers of acquisition
                              and possession
And the walls of Might is Right
And on the radio I hear
                    the immediacy mongers
Tell everything of all they felt
Like someone inspect the
                              peristaltic convulsion
Of an eviscerated deer
                              seeing, fascinated,
The intestines
                    of the dead still writhe.
"Tell us how you felt
As the dead and dying screamed around
And you were not sure you would
                         not be one of them.
                              Tell us how you felt."

And then the bewildered Pharaohs
Hear them howl 'round the decay
                    of these colossal wrecks'
Howl for vengeance
                    on the slaves who dared
Destroy the Images that are their Gods …
And midst the outrage
                         call on pity for the dead
To sanction new destruction
                              on the world,
The enemy is invisible
For the enemy is within.
It only is the magnet's other pole
Pulling its own nature to itself
And figures are the calculation
of a mind that has no heart
So four or forty thousand dead
Will justify as many
            Multiplied by X.

And there unheard
            the simple voice of innocence remains
And does not blame

but sighs with thanks
            that loved ones still are here.
And grieves for those who grieve
                    for lives cut short
Yet asks no recompense
            of Wisdom beyond wars and stars.

## *Lest We Forget*

Don't worry, Mr Blair,
No-one has forgotten the image
                of the twin towers.

Nor their names of vengeance
Scribbled on the American bombs
That blast the ragged folk to death
                    today and tomorrow
Nor the tiny tattered eight year old
Terror widening the eyes
That look for her family
                shrapnelled to eternity
By your
Blanket solution
        Evil for evil
Death for death when
The skies thunder destruction
                on the innocents
No one forgets, Mr Blair,
Nor do we wish our names
Enrolled as terrorisers of the earth

So, Mr Blair, do not you forget
That your memorial will be that
Shoulder to shoulder
            you stood with
                the biggest bully boys on earth
In the old testament
            of blood for blood.

A terrorist

## *Echoes*

They have invaded our sacred lebensraum
And so we as a people
The good,
Will colonise the earth.
Enlighten with our philosophy

No matter what it costs
                in bombs
Or other people's lives.
We will teach them
                what is good
Show them
what is good for them.
The end will justify
                the means
And then maybe like us
They too can have – democracy.

## *Identikit*

"Describe a terrorist".
One who hurts and kills and maims
Innocents.
For instance, brings blitzkreig
                        from the skies
Fills folk with fear.
"By George!
I recognise a couple."

*Surfaces No.24* by Steven Hood, courtesy of Merz Gallery

# Terrorists Inc:

*The Story of Timothy McVeigh's Much Smarter Twin Brother*

## Colin Mackay

Ever since he had been a little boy back in the days when the United States was being so painstakingly nice to everyone, Tommy McVeigh had wanted to commit mass murder. Maybe this was connected with the U S being so painstakingly nice. The niceness did not suit him. Nice was not his middle name. Whenever Mr President made a speech about human rights somewhere or other, Tommy went out into the yard and tortured insects.

The whole yard was a combat zone. Tommy had it partitioned out with military cunning. He sat on the porch with a pair of binoculars that had come with a cornflakes box and scrutinised the yard for bugs. Whenever he saw one he went into action singing,

> I don't know but I've been told
> Airforce wings are made of gold.

Bugs didn't last long around Tommy. Ants, cockroaches, spiders, beetles – the only good bug was a dead bug, so Tommy zapped them all.

He grew upwards murdering things – bugs, mice, rats, cats, dogs, birds, fish, rabbits, deer, Tommy zapped them all. Wherever he went, something nice happened in murder form. The teachers at school didn't like him. They thought he was a thuggish boy with enough brains to turn hamburgers. They thought he qualified for a role in a Stephen King novel – the school dipshit with button eyes and crooked teeth who makes life miserable for the bright kid who is going to grow up to become Stephen King and write novels about his schooldays, while the dipshit buys himself a one-way ticket to Palookaville. They saw him as a psycho McDonald's, turning McBurgers in his McJob all day, and committing axe murders at night. Actually, Tommy was quite attracted to the notion of doing homicidal things with an axe, so they got half of it right.

The only teacher who had any time for Tommy was Mr Bates the sports coach who had a baseball cap permanently sewn onto his big shorn head and wore the school team colours wrapped around his stocky body like the battleflag of a victorious army. Once upon a time, before the painstakingly nice days had set in, Mr Bates had been a fly-fly boy over the jungles of Vietnam. Those had been the days! He went up into the gold and blue and in one day zapped more Gooks than Tommy had bugs in the whole of his life. Then when he climbed out of his cockpit, American guys gave him swaggering salutes and swapped cigars with him, and he had plateloads of hamburgers and ice-cold beer at base, and respectful little Gooks stood up and called him "Sir!"

Tommy sat at his feet listening to tales of his Gook-zapping days. Looking at him and Mr Bates was like looking at an update of Millais' famous painting 'The Boyhood of Raleigh'. Tommy was sailing out there on seas of gold and blue. The morning wind brought him the scent of aviation fuel and napalm and burning things. It made him think of a world that was one big America with everybody high-fiving, and wearing baseball caps, and eating McBurgers, and calling him a great guy for zapping whoever needed to be zapped – and nobody looking at him sideways, and thinking he was a dipshit with crooked teeth and a one-way ticket to Palookaville.

Tommy's dad was an electrician and had made sure that his son was computered-up as soon as possible. Tommy took to the computer when he discovered that he could crash cars and play murder games on it, zapping space aliens and monsters and uglies and people who looked at you sideways and were different from you and generally un-American. He took to electronics too when he discovered that live wires were a really cool way of torturing things, and he even got himself a second-hand microwave to use on the neighbourhood kittens.

Tommy got to college on a Run-Round-The-Field-And-Kick-The-Shit-Out-Of-People-With-A-Crash-Helmet-On-Your-Head scholarship because he was good at anything stupid and violent, and gave too many people the creeps at school to earn good exam marks. At college no one knew him. He wasn't unusual any more because there were hordes of sinister boys who also loved power and violence and killing, and hordes of sinister girls who admired them and thought they were sexy. By day Tommy studied electronics and computers with professors whose language was bright and false as a set of dentures, at night he got stoned or drunk, and jumped around to music that sounded like gunfire. A couple of times a week he ran round a field and kicked the shit out of people with a crash-helmet on his head, and watching girls jumped up and down in tiny skirts, shook their breasts, did the splits, and shouted *rah!* Several times people kicked the shit out of Tommy and he got taken to hospital. Several times the people Tommy kicked the shit out of got taken to hospital too. It was cool.

The older professors, the dorks, nerds, geeks and jerk-offs, all thought Tommy a cultureless and sadistic lout incapable of expressing a sensible opinion about anything – but then what would they know? Leaving college with a roll of paper and a silly hat with a tassel on it, Tommy walked straight into the arms of the Airforce which was looking for big beefy boys with a knack for machinery and a lust to blow things up. Tommy sang,

> I don't know but I've been told
> Airforce wings are made of gold.

He sang this in the company of other beefy boys who knew all about wires you could kill things with, about running around a field with a crash-helmet on your head, drugs, beer, rape, kicking the shit out of people, and little else. They lived in dormitories whose walls were hung with humiliation. Men with shorn heads came and yelled at them. Every word was abusive, every act brutal. The men with shorn heads were quite frank about this. In their limited vocabulary, they talked about "takin you fuckin pussies apart and puttin you back together again", "knockin you faggots down and buildin you back up", and "makin men of you motherfuckin jerk-offs".

In their limited vocabulary, other men with shorn heads and greater importance said, "We are totally committed to creating a personnel who are incentivised to totally enter a combat-focused mode". In his limited vocabulary, the most important shorn-headed man chewed his cigar and said, "We're gettin em ready to kick some fuckin ass."

"Whose fuckin ass?" asked a reporter.

"*Any* fuckin ass!" said the shorn-headed man, chewing his cigar.

Christmas came. The mess hall was decorated like a department store grotto and a shorn-headed man dressed himself up as Santa Claus and went "ho-ho-ho". Everybody sang carols. Everybody thought about home and Mom baking nice things in the kitchen. There was a plywood sleigh, and stuffed reindeer, and a picture of the President. There was a real tree covered with stars and spangles. There was a fairy on top of it dressed in Airforce uniform with an American flag in her hand. Old Glory was everywhere and flowers of snow were aerosolled on all the windows. The boys had dreamy expressions on their faces. The shorn heads mellowed into fathers and husbands. For an hour or two. That night Tommy looked at the real stars. The winter wind came with blue hair and a long grey coat and sharpened itself on his nose. It rained. Tommy was the brother of the rain. He had never felt so alone.

When Tommy graduated from fly-fly school he was pretty far up. He had good marks in preparation to blow things to bits, and to fly very fast in an expensive aeroplane preparing to blow things to bits. He also passed his History of Killing exam with credit by saying that the United States had single-handedly won every single war that had ever been fought in the whole of human history from Vietnam to the fall of the Roman empire.

As the famous philosopher Hegel once remarked, there is such a thing as the Spirit of the Times, and the man who is destined for fame is he who best encapsulates it. Tommy arrived in uniform with a shorn head and wings on his chest at just the right time. The United States wasn't being painstakingly nice any more. The rebel generation which had concluded that creeping around in jungles looking for Gooks to zap was not as much fun as it had been cracked up to be, was middle-aged now, fathers working in offices, paying mortgages, and worrying about health care, mothers working in offices, baking nice things, and worrying about the violence levels on television. A new generation had arrived – Tommy's generation. It was in rebellion against all that goddam niceness. It listened to murder music, believed gang rape was entertaining, and saluted the flag. The shorn heads were back, and Tommy was in the midst of them.

It happened that in another country inhabited by third world queers with rags on their heads was a bunch of terrorists who were causing the United States untold harm. Based in two oppressively tall tower blocks they controlled companies whose toxic emissions were corroding the ozone layer over America. They controlled factories whose waste was polluting the seas around America. They were cutting down the forests and tearing up the cornfields of America for their fast food industry. They regarded American workers as handy cheap labour and American women as prostitutes. They were in league with extra-terrestial creatures who kidnapped Americans and brainwashed them inside their hovering space craft. And they weren't being very nice to the rest of the world either. They had to go.

"Like totally cream the mothers, big time! – Energise our response to touch base in a confrontation agenda! – Kick fuckin ass!" said the shorn heads of varying degrees of importance in their limited vocabularies.

In the movies it is easy, but not in real life. The Raghead city was stiff with anti-aircraft and anti-missile missiles. On top of the huge tower blocks, a quarter of a mile up in the air, were batteries of automatic anti-aircraft cannon which could fire four thousand rounds a minute. Radar scanned the skies around Ragheadopolis. Guards with automatic assault rifles strapped across their chests and rags on their heads patrolled all the approaches.

Military Intelligence assembled its data. Spy satellites showed the exact location of all the missiles. Men with shorn heads and lots of medal ribbons pointed at maps. They said, "Anti-radar missiles can totally negate radar installations."

"Yo!"

"Anti-missile missiles can totally take out missile launchers."

"Affirmative!"

"Anti-anti-missile missiles can totally deconstruct the anti-missile defence capabilities."

"Roger that!"

"Leaving the enemy's front door standing wide open."

"Huh?"

"Leaving the hostile's entry aperture totally accessised."

"All right!"

"And then we go in – "

"And kick some fuckin ass!"

And they all stood to attention and sang,

> I don't know but I've been told,
> Airforce wings are made of gold.

So that was the plan [codename Divine Intervention]. Waves of missiles fired without warning would destroy the defences of the enemy, who did not know that they were the enemy and were about to be destroyed. Then manned aircraft would go in with Smart Bombs, Dumb Bombs, Guided Missiles, Free Fire Rockets, Gun Pods [you name it, they had it] and destroy what hadn't been destroyed by the missiles.

Tommy's squadron of F-16 fighter bombers was given the task of destroying the Twin Towers. Other squadrons of F-16s would hit pinpoint targets throughout the city. F-15 long-range fighters would destroy anything that came into the air to meet them. Waves of B-52 strategic bombers would pound everything of economic value to the enemy in the vicinity. F-14 fighters and F-18 fighter bombers operating from navy aircraft carriers would take over when the airforce boys turned home to refuel and rearm. Then the F-15s, F-16s, and B-52s would go back and do it all again until Ragville didn't have two bricks left standing one on top of the other.

Everything humanly possible would be done to avoid collateral damage.

The beefy boys were very confident. They walked round the base high-fiving each other, drinking beer, and laughing loudly. They had violent sex with real women, with inflatable women, and with paper women. They listened to murder music and watched strangers having violent sex on television. And they talked about the Rags. The Rags were despicable. Their weapons were junk, their soldiers were gutless, and those of them who turned themselves into bombs and ran at the enemy with sacks of explosives strapped to their backs – they were ludicrous medieval fanatics who wanted to be martyred. The Rags wore beards and long hair and made women cover their bodies. They didn't drink alcohol and used football stadiums for public executions. They didn't talk American and had no McBurger franchises. The goddam Rags were just a bunch of savages who belonged in the desert herding camels.

"We will not disrespect their culture, but we will totally terminate any terrorist persons operating within the parameters of this combat environment," said a very, *very* important shorn head to the boys. He grinned knowingly, happy memories of medal-winning missions over jungles flooding back into his mind. "And any terrorist low-life son of a bitch who tries to first base the airforce on this thing with a one-on-one slug fest will get like totally martyrised!"

"YO!" the boys all yelled. The next day Tommy's squadron flew out, their long planes newly painted in camouflage colours. They flew with maximum fuel to a friendly Raghead country, where the Rags knew American, stood up respectfully, and called you "Sir!"

The days were hot in that country, but the nights were cold. There were no trees to keep the heat, and little grass – just sand and rocks, and more sand and rocks. The boys sat in base and watched fun murder movies. Radios blared hate and sex. A band of multi millionaire drug addicts came and jumped around on a stage and screamed into microphones about how sexy killing was, and how much money you could make doing it.

The boys weren't allowed to touch women. The Rag women were strictly out of bounds. The base soon ran out of tissue paper. The boys stank of semen. They walked around panting with the stuff ready to blow out of their ears. They spent their time whacking little balls hard with sticks, and running around in crash helmets kicking the shit out of each other.

Then orders came. 0600 hours. They would hit the target at first light, before the Rags had woken up. The boys whooped. They shouted "Yo!" and "All right!" and "Yee-haa!" They sang their silly pugnacious song. They made murder music in their huts. The night came down. The burning heat disappeared. Half an hour later it was freezing. Tommy stood and looked out over the lonely desert. On the other side of the perimeter fence an old man was walking his dog. Tommy waved to him. The old man did not respond. The moon came out and shone on the desert. Tommy looked at it. The night clung to him like a cold friend.

An important shorn head came and put his hand on Tommy's shoulder. "Scared, son?" he asked.

"No, *Sir*! I'm not scared, *Sir*!" Tommy yelled.

The important shorn head smiled benignly.

"I know just how you feel, son," he said. "But the job's got to be done."

"Yes, *Sir*! I know that, *Sir*!" Tommy yelled.

The important shorn head went off and left Tommy alone. Again the old man walked by with his dog. Tommy waved half-heartedly. The old man still did not respond. Bright birds sang in the trees of Tommy's memory. They were vivid as flying flowers. Then the door of the hut was flung open, and murder music came pouring out and chased them all away.

0600 hours. The day landed like a white crow on the roof and strutted about smacking the tiles with its beak. One after another the F-16s took off with their engines firing and roaring. They had snarling animal mouths painted under their noses which were supposed to look terrifying but actually seemed rather childish. The pilots all had their names stencilled on their helmets. They had their nicknames stencilled on their helmets too. Their nicknames were things like Gunslinger, Caveman, and Super Stud. Their faces were fresh, their eyes were blank, their teeth were dazzling white, and they made flamboyant gestures to each other.

The first wave went for the North Tower. Tommy was in the second. The South Tower was its target. His nickname was Bug Killer. On his control panel was a sticker of Bart Simpson and a sex-mag cut-out with a cunt like a canyon. "Way to go, baby!" he said to the cut-out as his wheels lifted off.

The first wave were ten minutes ahead. The second wave followed.

"Gonna fry me some bugs!" said Tommy.

The anti-radar, anti-missile, and anti-anti-missile missiles had done their work. There were fires raging on the ground as Tommy screamed over it above the speed of sound, and nothing came up to intercept him.

Up ahead! Ragville! Huge. Packed with millions of low-life terrorists.

Bug killer! The first wave had got their target. Above its ninetieth floor the North Tower was burning like a torch. Some tracer shells came at them from the roof of the South Tower. Gunslinger rocketed the gun emplacement into silence, then Caveman released his smart bomb. It sailed right through a window about the eightieth floor. The explosion looked like an orangeade fountain going *whoosh!* Bits of steel and glass and human bodies were blown out in all directions.

"Them Rags is spillin out like bugs!" shouted Caveman over the radio. "Yee-hoo!"

"Leave some'd fuckin muddahs for me!" shouted Tommy.

"Yo!"

"Megadeath!"

"Yee-haa!"

"Up for it!" Super Stud put his bomb into the sixtieth row of windows. "That's how Uncle Sam kicks ass!" he shouted.

It was Tommy's turn. He locked his weapon system onto the thirtieth floor. Pressed the button. The indicator light should have turned green. It turned red. The WEAPON MALFUNCTION sign flashed.

*"SHIT!"* he roared, and sent his spittle splattering over the panel.

His eyes dilated with anger and hate. "Shit!"

He was close enough now to see the main door of the Tower. Down there the bug horde was spilling out, running in all directions, tiny, dirty, useless insects. He put his plane into a nose-dive, glaring out through the windscreen of his cockpit the way he'd glared at all those other screens when destruction and murder and rape were played out for his entertainment.

"Bug Killer, what the hell you doin?" called Caveman.

Tommy's F-16 was in a dive that he couldn't come out of even if he wanted to. He didn't want to. He pressed his gun button. The gun raved. A splatter of 20mm shells slashed into the bugs and butchered them.

He laughed. Shrieked with glee.

"Yo!" he yelled. "All right! Go for it! Kiss mine, motherf …"

Deafening explosion.

"Go for it, Bug Killer," said Caveman quietly, circling above the carnage as all Tommy's weapons and fuel tanks exploded simultaneously, frying every living thing in sight.

The South Tower collapsed in an avalanche of steel, glass, concrete, smoke, dust and flame. The North Tower followed some minutes later, after the F-16s had turned for home, and before the first wave of B-52s arrived to carpet bomb the rubble.

America mourned her hero. Little *mention was made of the number of Rags dead. Few Americans seemed to care whether it was three, three hundred, three thousand, or thirty-three thousand. It was a just war in a good cause, they had a hero, and that hero had done it for them.

Truly, America mourned. People sobbed on television. Everyone who had ever met Tommy said what a swell guy he had been, and sold the story to the press for thousands of dollars. Tommy was a hero, a saint, a martyr in the cause of freedom. He was an all-American boy, a clever student, a sports star, a good friend. He had been kind, gentle, caring and affectionate. He had loved animals, and his Mom, and gone to church. Overnight his face adorned T-shirts, cola cans, beer labels, bras and panty-hose.

The President addressed the nation. The President was a stooge who had been hoisted into power through corruption, and three quarters of the nation hadn't voted for him, but everybody listened.

The President's vocabulary was so limited he sounded like a Bulgarian who has been learning the language for six weeks, but he had a staff of hard-working scriptwriters who had his speech written out for him on an autocue, spelled phonetically. The Presidential address played on all TV channels simultaneously. Picture of the White House, the American flag flying, and a voice-over saying, "This presidential address is brought to you by McBurgers. Wrap your teeth around a juicy McBurger. Yum, yum." Then the President, sitting at his desk in the oval office looking presidential.

The President read from his [phonetically spelled] autocue:

"My fellow Americans. Today we have begun to strike back in the war against terrorism. The freedom of the world depends upon us in this great country. The freedom of every man, woman and child of every race, creed and colour is in our hands, and we shall not fail them. Tommy McVeigh died in a noble cause. By his heroic self-sacrifice he destroyed the most important headquarters building of the evil that is threatening the whole human race. Tommy McVeigh, we will remember you as we come together with nations world-wide to fight terrorism and reassert our common humanity. God bless you, Tommy McVeigh. And God bless America."

Picture of the President sitting at his desk in the oval office, the American flag flying, the White House, and a voice-over saying, "That presidential address was brought to you by McBurgers. Wrap your teeth around a juicy McBurger. Yum, yum."

Tommy was a hero. Though nothing was left of his body, a ceremonial coffin containing that nothing was slowly lowered into a grave on a day of cold sunshine before a crowd of solemn celebrities, many of whom were weeping, 579 cameras, and an honour guard in full-dress uniform who fired blank shots into the air.

A hero.

Pop stars dedicated songs to him. "The Ballad of Tommy McVeigh" reached number one in the charts, closely followed by "The Tommy Rappers", and "Bug Killin Man". In towns and cities throughout the country streets were renamed in his honour. His photograph was hung in schools, mothers christened their babies after him, boys joined the armed forces to be like him, proud veterans commemorated him, and sweet little girls wept.

> They call it terror if you are few
> And have no B-52s.　　　　　　　(– old protest song.)

# Zekria Ibrahimi

## *The Defeat and Destruction of Afghanistan*

Let's bomb the goons and the geeks now –
A million missiles in the sky –
A fireworks show that is wow –
Red flames – red blood – in red, they'll die!

Gee whizz force! Some war, holy cow!
Riots of spark to singe the eye!
Explosions like stars, fire, and how –
Our humdinger Fourth of July!

A dirty mosque, a dusty street,
Nothing here organized and neat –
The shadow of smoke, of attack,
And corpses, motionless, bleak, dark,
Near which half-starved dogs whine and bark –
An endless night, ceaselessly black …

# W Gordon Smith

## *A Greenwich Girl*

Legs apart she stands
astride the mark, inclines south
and adjusts her loins
to the true meridian,
matches crotch with crack,
and sparks her electric hair
at northern darkness.
She feels the dying sun on
the western wasteland.
A girl of latitude at
zero longitude,
she knows how the river runs
and responds sometimes.
She knows that sailors alive
and dead compounded
the preference of left breasts
and eastern promise

W Gordon Smith (far left), Jack Vettriano (far right)
photograph by Rik Walton

# Jack Vettriano

In less than ten years Jack Vettriano has emerged from obscurity to become Britain's foremost contemporary narrative painter, a remarkable achievement because he received no formal art school training. Born in Fife, Scotland in 1954, Vettriano left school at sixteen to become a mining engineer. For his 21st birthday a girlfriend gave him a set of watercolour paints and, from then on, he devoted himself to learning to paint.

It was fourteen years before Vettriano felt ready to show his work in public. In 1989 he offered two works to the Royal Scottish Academy's annual exhibition; both were accepted and sold on the first day. The following year, an equally enthusiastic reaction greeted the three paintings, which he entered for the Summer Exhibition at London's Royal Academy.

1994 saw the publication of *Fallen Angels,* edited by Scottish playwright, broadcaster and art critic W Gordon Smith (Pavilion). This was a unique initiative establishing connections between Jack's work and that of Scottish writers. Contributors included Ian Hamilton Finlay, Norman MacCaig, Iain Crichton Smith, A L Kennedy and Joy Hendry, some of many who found his paintings stimulating and inspirational. His appearance as featured artist in this 100th edition of *Chapman* is also a tribute to Gordon Smith.

In the last nine years interest in his work has grown rapidly. There have been sell-out solo exhibitions in Edinburgh, London, Hong Kong and Johannesburg and New York. In March 2000 BBC Scotland produced a half-hour documentary about Vettriano for their series EX-S; aired initially in Scotland only, the documentary may be aired nationally later this year.

Vettriano's last major exhibition, *Lovers and Other Strangers,* was at the Portland Gallery in London in June 2000. The exhibition transferred to The Kirkcaldy Museum & Art Gallery in Fife. More people visited the Museum during the Vettriano exhibition than in the whole of the previous year. A new book (also Pavilion) was published to coincide with this exhibition, featuring over 100 paintings and biographical text by Anthony Quinn.

In September 2001, Vettriano donated a painting to a charity auction, which was held at Sotheby's in aid of *Help the Hospices.* The painting, *Beautiful Dreamer,* was the second-highest bid-for Lot, making £25,000. He is also about to donate a self-portrait to The Kirkcaldy Museum which inspired him so much as a 'trainee self-apprentice'.

Portland Gallery exhibited twenty-one paintings at artLONDON, an annual contemporary art fair, in May 2002. All twenty-one paintings were sold within the first hour of the opening night. Aside from his exhibitions, Vettriano has acquired a vast following through the posters and prints of his paintings that are distributed worldwide. This year the two best selling art posters in Britain are both Vettriano images. To date, more than 1,000,000 posters of Vettriano's paintings have sold worldwide.

Jack Vettriano's paintings appear with the kind permission of Pavilion/Chrysalis Books, © The Portland Gallery, 9 Bury Street, St James's, London SW1Y 6AB Tel: 0207321 0422 Email: art@portlandgallery.com

# Jack

*Self-Portrait (detail)*

*Fetish (Study) (detail)*

*Self-Portrait of the Artist (detail)*

*Chelsea Morning (detail)*

*Amateur Philosophers*

*The Billy Boys*

*The British are Coming*

*The Clouds are Gathering*

The Green Gown (Study)

Model in White

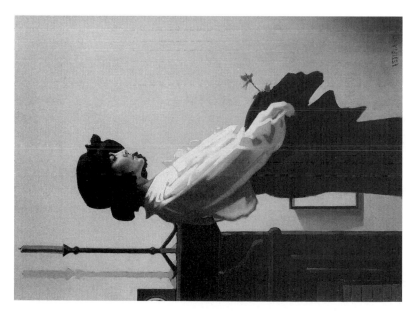

*A Valentine Rose*

*The Missing Man I*

*The Shape of Things to Come*

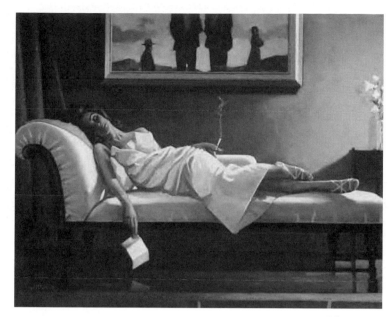

*The Letter*

*In Thoughts of You*

*A Brave New World (Study)*

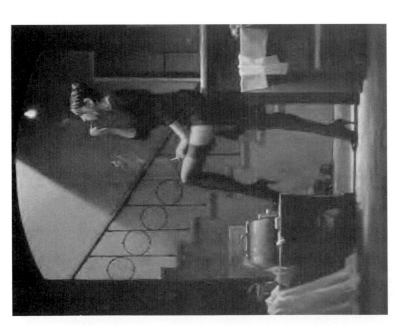

*A Dancer for Money*

All works reproduced by permission of Jack Vettriano
and The Portland Gallery, London

# Joy Hendry

## *Blood*

*prompted by an Anglo-Catholic friend incensed by the introduction of
women priests to his church due to the idea of 'blood' on the altar*

So. Blood makes us women unfit
to preside over the tabernacle,
the altar, the communion sacrament,
unfit to speak to the Maker
of souls, bodies – yea, matter itself.

It is blood makes us unfit
to be priests in your Catholic Church
It's all down to molecules1
atoms, the polychromatic notes
on the biochemistry scale.

God must not be besmirched
by the reality that procreates his own
universe.

Did Christ not bleed on the cross?
Did martyrs not die for the Blood
of the Lamb?
Was Abraham not ready
knife in hand
to draw blood on the altar,
to sacrifice the life of his son,
born of woman's blood in the begetting
and the birthing?

This was the man whose name gave title
to a legacy of compassion,
who lived to deliver the Tablets
from the High Mountain saying
that the son should happily forgive
the murderous, jealous impulses of the father,
who lived to say, honour thy father and thy mother,
not in the letting of blood,
but in the red glow of growing understanding.

My friend, mock not
nor fear the blood of women shall diminish thy altar.
The blood of women is like the cry of the herdsman
calling his udder-filled kye hame for a kind milking.
The blood of woman is shed, a black eye as she laments
her man going to a stupid, useless battlefield
where the blood of striplings stains the soil

with a red undiluted by torrents of tears
from heaven, leaving women bleeding monthly
with no men to make plants of seed.

The blood of women makes possible
the worship of the God you claim you own.
We do not, cannot claim him as our own.
We hope upon a moment he might listen,
might know the blood we shed in his name.

We cannot help our blood, but offer it
as a flower on his altar, as knowledge
that his aura will continue through our pain,
to light the future dawns and sunsets
of this world that we hope
He loves.

## *Another Kind of Love*

Alas, poor sod –
not sod but stone, bare stone,
I have you now, bald pate and all.

See, if you can, your devil bride
veiled in black, come to claim
your marbled contours:
death is not the only leveller.

How unwise to think
that blank white eyes alone
mirror the ancient secrets
with a kenning more than those
whose eyes still follow the sun.

No sun here, old boy,
for you and all your limbless friends.
Too much sun, and change
could be fatal.

I wear black, neck cut low
in honour of you, to make you
feel at home in a world coloured
only by blood-red lips.
You leer without eyes
down my front.

It's all changed, boy.
You're no puppet master now
to make me dance for you,
sing, laugh, open joyless legs
at your command.

I come in black, master puppet,
place my left hand, a lover's hand,
upon your right shoulder,
the better to whisper in your ear,
and my right hand, red-clawed
rests on your white brow.

See how I smile,
My body perfectly aligned to you,
roused and waiting.
If you could lift that veil
so close to your mouth
what would my eyes say …

Gently, my golden scarf
could wind itself around your neck
a silken rope to topple you
and strangle immortality itself.

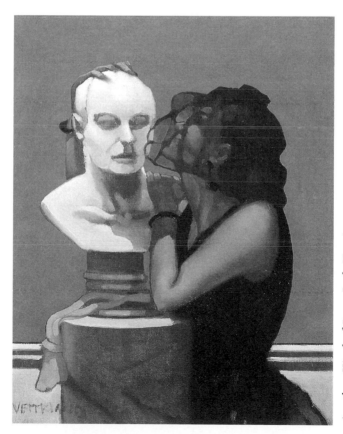

*Another Kind of Love*, Jack Vettriano

# pounpounFillip

## *Pete Fortune*

Phillip Murray haed been mairriet fir a whein o years an coud richtly blaw that he'd ne'er luikit at anither wumman. (Aiblins his anerlie faut in the een o his wyfe wes spennin ower mukkil siller on fags!). But na, he didna grie wi sic swickery, an asides, he jaloust nae ither weimen woud luik his road oniewey.

Houanevir, he wes at the bank biggins ane nicht, takin oot twantie poun frae the hole-i-the-waa, whan he tuik tent o this lassie smirlin at him in an ill-trickit kinna wey, syne fair govin at him. Neist thing he kent she'd flichtert owre an graipit him atwein the legs, stertit ti unsteik his breiks. She said fir twantie poun he coud dae ocht he wantit ti her. Phil didna swither at sic a fouth o pleisur, but oniebodie ava coud hae cam breingin inti the bank causie an caucht thaim, e'en tho he'd anerlie taen aboot a meinit. Whit a carfuffil thare coud hae been. But he'd got awa wi't, an the limmer wes awa nou tae, smoulin inti the mirk wi his twantie poun note. Phil wes left feelin gey thrawart – an pechin wi the brounkaities – but it wes the maist lousum wey o lattin gae a twantie poun note that he coud mynd on.

Aboot fower weeks efterhaun Phil becam gey ill-naitert wi sumthin fremrnit that wes gaun on wi his bank account. The maist raicent blaud shawed wi-drawins o siller he wes shuir he'd ne'er made. Twantie poun a week. Ilka bluidy week sen his knee-trummiler thon nicht. He coudna faddom it oot, sae buikit an appyntment ti argie wi the sorners at the bank.

But it wes hippit, kis the young chiel he speired wi gied him a sair tyme o't. He said Phil wes mebbe gaun doitert, that he maun be takin siller oot an nae kepin a richt note o't. Syne he gaed a bit kekkil an tellt Phil that the bank was gey nakkie wi thair security nou-a-days, which wes the raeson they'd thon fantoush CCT cameras in the bank causie. He askit Phil gin he wantit ti tak the maitter up wi sum o the heich-heid anes, an syne fordilt the norie that he shoud aiblins lecter his wyfe. Mebbe *she* wes takin oot siller an no lattin on ti him?

Phil whyles sees the sleikit loun frae the bank wi a bit lassie, a richt guid luiker she is tae. The furst tyme he saw thaim thegither he jaloused that he kent her frae sumwhaur, but suin puit that norie oot o his heid. Phil's mebbe no aye gleg at the uptak, but slawly it seipit throu … an syne he made up his mynd aboot whit he wes gaun ti dae. It wes sempil but perfit! He wes gaun ti cut the fags doun ti a poukit twa-thrie a day, but no lat on ti the wyfe. The bawbees he'd hae ti spare! It wad be at laest twantie poun a week.

Phil jalouses that he's been gey chancie – that the daftlyke cairrie-on wul be ti his ayebidin guid – kis cuttin doun on the fag reik maun be ti the betterment o his neglekit health. His wyfe woud hae been sae gled an prood o him. It's juist a peity that she'll ne'er hae the wittins o't.

An Phillip howps that it wul aye stey that wey.

# A Beautiful Restoration

## *Dilys Rose*

– Before the Nazis and the Communists, pani Anna says, this place was a palace.

I nod and go on with my work. My boss is not really talking to me about the hotel, she's just thinking aloud. Though the exterior of the building is soot-black, it is still beautiful but the interior has suffered and, for pani Anna, restoration has become something of an obsession. She has spent so many thousand *zlotys* on restoration – the cost of wallpaper alone would have been enough for me to buy a small apartment – and renovation too: The bedrooms are modern and comfortable – I know people like the rooms, especially foreigners. If I meet them in the corridor as they're going out to find breakfast and I'm off home to sleep after a night shift, they smile and say hello. In the place I was before, which hasn't changed at all since independence, I was only ever greeted by grunts and groans.

I like the night. I can get on with my work without too many interruptions and, when I'm done, there's no need to pretend to be busy. Mostly it's ironing, folding and stacking linen and filling up the trolleys with soap, bottled water, shower gel and shampoo, toilet rolls and bin bags. Tonight I also have a frilly shirt to wash, buckled boots to polish. I make extra money from washing. Good enough money. There's always the chance that a light bulb might explode, the batteries of a TV remote run down, a toilet become blocked. On night shift I don't like guddling around with toilets while the guests, in their night clothes, stand over me and get in the way, or sprawl on the beds and behave as if I'm not there.

Worse can happen. There's illness – for some reason guests need a doctor much more often at night than during the day when it's a lot easier to get hold of one. During the small hours I've witnessed a birth and two deaths; one simply from drink, one from drink and sex and heart failure combined. Drink causes a lot of trouble and mess, spilled or broken bottles, blood and vomit on the carpet, the bed, the wallpaper. Mess and fights. I deal with the mess but for fights I call Dmitri, the night porter. He's big and strong and doesn't waste time, just barges in. If the door is bolted on the inside, Dmitri presses his bony forehead against the door and says:

– You have one minute, starting from now, before I break in. So far, Dmitri's threat has always worked, which is just as well. Pani Anna wouldn't be too happy about a broken door. In fact, I think Dmitri would be more likely to lose his job over a broken door than a smashed nose.

And visitors: I see the girls in their narrow heels and split skirts flitting down the corridors like moths. I see them sneaked into the lifts and, later, hustled down the back stairs and out into the night. I see the rooms the next morning. The girls are better fed these days and probably own prettier underwear now that there's more than black market goods to choose from. Pani Anna knows this kind of thing goes on but as long as guests and visitors are discreet, it means nothing to her. For Housekeeping it means extra work – more linen and towels to be changed, more airing of rooms and scrubbing stains off the new, soft carpets.

Pani Anna cares a lot about carpets, wallpaper, about furnishings, and dreams of restoring downstairs to exactly how it was before the Nazis and the Communists: marble columns, gleaming wood panelling, flashing chandeliers and heavy damask drapes. The work is a long way from finished and she worries constantly about running out of money. The new government has given her some financial help – the hotel is an important historic building – but not enough.

– Not nearly enough, says pani Anna, with the costs of materials and labour rising every day. And just look at the news: *Deficit may sink zloty.* Where will we all be then?

The *zloty* is not a ship. How can it sink, or float? All I know is that I need every shift to make ends meet. Pani Anna has a friend in Germany, a man who makes money from money. He has promised – for what reason she hasn't said, though Dmitri and I have our ideas – not to let her plans for a beautiful restoration collapse into tragedy or farce. But often, after a phone call, pani Anna is angry or gloomy, or both. She sits at reception, rests her pale, round elbows on the newly varnished horseshoe desk and drinks scotch soda. She won't touch Polish vodka and don't even mention Russian! A good-looking woman, though the whisky and the worry are making her grey and puffy around the eyes. She should go out more, sit in the sun. Summer will not last forever.

Of course the hotel has always had more interesting guests than drunken, whoring businessmen. Its fame comes not only from its frozen music, as pani Anna calls the architecture of the building. These are not her own words; they belong to to somebody famous, I don't know who. The hotel has been host to many famous people. It was here that, in 1948 – the year I was born – an International Congress was held. Writers and artists, film stars and philosophers gathered in this very building to discuss what to do about our poor, devastated country. People say pan Picasso first drew his famous fat dove of peace here, in this very building.

At that time, the interior was in a very bad condition, smashed windows and furniture, charred walls. There was a paper shortage too – well, there was a shortage of almost everything. People say that pan Picasso first drew the dove on his bedroom wall. The register from the congress disappeared – some say it was confiscated by the secret police, others that it went up in flames but anyway, it's gone, so nobody knows who slept where. Maybe the story of the dove on the wall is just a legend. A place like this has many legends, one on top of the other.

Now, after a long absence, we have international visitors again, for the festival. During the day, music spills from the bedrooms, bright and clear as mineral water, vodka. From room seventy-seven I've been hearing heavenly singing. The voice belongs to a young Italian who even after being up very late – I know how late! – will stop in the corridor, sweep back his hair, put a hand on his heart and bow. This is an act: I know he is practising and I am a substitute for his audience but still I blush and simper and scurry off to my housekeeper's room as if I'm very busy, as if I've just remembered some urgent task. Really, I'm embarrassed and ashamed of my dry, colourless hair, my cheap shoes.

Dmitri says he's a gay. He says this because the singer – whose name, I think, should be Angelo but is Giuseppe – doesn't sing in his deep speaking voice but high as a woman.

– Sounds like a castrato, Dmitri says. And the costume! Have you seen his costume? High-heeled boots, frilly blouse. A gay. Crime against nature, he says, pleased with himself and his certainty.

God, everybody knows this country has seen real crimes against nature – and not just seen them. I don't argue with him. On the night shift, I have no-one else to call on and sometimes I really need big, bison-headed Dmitri to help me out.

And yes, I've seen the singer's clothes. I have some of them with me at this moment; the shirt with the lace cuffs, the high boots with the silver buckles. He called me to his room, around one. He had changed out of his costume into jeans and a white t-shirt. His chin was blue with stubble and his arms were covered with thick, dark hair, like fur. He is not tall and his nose is too big to call his face perfect but what does perfect mean but a set of rules? He was tired and a little tipsy – not drunk, not like the stringless puppets you can see on every street corner – but bright-eyed, lit up. His bedside table was strewn with bouquets of flowers, still in their cellophane.

– Please, one moment, I said, and rushed out of the room.

All I had in my supplies cupboard was an ugly ceramic jug, not nearly big enough and with a crazy slogan on the side: *The Flowering State*. That jug would not do. I phoned reception.

– Dmitri. Bring me vases, Blue ones. Two or three.

– Blue ones are only for reception.

– Blue vases, Dmitri. Please. And please hurry.

Dmitri never does anything quickly. I went out into the corridor and paced about in front of the lift. How slow Dmitri was! I should have fetched the vases myself. The flowers would be in water already, the singer would be bending his head, his hair falling into his eyes, burying his face in the blooms, turning his big nose from side to side, breathing in the perfume … Dmitri's head appeared in the glass window of the lift. The door creaked open and he stepped out, a blue glass vase wedged in the crook of each arm, his broad face pressed between them. Good vases he'd brought me, with heavy, swirly bases. Hard to knock over.

– Who puts flowers in water at this time of night?

– The Italian, I said. Thanks. Have to go.

Dmitri noisily sucked air through his crowded teeth, then clumped back into the lift, slowly shaking his head.

By the time I reached the singer's door I was out of breath and, I expect, red in the face. It's still so hot, even at night, though the leaves on the trees have turned gold and begun to fall. I knocked on the door with my elbow. When Giuseppe opened it and saw me standing there, half-hidden by blue glass, he gave me such a smile that I thought I would drop the vases and break them as well as my toes but then … then … he took my face in his cool hands and – I still don't quite believe it – kissed me on both cheeks and ushered me into his room.

Giuseppe, the angel Giuseppe filled the vases with water and asked me to help him arrange the flowers, one vase each. This is not normally part of my duties but who would refuse such a sweet-smelling task? It was more of an honour than a chore to sit at the oval, glass-topped table, selecting stems from the bouquets spread in front of me. Roses, lilies, chrysanthemums; the perfume rising from the table, curling around us, drifting into our nostrils, mouths, our hair. The angel Giuseppe didn't squeeze the stems the way Dmitri does when pani Anna asks him to arrange displays for reception, he balanced them on an open palm and used his fingertips to guide them into position. Stems matter. Stems are like arteries. I've told Dmitri this but he continues to clamp them in his big fist. So, I suppose, he doesn't look like a gay.

While we were filling the vases the angel Giuseppe spoke to me, in Italian. I know the sound of the language because, on night shift, I sometimes listen to opera on the radio: it makes a change from the American pop music people can't get enough of these days. I couldn't understand a word but I could hear the angel's voice squeaking and grating, his throat hurting.

– Too much singing, he said, pointing to his open mouth. His lips were red from wine, teeth white: no gaps, no twisted stumps. His tongue, I could see his tongue, pink and curling. My ears burned; I was blushing again. I slipped the last few stems into the vase and stood up. Excuse me, something else you want? I said, in my horrible English. I know my English is horrible but Italian for me is no more than a wish, a dream.

– Yes yes, I forget …

He stood up, praising my flower arrangement over his own, went into the bathroom and came out with his boots and shirt.

– Please, can you clean, for tomorrow?

– Of course, of course. No problem. Thank you, please, I said, nodding, backing out of the room like the grovelling servant in too many bad films.

Earlier tonight, before the singer distracted me, I was ironing pillowcases and looking up from those endless bleached squares at the old, stained wallpaper which was jumping with red and green dots after all that white linen. I was thinking about pan Picasso and his fat dove, and wondering how many times the walls had been papered since the year of my birth.

In my housekeeper's room, the door is locked and I'm alone with my magazines, my kettle and tea bags, the stacks of ironed linen and towels. The linen is, of course, white, the towels too. There are plenty of good enough red (now pink) ones from before independence but pani Anna won't have them used unless a guest disgraces him- or herself. (I don't think many guests understand pani Anna's towel code.) Nearly always, it's a man who slips up, or a man and woman together but I try to be open-minded, not to discriminate.

There has been – and sadly still is, too much discrimination. Already, in the newly restored old town, over fresh, cheerful paint in colours we haven't seen for decades, the spray can and stencil graffiti are again making their ugly, hateful marks. After living with grey crumbling buildings for so long, with broken windows, broken promises and captive spirits, could we not, for a short while, enjoy the cheeriness of fresh paint, the calm sheen of unsmashed glass? It's a small improvement, not important, I know, but this country has seen so much destruction. Too much, too many lives crushed by one set of rules or another, this country which has the shape of a jellyfish – out and in, here and there, stretch and squeeze – a strong, stubborn jellyfish all the same, one which refuses to die no matter how many times it's stamped on. But what must it be like to live in a country with fixed, definite outlines, borders which haven't strayed for centuries, like Italy, say, a shapely high-heeled boot dipping its toe in the Mediterranean?

Carefully I put down the angel Giuseppe's boots, so as not to mark the leather which is soft and supple and smells like money. It does, it really does smell like banknotes – or else banknotes smell like good Italian leather. I pick up the shirt; such fine cotton, it's almost transparent, weighs nothing. I press it to my face and breathe in sweat and cologne; olives, sun, salt. I breathe in and in until my head spins and I have to sit down on the old battered chair in which I've passed many quiet night hours.

Most of the guests will be asleep by now. Dmitri will be dozing at reception, hoping that none of the stragglers falling in from the casinos will want room service – vodka, beer, champagne, cheese, ham, caviar. The angel Giuseppe will be lying on his big bed, naked I expect, naked I'm sure, in this heat, on his back or his side, his head resting on the pillowslip I ironed last night. How differently I'd have ironed the linen, had I imagined this: I'd have pressed it smooth with the flat of my hand, the weight of my body.

It's quiet now, except for the generator from which there is no escape. Even if I doze off in my chair I can hear its eternal grumble. No silence here, even in sleep. I fill the sink. The water mustn't be too hot, only warm, and the soap mild. I test the temperature with my elbow. Too hot. I leave it to cool down. In time it will reach the ideal temperature – blood heat. The room, too, is hot, airless, a tatty box. I toss my cardigan on the chair. No need to be tidy. Nobody ever comes here. Soon I'll wash the shirt, polish the boots …

Taking off my cardigan wasn't enough; it felt like another half-measure, another compromise and now that all my clothes are on the chair it's easy to pull the shirt over my head, slip my rough, blunt fingers through the lace cuffs and let the fine white cotton slide down and cover my nakedness, cover but not obscure the neglected architecture of my body, its frozen music, as pani Anna would say. The boots stand beneath my ironing board, a little dusty, of course, you can't have restoration without dust … the boots too. Only a little too big. Not heavy at all and cool against my hot legs. I unpin my hair, let it fall around my shoulders. It doesn't exactly swing when I turn my head, it doesn't fall over my face like a curtain when I place a hand on my heart and bow. No sound comes when I open my mouth but here, in my ugly little room, dressed in the angel Giuseppe's shirt and boots, it occurs to me that this could once have been a bedroom. Anybody might have slept in it, even pan Picasso. With the spatula I use to shift stubborn clots of mud from the shower cubicles, I pick loose a corner of wallpaper and begin to scrape. The strip peels off quite easily at first, right down to the yellow plaster. Then it becomes stubborn and clings to the wall. In the top corner of the plaster, a faint curving line swings between two raw edges of paper. I go back to where I started from and loosen the next strip. It, too, curls away. The curving line continues across the newly-bared patch of wall. Above it, I can now see a small black dot. I keep scraping. With the angel's voice in my head, the memory of his mouth on my cheeks, I too become part of a beautiful restoration.

# Brian McCabe

*from 'Wild Numbers'*

## *1. Counters*

Tiddliewinked into the inkwell,
– that thimble of pale enamel
like an egg's shell, nesting
in an ancient wooden eye –

they were the counters
and we counted them: one
two, three – but who was this
cross-legged abstraction: 4?

We added them into a column
which leaned towards infinity
before it spilled and scattered
its random pattern on the floor.

Soon they'd have us lined up
in columns: human logarithms
chanting an ugly prayer
to the god of Multiplication.

The chaos we came from
would always be there –
whatever was done
with the counters.

Those buttons of colour
we placed on our tongues,
to taste the smoothness
the thinness of 1.

## *0. Mow*

All those men who went to Mow,
went to mow a meadow –
were they mad?

Had nobody told them
that their job was pointless,
that the meadow was endless?

One thing is clear:
they did not go by choice.
They went because they were sent.

Maybe it was no co-incidence
that the place they mowed in
was *called* Mow.

No doubt it was named after
its reputation: all that mowing
day and night, neverending.

The problem was the grass
kept on growing and growing
and the owner despised daisies.

Then one man – deafened
by lawnmowers – shouts to his dog:
"I've had enough! Let's go!"

Then two men – the two
who followed him to Mow –
stop, wipe their brows and go.

Three men, four men, five men...
Very soon there is an exodus
of men from the meadow.

Before leaving, the dog
cocks his leg at the infinite
and pisses a zero in the grass.

## 216. Three Lives of Pythagoras

### 1. A Free Slave

Understand this Zalmoxis:
I bought you in order to free you.
Let me show you the hieroglyph
which explains the flow of rivers.

You must join my semi-circle.
The apprenticeship is five years
of silence, worship of Apollo,
and eight hours Geometry a day.

Here is what you do: go to Thrace.
Hide in an underground chamber.
I will follow you. You will hear me
singing the music of the spheres

That's your cue: rise from the dead.
Don't worry about the town elders –
they will express surprise and wonder.
Then I will begin my discourse:

*This is my sacred discourse.*
*Everything is part of one soul.*
*The gods are stars and numbers.*
*We should not eat animals, or beans ...*

## 2. The Miracle of 6 $^3$

We were hauling in the catch
when he appeared on the shore.
He was something else to look at:
the trousers, the long hair, the turban.
He didn't look like a Greek to me.
More like an Egyptian or a Persian.

When he showed us his golden thigh
and said he was the son of Apollo
I thought I should pay attention.
I listened to what he had to say
this prophet of earthquakes
this charmer of triangles.

He told us we should sacrifice
to Aphrodite on the *sixth* day.
Six was perfect, he said: the child
of its divisors: one two and three.
Moreover it was circular,
since all its children ended in six.

It didn't make any sense to me.
There were only five of us there –
unless you counted Pythagoras.
To give him his due: he predicted
the size of our catch. Mind you,
he did supervise the count.

When he bade us set the fish free –
we did. This shaman from Samos
this cave-dweller who hears
the pure music of the spheres –
his fame has come before him –
who knows what powers he has?

When he paid us for the catch
we'd squandered, he said:
'Two hundred and sixteen.
Six *cubed*, six to the *third* power –
or the number of years between
your death and your rebirth.'

We nodded and we applauded.
He was a very good speaker.
I mean – he knew when to stop.
I was coming to the miracle.
The miracle was the fish:
during the count, none died.

Is this all the bread there is?
Let me share it out equally.

## 3. The Future of Geometry

When Pythagoras crossed a river
it said, 'Greetings, Pythagoras'.
At the same moment he'd been seen
freeing his slave at the market

He was crossing the border
between one life and another
under the ten heavenly bodies
and he wasn't looking back.

Out on the boat with the brotherhood
he had his right-angled triangle
and his table of opposites with him.
And his kithara. He'd demonstrated

that when you stretch the strings
in a simple ratio: 2:1, 3:2 or 4:1
they'd make consonant notes
when they were plucked.

He was also going to show them
what he'd found out in Babylonia –
when the flood waters had receded,
the demarcation of the fields:

that in a right-angJed triangle
the square of the hypotenuse
is equal to the sum of the squares
on the other two sides. Always.

Trust that loudmouth Hippasos
to bring up the square root of two.
Him and his 'irrational' numbers.
They're *expressible*, he'd said.

So be it: the boat would return
to the shore with one student less.
(Some sacrifices were necessary
for the future of Geometry.)

## 164. The Romans

Listen up. This is how
we're about to count from now on.

We got a one: I. We got a five: V.
We got a ten: X. We got a fifty: L.
We got a hundred: C. Maybe a five
hundred: D. We got a thousand: M.

That's it. That's all we need.
The fuck with dealing out letters
to two three four six seven eight nine,
eleven twelve thirteen etcetera.

Those motherfuckers can go eat shit.
The rule is you add the little fish
if it comes after the big fish
because the big fish eats it, right?

When the little fish comes before
the big fish, you take it away –
on account of the big fish aint
ate it yet, okay? Any questions?

Whaddya mean howdya write
one hundred and sixty-four?
Am I talking to myself here?
CLXIV. Dumbfuck.

This means Tony the Scribe
only needs to know seven letters
to run any number we tell him.
Okay let's go eat Chinese.

## 666. Gematria

Pope Innocent IV
signed the papal bull
authorising the use of torture
in the Spanish Inquisition
and finished his breakfast.

The sun came up as usual
according to certain laws
– religious or mathematical,
did it really matter which?
In any case it had no choice.

Even if what they were saying
was true: so his cryptograph
was the number of the beast

in Revelations 13:18 – the case
against him was preposterous.

An agitated cardinal entered
bearing a message from Batu
– the grandson of Ghengis Khan –
declaring war and telling him
that his heart would roast in hell.

– Tell him he can kiss my ring.
There was nothing like a war
to spread the word of God.
Today's sermon would be:
Prester John Destroying Islam.

## 3, 5 etc Twin Primes

They show up every so often,
these shivering refugees
of the known infinite.

In their pockets they hide
stolen candles, calculators,
indecipherable calculations.

After the search, we begin
the endless interrogations:

What are your names?

Where are you from?
Who do you represent?
What is your purpose here?

Words fail them: they can never
put a name to the catastrophe
they have left behind.

In isolation, they deny
all knowledge of their contact
and come out with the same alibi.

Only in the observation room
when they think they are alone
do they glance at each other

with something like pride.

## 997. The Reckoning

This is what you have to do:
write their numbers in this book.

The taking away of the living
the adding up of the dead –

a strange arithmetic isn't it?
They were numbers in life too.

Something I've noticed: orifices.
Human beings have nine.

This one is nine nine seven.
His only significance now

is his number: the last prime
before a thousand.

I don't suppose it matters to him
that he has that distinction.

You'll get used to it. I did.
Go on from where I left off.

After the next two, of course
you'll need another column.

Now I have to go over there
to count the living.

*Literary Life in Edinburgh #6: The Small Hours chez MacCaig*
(L to R: Norman MacCaig, Brian McCabe, Tom Pow, Alan
Taylor and the cartoonist Gerry Mangan)

*Jedburgh Town*

# The Spread Eagle Hotel

*Scotland's oldest continually inhabited hostelry*

20 High Street, Jedburgh,
Scottish Borders, TD8 6AG

Tel. 07958 22418 / 0131 662 0455

# Tom Pow

## *At La Poivière*

At La Poivière, the old words come to me –
the soft plosives of bower and bough –
as I stand below a fiery vault
of cherries. In the filtered sunshine,
first I hold the ladder for my son
as he reaches up to another bright cluster
and drops them in the bowl. And as he does,
so I reach out from the heart of the tree
and feed on those perfect little planets,
coldly burning, which orbit his ankles.

But you're clamouring for your chance too
to harvest plenty, to pluck a treasure
so willing it makes us needlessly laugh.
Soon, your industry's sending our son
running for "Something! Anything!" Nothing
will stop you now, as you toss down
handfuls for me to hold for the coming bowl.
Only I don't. Part-hidden from you
by one of those leafy boughs, I slip
the cherries, one by one, into my mouth.

With tongue and teeth, I ease out the stone
and the sweet flesh is gone by the time
I spit the pit into the dry earth
or at the crumpled green handkerchiefs
of lettuce. You will, after all, pick more
than my hand or a bowl will bear.
And when you do, I'll reach out again
around your skirts to harvest whatever
falls within my reach; thinking, somewhere here
is a parable concerned with love or beauty.

## *The Garden at Bel-Air*

Once you've trimmed the grasses down,
a lattice lies across the lilies of the pond.
Goldfish mouths, like bright rimmed coins,
are scattered between them. That's a start.
Now you clear the ground round two huge limes
that nurture a cherry in their shade, and so free
for uselessness the broken swing that hangs
like two clappers from one lime's bough.

More thrillingly yet, you excise a path
from the arch of the hedge to a green slatted
garden seat. On each side of this track,
twenty yards of briars, of softly dying
roses; a medley of grass heads that dissolve
as they meet the light. "For the children,"
you say, "their secret garden." So is it
the child in me who sits on that bench
in the evening's bosky sunshine, fresh-eyed
and isolate, as the last light dusting
a dragonfly's wing brings me to the edge
of revelation? Could be. But later,

while our children play rummy downstairs,
laying down their cards as chance would have them,
through the dark gate, my love, I'll take this
one shorn road into *our* secret garden
as into a place of meditation or prayer.
Two goldfish under the wings of lilies we'll lie –
and though I'll rarely linger as we'd wish,
our pleasure is in knowing it's always there.

## *Alabama*

### *(sequence of photographs by Walker Evans)*

In the first of the sequence, top left,
there's a corner of leaves like congealed
light. Evans crops them, his camera
clipping the top of the father's hat
till there's nothing of natural beauty
suggested here: if it's not a fragile

choreography – the echoing
elegance of gesture, the rhombus
of arms lifting hair from a damp neck,
the tilt of a man's head, as he draws smoke
through the parched air. For richer
or poorer, an image of family.

Evans takes us down, down to the dust
of the earth. Look! it's to handfuls of dust,
not to light, we're all headed. Down
to the crook of wall and stoop, where a patched
mongrel pants away the day. Down
to bare feet, rough as tools, as planks –

planks on the stoop, their ends like ragged nails.
Down to the chancy boulder stones, perched

precariously one on the other,

*The Drifter* by Jack Vettriano

which hold for now the weight of family.
But if you advance too far on the stoop,
like the youngest, you'll be screwing up

your eyes against the light – the light
which even in shadow holds the deep folds
of their sack-like shifts, the watchful faces
of children, the lean planes of the face
of the father. It's mostly where they live,
out here, between darkness and light.

For through the window, through the doorway,
darkness waits for them to entrust one more
small part of themselves into its care.
There's a simple wooden table there,
with little, God knows, to put on it,
but each evening laden with prayers.

## Rainy Day, Mayenne

Rain falls on the brindled cows

composed within their loose pen of poplars;

on the empty duck pond with its square,
flat-bottomed boat. While quadrilles of chestnuts

and limes shoulder the storm, you
blow soap bubbles into the sherry-dark.

Sizeable fruits they are, each one at least
an apple, though now and again, a sweet

little cantaloup, almost wasted, falls
from your hooped lips. We marvel

at your steady puckered breath; at the soft
watery explosions, the meaningless

blessings we reach for with our open palms –
"let it come! *let it come!*" – as outside rain falls

on the lonely old roads, on churches spaced
like stations – see, in each, St Joan rising

cleanly from flaming tracks. And rain falls
on the war memorials, each name a prayer –

*never again* – and on the villages
where geraniums disburse their brilliant mould

round windows, doors and walls. I love you
unencumbered like this –

lost in what you do.

           Outside a buzzard,
carved from a fence post, takes off

in the drizzle and looks down on a landscape
held by the seams of Roman roads

and by the ramparts of chestnuts and limes,
now shimmering in a rain–stopping light.

# Scottish Culture and the End of Britain

## *Angus Calder*

I'm writing in the aftermath of two big Scottish deaths.

Hamish Henderson was an astonishing figure, central to Scottish cultural development from World War II on, and crucial to the achievement of our new Parliament in 1999. Out of his service in North Africa with the 51st Highland Division came *Elegies for the Dead in Cyrenaica*. This sequence, with its learning, reflection and passion challenges comparison with the biggest men of Modernist verse in these islands – Yeats, Eliot, MacDiarmid. It was at once recognised as a startling achievement, making poetic sense out of a terrible war. But Hamish also emerged as the balladeer of the 8th Army and in the '50s he was the major collector and scholar of the Scottish Folk Revival. This had immense political implications, and Hamish expressed in song as well as in prose his detestation of nuclear weapons, imperialism and racism and his non-sectarian Marxist socialism.

Since he was a republican, it must seem odd to set him beside Elizabeth Bowes Lyon, born in Glamis Castle near Forfar, who became Queen of Britain and co-head of the British Empire (which she most certainly didn't oppose). But her 'common touch' which helped to rally Britain in the dark days of Blitz clearly stemmed from a Scottish environment where her father, Earl of Strathmore, had the time of day for every tenant; and after George VI's death she baffled her English courtiers by choosing to acquire Mey Castle in Caithness, a county notable not for 'lovely' glens apt for the persecution of grouse and stags but for bracing winds, stark wee cliffs facing cold dangerous seas, heelstergowdie cloods and dour folk. (After she died, a couple of these courtiers turned up on TV admitting how much they'd hated it, and I fell about laughing…) History moves on. She was as Scottish as Hamish. But her year was 1940. His was 1999.

'British' as a word defining cultural identity was always of restricted application and is now terminally infirm. But it has served a valuable end, heuristically, in defining and marshalling at certain junctures – the Battle of Waterloo, the Battle of Britain – the commitment of people from various parts of the island to a common cause. In both cases, 'liberty' was on the agenda.

Since sport matters more than politics to a high proportion of the populations of these islands, I'll begin considering Scotland and Britain historically from that perspective then move back to songs, remembering Fletcher of Saltoun's remark that "if a man were permitted to make all the ballads, he need not care who should make the laws of a nation".

The rules of many sports were codified in Britain in the 19th century. Accordingly the first international contests in association and rugby football were between teams from different parts of the British Isles. Interesting anomalies result from this. Five teams from the islands are allowed to compete in European and World Cup soccer competitions. In Rugby Union, the arrival of the Irish Free State in 1922 did not disrupt the practice of selecting Irish rugby teams from both South and North, including Protestants along-side Catholics. Touring in the Southern Hemisphere, the best Irish players have been happy to represent the 'British' Lions. Since the First World War, the Five Nations Championship has brought together teams from all the territories once claimed by Plantagenet and Tudor monarchs.

In Scotland, unlike Wales, Rugby Union was the 'people's game' only in the Borders. Elsewhere, like the south of England, it had a small base consisting chiefly of men educated in fee-paying schools, and soccer was dominant as the sport, effectively the religion, of the Lowland Scottish masses. Nevertheless, rugby internationals attracted huge crowds. There were surges of national pride in 1984 and 1990 when Scotland, with the smallest pool of players, beat the other four nations to achieve the Grand Slam. On the second occasion, captain David Sole famously terrified his opponents in the shoot-out at Murrayfield, when the English also might have achieved a Grand Slam, by leading his team out in a slow march rather than the usual brisk gallop as the crowd howled out the recently composed anthem 'Flower of Scotland'. Around the Millennium, each other nation in turn, as if in conspiracy, denied England four successive Grand Slams.

English fans, like their TV commentators, are not noted for their sense of humour. They find Celtic solidarity against them rather upsetting. They are dismayed by the fact that Scots tend to support anyone, including Iraq, Botswana, Fiji or North Korea, competing against any English team inter-nationally, whether at football, cricket, or tiddlywinks. "But we always sup-port *your* sides," they whine, before the more erudite of them, who read *The Guardian* (which covers Scottish affairs especially badly) digress into their fantasy that ethnic cleansing of the English will occur if Scotland ever votes for independence. But ethnicity has nothing to do with it …

The fact is that no sane Scot believes that there is a Scottish 'race'; or anything which could be defined as a Scottish 'ethnicity'. Geographically, Scotland has the most stable borders in Europe, identical since the 1470s, when the Northern Isles were acquired from Denmark. The population was of diverse Welsh Brythonic, Irish Gaelic, Pictish and Anglo-Saxon stock. When some of us set up the Scottish Poetry Library in 1984 we announced our intention to include verse in all 'the three leids' of Scotland – Scots, Gaelic and English. I have since come to think that one could argue that Scotland has more than three languages, since North Eastern Doric and Norse-based Shetlandic might claim as much autonomy as Por-tuguese has from Spanish, leaving aside the distinctive patois of Glasgow, Lothian and Fife, which might be considered mere dialects.

Cultural differences related to this are so pronounced that one could imagine Scotland dissolving, along lines favoured by Fletcher of Saltoun himself, into a set of city states within the expanded European Union. Recently, after she gave a reading in Edinburgh, I put up my friend Sheena Blackhall from Aberdeen, the leading writer of poetry and stories in Aber-deenshire Doric and also a fine unaccompanied singer in the tradition of the travelling people. Visiting Shetland she detected great prejudice against Aberdeen, which has functioned as a metropolis for those islands. People there preferred their close Norse cousins, Norwegian trawlermen, to crews from the Northeast of Scotland. She has found that the Doric is in steep decline in its historic rural heartland. The peasant culture of the Northeast has waned since the cataclysm of the First World War, and now incomers, often English, have been attracted to work in and around the North Sea oil industry. So, in rustic Aberdeenshire, English and Anglicised speech have gained ground, and the epicentre of Doric is now found in working class areas of Aberdeen itself, reversing the former pattern. Anyway, after the success on TV of *Rab C Nesbitt* and of the film of *Trainspotting*, young people regard Glaswegian or Leith patter as cool, whereas Doric is old fashioned.

However, Sheena would agree that Scots language(s) will survive. Apart from the rich body of literature produced from the middle ages onwards in various forms of Scots, the country has the strongest tradition of folksong in Western Europe. The status of Burns as cardinal national hero, and the rituals of Burns Night are significant. So is the Folksong Revival led in the 1950s by Hamish Henderson and Norman Buchan. Henderson moved around Scotland recording non-professional singers while Buchan and others were vividly interested in songs to traditional tunes as a motor of up to date radical politics. Songs old and new, in any and every version of spoken Scots, passed from singer to singer, accompanied CND marches and helped to inspire the turn of fortune which in the late '60s transformed the SNP from a fringe organisation of eccentrics into a major contender in local and national politics. Music can be said to provide a surrogate for an otherwise indefinable 'Scottish identity'. This provides reassurance that a multi-ethnic, multi-cultural Scotland can work, in so far as immigrants from Europe, Asia and Africa have adapted to and added to the Scottish repertoire of entertainment. I know personally a performance poet whose father was a Yoruba coalminer in Cowdenbeath and a singer called Andy, also from Fife, who looks like a full-blooded Polynesian but will belt out 'Scots Wha Hae' with the best of them.

As they pick up Scottish mindsets, such people are less and less likely to think of themselves as British. A survey published towards the end of 2001 revealed that 37% of Scots now consider themselves to be Scottish not British compared with 19% in 1992. Asked to make a straight choice in 1992, 57% affirmed that they were Scottish *rather than* British – in 2001 80% decided to be Scottish, (*The Times*, 17 December, 2001). One will still encounter people who reject what they conceive to be a parochial Scottish identity in favour of being British. But their numbers seem set to dwindle, despite low support for independence – the SNP in opinion polls only very rarely attract more than a third of the electorate – and lack of much enthusiasm for the performance of the new Scottish Parliament.

The late '60s were when the hinge was swung. The Folksong Revival intersected with the end of the British Empire. Colony after colony was relinquished. Young Scots who would formerly have looked forward to employment under the Union Jack overseas now had to consider their chances in their homeland. Meanwhile, 'nationalism' was in fashion all over the world as ex-colonial countries experimented with independence. Minority rights were an important issue. Beside the surge of Black Power in the USA and the Civil Rights movement in Northern Ireland, Basques and Catalans in Spain, Bretons and Occitanians in France, Sardinians in Italy, were seeking political clout. Left wing activists joined the SNP from the marching ranks of the Campaign for Nuclear Disarmament, and electoral success began with Winnie Ewing's famous by-election victory over Labour in Hamilton in 1967. The exploitation of oil in North Sea waters gave the SNP a specious slogan – 'It's Scotland's Oil' – just as the great postwar world boom was ended by the muscle-flexing of oil producing countries in 1973. In Westminster seats and share of the vote the SNP hit its all-time peak in 1974, since when it has settled down almost as a regional party in Northeast Scotland, but that success spurred Labour towards producing a weak devolution bill which failed in the 1979 Referendum yet gave Home Rule a place on the left's political agenda.

Meanwhile, there is general agreement that Scottish culture had entered a remarkable period. Scottish writers, artists and musicians related themselves directly to developments in Europe and America; English culture seemed tame and unfocussed in comparison. It can be said that this newly assured sense of cultural distinctiveness converged with the 'democratic deficit' established in the 1980s, when Thatcher's government was deeply antipathetic to most Scots. Gradually voted out of Scotland, the Tory party nevertheless continued to impose its policies, with the Secretary of State looking more and more like a colonial Viceroy attempting to subdue fractious natives. The Tories were wiped out in local government in 1995 and lost every Scottish seat at Westminster in the 1997 General Election, after which the Blair Government simply had to accede to the settled will of the Scottish people.

Paradoxically, there seems to be growing consensus among historians that the Scottish 'nation' which now seems to be established, like Catalonia, as a distinctive component of the new Europe, originates historically in and through the Parliamentary Union with England in 1707 which gave Scots the chance to achieve prosperity as collaborators in the British Empire.

To accept, or swallow, this proposition, one has to distinguish between the medieval meaning of 'nation', applying simply to people coming from a certain geographical space and sharing quasi-familial bonds, and the modern sense of the word, implying 'nation state', which supersedes the old sense of the word 'empire', as when James VI & I asserted that Britain – the island he now ruled – was an 'empire', meaning a noteworthy expanse of territory under a single powerful sovereign. Scotland before 1707 was the Kingdom of the King of Scots, who since 1603 had been King of England also. Its parliament met intermittently and had established no significant traditions of debate or lawmaking, its bureaucracy was sketchy, judicial power was devolved to local magnates whose rights were secured by a chaotic mixter-maxter of feudal laws.

Scots anticipated the thrust towards popular representative government which was consummated in the American and French Revolutions in the Declaration of Arbroath of 1320. Scottish barons assured the Pope, firstly, that they followed Robert Brus as their King, as against Edward of England, and secondly that if Brus betrayed the Scottish interest at some future date they would depose him. This right to depose unjust rulers was reaffirmed by John Knox and George Buchanan, in the name of the common people, at the time of the Scottish Reformation when the new Protestant Church of Scotland might have become, as in England, the basis of an emergent nation state. But it didn't. Presbyterians opposed the attempts of Stuart Kings to establish bishops as agents of royal control. Landed magnates joined them in the National Covenant of 1637 when Charles I attempted to anglicise the forms of the Church of Scotland along with its organisation. After this movement fell apart in the late 1640s, Scotland became easy prey for Cromwell's army, which established by force such centralised rule as Scotland had never previously experienced. Something like an emergent modern 'nation' can be seen after the Restoration of Stuart rule in 1660, with a great systematisation of Scots Law, a role for the Scottish Parliament in economic affairs, and developments, largely inspired by the achievements of Calvinist Holland, which prepared the way for intellectual Enlightenment and agricultural improvement in the next century. The establishment of a Presbyterian Church of Scotland after the fall of James VII & II in 1689 was a further step towards coherent modernisation. But the collapse of Scottish aspirations to an independent overseas trading empire with the abortive Darien project of the 1690s helped ensure that arguments for Parliamentary Union with England prevailed with the ruling elite in 1707, when the Scottish Parliament voted itself out of existence. Scotland emerged as modern nation in the 18th century.

Scotland retained a distinctive national church, and independent legal and educational systems. European contemporaries deeply impressed with Scottish achievements in thought, science and literature easily saw that these were not 'English' and indeed the prowess of Hume, Smith, Macpherson and Burns was definitely not a product of the Union. These men and other pioneers in thought and culture drew strength from distinctive Scottish traditions traceable back to much earlier centuries. In return for supplying parliamentary votes *en bloc* to whichever government held sway at Westminster, the 'managers' of Scotland – first the Dukes of Argyll, then the Earl of Bute, then, most successfully of all, the canny Lothian lawyer Henry Dundas – controlled patronage in Scotland and governed the country as much as its influential people thought it needed. By this means the old power of the regional magnates adapted to the new politics.

Middling Scots on the make swarmed into England's overseas colonies and trading posts, taking over whole sugar islands in the West Indies, seizing control of the Virginia tobacco trade, the Canadian fur trade, and establishing from the 1720s onwards a wholly disproportionate stake in the successes and rich spoils of the East India Company in India. The fortunes brought back by Scottish merchants, administrators, soldiers and sailors furthered the agricultural improvement of what had been an habitually half-starved country and fuelled sudden industrial revolution, with the help of rich local deposits of coal and oil-shale. Highlands and Islands were opened up to modern economic development. Walter Scott projected the romantic history of his homeland to the delight and astonishment of the Western World, not forgetting All-the-Russias and modernising native élites in India. But it was now the most up-to-date of all nations, its scope extended by the conquests of the British and Indian Armies backed by the omnipotent Royal Navy, for which the Clyde came to supply ships while South Wales provided the steam coal. Scottish capital was rampant in spheres as far apart as the tea and opium trades of China and cattle ranching in the USA's Wild West. By 1900, Glasgow was a model for the modern city and Scotland was probably the richest country in the world.

Linda Colley has demonstrated, in her seminal book *Britons*, how the idea of Britishness came to prevail between the Union of 1707 and the accession of Victoria in 1837. The long series of conflicts between Britain and France, between the great Protestant sea power and the big continental Catholic military power, forged the invention of Britishness. A Scottish poet, James Thomson, wrote the words of 'Rule Britannia'. Britons, whether English, Welsh or Scottish, defined themselves, as Colley puts it, "… against the French as they imagined them to be, superstitious, militarist, decadent and unfree. And, increasingly, as the wars went on, they defined themselves in contrast to the colonial peoples they conquered, peoples who were manifestly alien in terms of culture, religion and colour." Even some Irish Catholics became British patriots, before and after the Union of the Irish Parliament with Westminster in 1800. But the cultures of the archipelago did not blend. As Walter Scott showed, one could preserve the most intense passion for Caledonia stern and wild, one's own, one's native land, while rejoicing in the triumphs of the British armed forces over Napoleon and expressing devout loyalty to the Hanoverian dynasty which, despite the madness of George III and the profligacy of his son and heir, had come to represent for Britons not only the virtues of sturdy monarchy under the sublime British Constitution, but, most improbably, family values.

The climax of the new Scottish combination of innovation, prosperity and small-n nationalism with proud acceptance of British identity came in the era of Scott and Byron, when Scottish thought and literature awed Europe, Edinburgh vied as a centre of publishing with London and Paris, and successive British prime ministers – Melbourne, Palmerston and Russell – studied at Edinburgh University. This didn't last.

The death of Scott in 1832 coincided with the departure of Thomas Carlyle to London, the development of the railway and the reform of national and local government which destroyed Scotland's oligarchic system.

Though Edinburgh still had many decades ahead of it as a major centre of publishing, Scottish writers now sought fame in London. The railway drastically reduced travelling times between Scotland and the south-east of England. In the 18th century not one English man had represented a Scottish parliamentary seat (though many Scots had been elected in England). Now prominent English parliamentarians found constituencies north of the border. The triumphant liberalism of free trade, with its dehumanised version of Adam Smith's political economy, had no time for romantic nationalist ideas. Scotland might as well be 'North Britain', as many of its people came to style it as they addressed letters adorned with stamps which did not mention Britain at all, as they still don't.

Early in Victoria's reign, the term 'British Empire' still referred primarily to the United Kingdom of Great Britain and Ireland. 'Imperialism' was a nasty thing which boastful French popinjays indulged in. By the time the old queen died, it was the proud creed of most Tories and many Liberals; she herself had been created Empress of India by her clever prime minister Disraeli. Half-baked Scottish nationalism in the 20th century would put it about that England, having subordinated Scotland and in some sense 'colonised' it, sent the country's active males out into the worldwide Empire to do its dirty work as policemen, soldiers and administrative and professional dogsbodies with the connivance of a Scottish upper class deracinated by attendance at English public boarding schools.

That in every part of the Empire Scots were prominent and important surely belies this caricature. In some – the economy, culture and politics of Canada, African exploration and missions, Bengal jute, Hong Kong banking and trade with China – Scots were quite simply dominant. Michael Fry, in his important book *Scottish Empire* (2001) has argued forcibly that Scots used the empire for their own ends. They were not interested in acquiring vast new territories but in commercial profit and social improvement, at home and overseas. Coincidentally Martha McLaren, a Canadian scholar, in a study of *British India and British Scotland* (Akron, Ohio 2001) has emphasised the importance of their origins in the Scottish Enlightenment of three administrators whose doctrines and practices had a cardinal influence on the development of the British Raj in India – Thomas Munro, John Malcolm and Mountstuart Elphinstone. They were not, as previous historians saw them, conservatives of the Edmund Burke school – '…they required land tenure and revenue collection systems that encouraged rather than inhibited progress; they required the creation of economically and politically active "middling" social groups to function as the agents of improvement; and they required, as a counterpoise to the inevitably authoritarian nature of imperial rule, liberty for Indians to participate in the administration, if not the legislation, of their own country – particularly the administration of justice.' Both Fry and McLaren reinforce the view put forward some years ago by John Mackenzie, Professor of Imperial History at the University of Lancaster, that a distinctive 'Scottish social ethos' informed the activities of prominent Scots in the Empire exemplified, for instance, by David Livingstone.

Livingstone thought that poor Scots would gain from emigrating to central Africa – but believed that local Africans wherever these emigrants settled would be brought as equals into the modern world by trading with Scots and learning from them. When presenting himself to English and European people in Africa, Livingstone was happy to call himself 'English'. When writing about his dreams and schemes to fellow-countryman Sir Roderick Murchison, head of the Royal Geographical Society in London, he reverted to being a patriotic Scot. I think such double identity was characteristic of Victorian Scots. It went along with Carlyle's notion that the English were great doers but needed others – presumably Scots like himself – to perform their thinking for them and with the smug conviction, rarely voiced in public, that the Empire was really run by Scots.

It was a Scottish politician, Lord Rosebery, who first, in the 1880s, put forward the idea of a British 'Commonwealth of Nations'. This re-emerged after a disastrous Great War in which troops from White Dominions had acquitted themselves most notably; its presence in Scottish debate in the 1920s has been generally overlooked. No one could miss the enthusiasm of Scotland's leading intellectual imperialist, John Buchan, for the white Dominions. It went along with a passionate attachment to Scots language and strong sympathy for Scottish Home Rule. Hence his encouragement of MacDiarmid's project to promote a new Scottish Renaissance in the arts.

If the Great War was a calamitous watershed for Britain as a whole, it hit Scotland particularly hard. Through the Scottish regiments, used as shock troops and in forlorn-hope actions, the country suffered the heaviest per capita casualty rate in Western Europe – one has to go as far east as Serbia to match it. Scottish heavy industry – coal, engineering, shipbuilding, iron and steel – had a spasm of climactic activity. Then after the war export markets dwindled or disappeared. In a spate of nationalistic thinking, related to the appearance – within the Commonwealth, be it remembered, until 1949 – of the Irish Free State, the idea that Scotland should have Home Rule as a Dominion, equal in status to Canada, Australia and Eire, commended itself for a time even to such an extremist as MacDiarmid.

The emergence in 1927 of the National Party of Scotland which MacDiarmid co-founded, and which became the Scottish National Party in the 1930s, was a natural outcome in a period which saw a Constitutional Convention in Scotland involving Liberal, Labour and non-party elements, the failure of several home rule bills, and the creation, by public subscription, of the magnificent Scottish National War Memorial on Castle Hill, Edinburgh – a direct result of the Duke of Atholl's angry response during the war when an English MP had suggested a British National Memorial in Hyde Park. This was formally opened in 1927. The popular writer whose pseudonym was Ian Hay, formerly Major Beith of the Argyll and Sutherland Highlanders, proclaimed in a souvenir book that "Scotland alone among the nations has erected a National War Memorial commemorating in detail the service of every unit of her Arms, and the name of every one of her hundred thousand dead". (*Their Name Liveth*, 1931) Hay underestimates casualties greatly, but his point is clear. Along with other right-wing Scots he wanted to celebrate the special military sacrifice of a very special nation. I'm sure Elizabeth Bowes Lyon went along with that.

What sidelined this nationalist upsurge was the great slump of 1929-1931, which came near to wholly destroying what was left of Scottish heavy industry in a period, furthermore, of severe agricultural depression. Scotland in 1914 had been a proud and wealthy co-partner in the Greatest Empire the World Had Ever Seen. In the '30s, high unemployment persisted even while the Southeast and Midlands of England made a sparkling recovery through the new light engineering industries. Daunted and demoralised, Scots began to blame the English for their troubles, and a tradition of whinge began which sadly persists in some quarters to the present day. Meanwhile, however, the Scottish Office was devolved from Whitehall to that huge new building on Edinburgh's Calton Hill, so that in a sense, up to a point, the government of Scotland came home to Scotland.

In Churchill's wartime Coalition Government, the Secretary of State for Scotland was Tom Johnston. This left wing veteran of the Red Clyde had promoted in the '30s the London Scots Self Government Committee, creating the impression that the Labour Party favoured Home Rule. Johnston himself was unquestionably a patriot, and used the then-fictitious bogey of rampant Scottish Nationalism to persuade Churchill to let him introduce, through quangos and by administrative fiat, striking reforms in his homeland even in wartime. Labourites were duly convinced that administrative devolution was enough. The senile arteries of Scottish heavy industry were flooded again with war contracts, it staggered to its feet and unluckily kept going after 1945, aided by the subsidies to regions handed out by Labour and Tory governments. Scottish nationhood reached an nadir in 1955, when over 50% percent of the electorate voted Conservative, followed a few years later by the Labour Party's abandonment of a traditional commitment to Home Rule which dated back to Keir Hardie.

This is easily explained. The heroic and successful war created a new focus for pride in Britishness. Scots had served alongside fellow-Britons in the armed forces, and Scottish females had flooded south to work in English centres of war industry, often marrying Englishmen. The populations of the island had been scrambled together as never before. Full employment and handouts from Westminster afterwards mitigated anti-English grievance. The unravelling of Britishness commenced only in the 1960s.

In a very simple way Scots must always be British, since we mostly live on an island called Britain. Our bit of it was never purely British ethnically, since the Brythonic Celts occupied only the south of Scotland. However, Scotland, even Orkney, featured in 'the Matter of Britain', the body of Arthurian legends stabilised by Geoffrey of Monmouth in the 12th century. Recent studies by Robert Crawford and others have emphasised the great, even dominant influence of Scottish writers on English literature since the 18th century, but only an idiot could fail to notice that Robert Burns idolised Alexander Pope and that Scott's momentous achievements in fiction drew on those of Shakespeare and the English Restoration dramatists, as well as the novels of Defoe, Richardson and Fielding. For that matter, sorting out – as Michael Fry has tried to do – a distinctive Scottish presence in the Victorian Empire will always be complicated, if not sabotaged, by the very success of Scottish Enlightenment thinking south of the Border, producing Anglo-Scottish, or if you like, 'British' ideological soups. Both John Stuart Mill and John Ruskin had Scottish parents and would always have been fully qualified to play soccer or rugby for Scotland, but to claim that their thought is 'Scottish' would be pettily chauvinistic.

I return to sport, where I began. It illustrates surviving anomalies and contradictions. Scotland, along with the Channel Islands and the Isle of Man, has its own representation in the Commonwealth Games, but its competitors become British, if picked, in the Olympics, even when they are curlers, adept in a sport not practised at all south of the Border. Any Westminster politician wishing to ensure that Scotland immediately declares full independence will seriously follow up and enforce somehow the idea put forward a few years ago by a temporarily insane Labour Sports Minister that there should be an All-British football team. Scotland will never give up the right to beat San Marino and draw with Faeroe in World Cup and European competition. But our biggest teams, Rangers and Celtic, want to play in the English Premier Division …

Only a huge political upheaval involving violence will unite the Basques of Spain and France in a single homeland. The people of Catalonia, we are told, like the Spanish better now that they have achieved a substantial measure of Home Rule and are mostly content to be Spanish as well as Catalan. Such notable historical entities as Brittany, Flanders and Bavaria, now merely regions or *länder*, are incorporated into a European Union which will probably soon include independent countries – Latvia and Slovenia – which had not the merest ghost of existence before the twentieth century and others – the Czech Republic, Poland, Lithuania and Hungary – whose present boundaries have been arbitrarily determined by the outcomes of appallingly brutal wars. 'Scotland in Europe' has been a recent SNP slogan. In so far as Scotland is and always has been a European country, this gets one no further than 'Scotland in Britain' would. In so far as it points to the same status as Denmark and Finland, countries of similar population, it implies no more, if no less, independence 'in Europe' than these currently enjoy. Since England has ten times as many people as Scotland, democracy insists that it will always weigh more in Europe.

Two decades ago, when I was editing an anthology of 20th century poetry in English from Britain for a publisher in the old East Germany, she insisted that it had to be called *Englische Lyrik*. Her argument was that Britain is a merely bureaucratic concept, like 'European Union'. Right enough – the *Wehrmacht* in 1940 sang that they were marching 'against England', not Britain. The only context in which the adjective British had cultural, rather than just bureaucratic significance, was in the terms 'British Army' (but note – Royal Navy and Royal Air Force) and 'British Empire'. Recently attempts have been made to use British and Briton as words to incorporate recent immigrant groups – as in 'British Asians' and 'Black Britons'. But black footballers born in England insist that they are English and want to play for England, and the Scottish Sikhs who invented a Sikh Tartan for the new Millennium were subscribing to Scotland not to Britain.

The British Constitution, which is supposed to enshrine this great British tradition, is notoriously unwritten. I hope that Mr. Blunkett will give all of us, not just immigrants, the chance to swear an oath to register ourselves as citizens of Britain. As things stand I am not myself a citizen. I am a subject of Queen Elizabeth II of the United Kingdom of Great Britain and Northern Ireland – Queen Elizabeth I of Scotland, as it happens – which means that I am completely at the mercy of the sovereignty of the Crown-in-Parliament. Equipped with my rights as a citizen at last, I could use them, along with my hereditary liberty, while pursuing my aim of freeing Scotland from that sovereignty, as vigorously as Bruce defied the claims of Edward II, and consolidating a Scottish Republic.

If the British Monarchy had crumbled in 1936–1941, as it might well have done, a people, or rather, a set of peoples, amongst whom republicans were a tiny minority, might have fallen into confusion and demoralisation and caved in before Nazism. Elizabeth Bowes Lyon, clever and beautiful and genuinely sympathetic towards ordinary subjects, saved the monarchy, with all its symbolic potency. Born in 1942 to leftwing parents, I simply might not have come into existence without her. Without Hamish, his songs and their spirit it is hard to imagine how the almost indistinguishable political and cultural movements of the 1980s could have created the momentum for our new Parliament.

Now we need a new momentum, a new cultural movement which can focus the fact that Scotland is not basically about Tartan, as the inane creation of Tartan Day in New York seems to propose. But what are we 'about'? We can't be 'British' any more. I suggest that we are, as we always have been, 'European', whether or not we are steered into ever-closer union within the EC, or, as an independent republic, decide to get out. What is our distinctiveness to be?

The era of MacDiarmid is over. May the era of Henderson begin. 'Freedom come all ye' has the implication of full-blooded internationalism. Our population is falling, and ageing. We need young workers and fresh genes in our always-mongrel mixture. We should aim for a Scotland in which immigrants are welcome and every school is multicultural. I think the new movement must be towards getting it to help us destroy racism and promote new syntheses with whatever customs and cultural forms new Scots – from Kosovo, say, and Afghanistan, from Sierra Leone and Somalia – bring when they come to join us. Frankly, with a declining population and good economic prospects, Scotland could do with plenty of Asian and eastern European immigrants just now, illegal if necessary.

# filmmusic
# theatrecomedy
# clubsartkids
# booksgay life
# travelshopping
# foodvideo
# comicsinternettv

**THE LIST**

GLASGOW AND EDINBURGH
EVENTS GUIDE

## Entertainment made easy

Magazine out fortnightly, weekly during August.

# Colin Donati

## *On a High Bridge*

Our cast shadows change the surface of the firth,
we move by day across the water in an absence
as shadows of clouds which touch the distant foothills
flow over the land and the green fields
and are cast upon everything.

Lichens and bracken clutch on emptiness,
shoots spire from fields of absolute uncertainty,
a dog on a chain is a car on a bridge
lifting its leg against a pillar on the bridge
which every second moment can never be a bridge.

Our shadows change the surface of the firth,
we move across water in an absence
towards a certainty that never comes until,
laid to rest by the advent of the night,
we become one shadow.

The water is emptiness,
the light cast on its surface
is cast into an emptiness.

## *Rent, Totorn ...*

We stood on the cliff's edge
　　you looked to sea, I to land,
　　　　I thought of stars, you of buses,

life's like that: the mind
　　all false correspondences and
　　　　juggled words preferred to silence

the constant wordless gaze
　　of all that's real round us we
　　　　don't connect with, split by rancour

standing at the cliff's edge
　　looking to land and thinking
　　　　of rents, or to sea and buckets –

this was what happened, this
　　was what was impossible
　　　　to let go of at time of death

but at time of death let
　　go of it we do and must
　　　　at time of birth let go again.

## An Uncanny Translation

I met Catullus in heaven
but he wasn't speaking to me,

I didn't understand at first;
I wanted to be friends with him,

When finally he turned and smiled
patient, wry, loveless, level, cold,

everything was explained: I knew
he wanted to know why I'd done

what I'd done to his poetry –
wanted to, and yet didn't care.

## Generated from the Sun

Rock is shade,
shade is cool,
cool is water,
water is life,
life is rock.

Rock is cool,
cool is shade,
shade is life,
life is water,
water is rock.

Rock is water,
water is cool,
cool is life,
life is shade,
shade is rock.

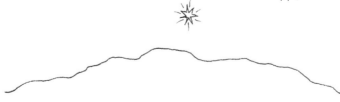

# Gordon Meade

## *The Shark*

To have a life so well honed down
As a shark's; where the merest whiff of blood
Acts as a trigger to release one's

Non-thinking, totally instinctual,
Predatory gifts. To be able to dismiss
Thought; to get rid of all one's

Psycho-babble, the white noise
Of the human species; and just exist. No Freud,
No Jung, no Melanie Klein, just

The pure line of a fin through salt.
To offload Shakespeare and unplug Bach; to have
Never seen a Rembrandt, nor a Monet,

Nor a Braque. To be one's own work
Of art, a one-man show, a performance piece, a wordless monologue of cartilage and teeth.

With no beginnings to be grateful
For, and no endings to fear. To be able just
To live; right now, right here.

## *The Bat*

The song of the bat is silence
Or at least it is to our ears.

Whosoever can hear it, is driven mad.
For what it sings of is the ineffable joy
And despair of life. It works on a frequency
We can only dream of. We can

Pick it up on our machines but when
It is played back to us, it loses all meaning.
It sings of a state from which few have returned.
And those who have, either have

Too little to say, or too much;
And, anyway, are usually ignored.

## The Song Of The Swift

The song of the swift is concise and direct.
It goes straight, to the heart of the matter

Which in its case, is speed. It is as if all
The colours; all the deep blues, the crimson
Reds, and the brilliant whites of the swallow
Had been burnt off by an almost suicidal flight.

For what it says is: *Go! And not with the flow,*
*But beyond. Go as far as you can and don't come*
*Back! If you can't hack that, then don't bother.*

For it, the sky is not the limit; it is just
The start. It is dying to be a rocket, and is
Headed for the stars. If, indeed, there is life
On Mars, it will be the first to find it.

## Prometheus and the Eagle

For me to say that she caught
His attention, would have to be
The biggest understatement

Of the year. For who wouldn't have,
With her beak buried in his liver, with her
Talons hooked inside his chest.

But to say that she earned his respect,
I would have to be a little more circumspect.
For how could he respect her, she

Who had shown him, so blatantly,
The extent of his own ambition. And yet, she
Gave to him what only an eagle

Can give. Not what he was looking for;
He thought he had already found that;
But what might happen to him if he ever did.

# Fancy Dress on a Theme of Sea

## *Morelle Smith*

### Skincity

Smudgy sunlight, soft and hazy, faces blurred, shadows softened, a slope of a street and the Dix-sept Café, with its wicker French chairs, seats and tables outside, this feels like Paris, this light and those café tables and the smell of morning coffee. Location is not geographical at all, it is stored in some library of perception, not entirely body nor completely mind, but somewhere, somehow – Paris perception is not confined to a remembered place in the imagination or a geographical location. No, Paris perception includes the imagination as well as the sight of these wicker chairs outside the Dix-sept Café, and spring sunlight filtered through a faint haze.

Perceptions perhaps listed under weather conditions. Haze being the vehicle of imagination. Blurring memory and the present. Letting in possibilities. Maybe this is what its like when you die, skimming though familiar streets. Do you make appointments then, with friends? Do you make phone calls and arrangements? Or do you feel time as pressure on your skin, or deeper inside you. Do you feel it as a kiss of magnetism, a direction-finder, steering you this way or that, the compass of emotion, light-fingered, light-footed, like the thin web of dance of the morning birds on the roof slates.

"Our culture is welded to time," the man in the stripey jersey had said, the night before. "We are welded," he said, "to clocks." Imagine clocks on the perimeter of our world – spires of clocks, like the one towering gracefully above the railway station; the mural clock in Clusone with its moon phases and its zodiac signs, as well as the day's hours and the sun's zenith, rise and decline. Plastic alarm clocks that buzz and push you out of sleep, like heartless gaolers. Musical ones, like mine; waking to electronic Mozart. Church clocks and railway clocks; neon digital clocks, clocks without numbers, or with Roman numerals; ticking clocks and silent clocks; rimless clocks and wooden-framed clocks.

The stripey-jersey man showed this most clearly by describing a culture with a different perception – a mixture of lunar rhythms and calculation – and interpretation of what is good or bad, encouraging or conflicting. By mixing these together, one came up with a very different kind of calendar. One could have two Sunday the 16ths for example. One could miss out Tuesday the 3rd. There could be 12 months or 13 in a year. This was not arbitrary, it was calculated with exactitude, then meaning, purpose, the movement towards auspicious and away from inauspicious, were added. Religion was interpretation, resulting in a perception based on harmony and balance. The ground belief was harmony and balance. Not the pursuit of the clock hands, some Sisyphean endeavour to catch time and overpower it, once and for all, so that the stone-pushing effort would not have to be done the next day and the next, into oblivion. Our culture gives a lot of power to time. The master. Time has to be obeyed.

But this other culture, other perception, alters it in the interests of peace and equilibrium; in the interests of harmonious relationship between the human and the divine. Which is after all, what religion is supposed to be. This culture adapts time, to serve the greater good; to shrink suffering and enhance balance and harmony. This shocks us. Time – God toppled from his throne. How could this be?

The hazy light softens everything. People's faces have a wondering look to them, faintly smiling. The big clock over the train station says that I am late, though I do not feel late. I dip down past the tour buses parked outside the station. Arriving tourists are caught in the city web of buses and taxis. Someone plays the bagpipes outside the station. He – or some-one like him – will be there for all the summer months and the autumn ones as well. He will be endlessly photographed and his cap will fill with coins. He's not the only one. Up in the High Street there is another, in less formal dress, a plaid thrown over his shoulder, leather thongs round rough cloth from his ankles covering his calves. His hair is long, curly, thick and wild. Sometimes he ties it back. It bursts out from the leather tie, surrounds his face, like the stylised glow around the sun in medieval paintings, faintly curling yellow licks of light – emanating flames, leaping out. His hair streams out as if his face is the source where all the winds are born. As of course it is, for all of us, who live in windy climates.

But today is still. As if the weather-mongers are asleep and holding their breath, or gone off on holiday. Businessmen all, the weather-mongers are concerned with profit, economic growth, improving returns and minimiz-ing outlays. Like time, we have linked ourselves to these strange laws of loss and profit, outlay and returns. Coming to the top of the hill, I cannot believe in them. I leave the vestiges of my lip-service to grey-suited gods at the roundabout where Hanover Street meets George Street. In the mid-dle is a statue of George IV. There is one god only, in this muted sunlight, stroking my hair back from my face. Both she and he, this god is within me and without. Within me and without I hum quietly to myself, walking over the black and white pedestrian crossing, down towards Princes Street.

Sorry I'm late I say to Brenda, as I arrive in the café. Time again, stalking us, pursuing us, prostrating us. My most persistent lover. My feelings towards him are ambivalent. Any love I suspect sometimes, of being a tyrant in disguise. A trapper. After my pelt or my conscience. After my store of nuts, or the kind of time that's left after the clocks have done with it. This is called freedom time and I cannot touch it or see it, cannot really describe it. Its not something you can store in a room, turn the key on and come back to. If you have some, it comes with you. Even if you forget that it is there. It disassembles your atomic structure, alters it, fills it with space and sunlight. It is the most powerful thing I've ever known. I cannot talk about it, not directly.

Words make it itch and edge away. 'Don't try and pin me down' it says, truculent and tetchy. 'I'm not for owning, not for defining.' Or I imagine it would talk that way. In reality, it simply tunes out, lost in background chatter, traffic hum, the layers of sound that wash over us. Beachcombing in this sea of sound we find shells and bones. Once, only once, I found a starfish on the beach at Senegalia, Italy. We are often shore, but, in the times when that indefinable, disassembling energy is with us, we are also sea and the inhabitants of the long-abandoned shells; we are horizon and the warmth of sun on skin; in short, we can unlock time's secrets if we let that disassembling energy come so close to us that we remember – for a moment or a season or a day – that this 'free time' or time-free essence is who we really are.

It is, you could say, the Source Perception in the library of Perceptions – and, more than that, you cannot say about it. But with it, with it – with it turning your bloodstream into sun- stream, with the diamond energy within you, there is nothing that you cannot say. You're not late, Brenda says as I sit down. Funny that for it agrees with my perception. I hadn't felt late. It's those clocks again. The clock in this café is a light, reflected on the wall. It is nothing solid. It's a projection, or that's what it looks like. Brenda's drinking a double espresso. Her eyes are blue. She leans into the morning, a quiet boat. A light sail, rippling in a benevolent breeze. Thick canvas. An occasional thump, like a drum. Rough texture, aching the fingertips, waking them, wanting more. Make rips in your canvas, fray them and dip your fingers in sand, broken sea shells and charcoal. I think this, but do not say it. Instead, I say, This city is Paris today. Will you have half of this chocolate muffin? she says. I didn't realise how big it was, it's too much for me, please have half."

As I eat the muffin I say – I'm wondering if habits and expectations are what make a relationship. If you take the habits away, there might not be anything left. That reassembled part of me cannot bear habits, they're mud and glue and limit me. Brenda chews the chocolate muffin. Like an illness you mean? Maybe. Habit as illness. I don't understand why people get ill. I know someone who's had this bug for two weeks now and she's not really better. I don't understand why she lets it happen. I order a regular coffee. The lemon light falls through the plate glass window. It could be I suspect all lovers of being time's accomplices, covertly trying to steal something from me – my store of time, my selkie skin, that symbol of freedom – they want to tether you. That may be your perception and not them.

Yes, it is my perception. Maybe it is not them at all. But where do these stories come from? Of men hiding seal-women's skins, for without their skins they cannot go back to their true element and their real love, the sea. The only way men can make them stay is by stealing the thing that enables them to be who they really are. But yes, we collude on some level. Until we don't any more and we find the skin, the lost freedom. Like an illness maybe. Why might we want an illness? Still, at some point in our lives, our bodies get mortally ill. Most people die, at some point. Unless, she says, you're one of these spiritual people who live for hundreds of years. Would you want to be one of them? I don't know.

Do you think you've lost your skin? Is that why you went to Newcastle, to do this course? Maybe. But I didn't find it there, in the post-modern art department. It isn't me. I argue with the tutors and they don't like my work. They're the orthodoxy. If you don't agree with them, then you must be the heresy. So of course they won't like your ideas. More, they will be utterly opposed to you, on some deep level. Which they will rationalise, into this or that concept. No, I don't suppose your skin is there. She smiles. The young man behind the counter comes and fills our coffee cups.

## II – Seaskin

The sun blares out like a trumpet from the clear blue, then a shelf of cloud moves across the sky, a bit like one of those sliding glass partitions you get in certain reception areas where people who you can still see moving about and talking to others have just announced they're closed and have ceased communication. You can thump on the transparent screen all you want, they're going to ignore you, so you're wasting your time.

The cloud slides across. The procession along the Fishquay begins with brass bands. Everyone is dressed up in some sea- theme. Some blues and greens are easy enough to recognise, other orange and yellow ones, not so clear. One of the bands is dressed in light brown, beigey colours, so I figure they're the sand. Sand band have hats on that remind me of nine-teenth century explorers, hard, shady, protective, so I wonder if perhaps they're the crab band, in subtle camouflage.

People on stilts wear flimsy fish-net over skimpy swimming costumes, hats on their heads like pies, with wiggly black snake- like things hanging from them. The octopi or squid squad do a carefully choreographed waltzing march, one of them, with a painted cardboard boat around his middle, floundering desperately and the others weaving an agitated motion round him, spreading their alarm around in increasing circles. Can you help him? they ask the children on the outskirts of the crowd. A few move forward tentatively, take the rope offered by the stilt-walkers, help to pull the wounded boat to shore. The boat man rocks and heaves, but the stilts never stumble. The children get into the game and the wounded boat moves on, the stilt-walkers swallowed in the crowd.

I'm sitting outside Joe's café, drinking a 50 pence cup of tea, in a sty-rofoam cup, brown plastic container of milk – about the size of a thimble – and a plastic stick, slightly thickened at one end, like a miniature fly-swatter, to stir the tea with.

There's a poster on the inside of the window, displaying a gas mask and advising people to keep one with them at all times, for one never knew when Mr Hitler might strike. Another poster asks for women to take in evacuated children. There's a picture of a very slim and elegant woman bending to embrace a child, one of several who have just come off a train. The children look clean, tidy, shyly expectant. Another holds his hand out to a friendly dog. A picture of safety, warmth and welcome. An old wooden wireless in the window. Mr Joe wears a navy-blue apron, with thin white stripes and a broad brimmed straw hat.

The procession brought a wave of people with it, which thins out after it has passed. There are stalls selling hot dogs, fish and chips, hamburgers, sausage in a bun, chips and curry sauce, kippers being smoked on a grill, right before your eyes. There's also stalls of candy floss, ice-cream cones and the usual gaudy array of plastic trinkets and unbelievably ugly syn-thetic-furry toys. Lindy Lee, Gypsy Rose Lee's grand-daughter, has her own psychic wagon, brightly-painted in green and red, with gold lettering on the board that lists her abilities to tell your fortune, tell your future, give clairvoyant readings, read the cards and the stars for you, as well. Every-thing, it seems, is readable by her. Faces, hands, eyes, tea-leaves, flower-petals, stones and clouds. Entrails are notably absent from the list, but she could probably ply a fast trade in reading fish-bones.

The smoke from the sizzling kipper-fires lunged up the steps from the Fishquay to the studios, lingering in hair and clothes and nostrils. Inside the building, the kipper smell has sunk into the stonework. On the wall of Brenda's studio is a blue spattering of spiral broken up like water pat-terns gathered on a pane of glass; blurred vision seen through rain or through emotion.

On another wall are self portraits in monochrome. These selves are shadows, sometimes dark and sometimes pale – mere outlines, barely dis-tinguishable from their surroundings. In one of them a few drops trickle down the white outline, so the effect of looking through an invisible, but impenetrable barrier, is increased. Its what I feel, Brenda says. Effaced, almost invisible.

From her studio window you look out onto the quay and beyond it, the water. A liner slides out from the mouth of the Tyne, heading out to sea, bound for Scandinavia.Later, when we walk further round the sea-edge, leaving the raucous music and crowds and whistles and shrieks of chil-dren, all behind, we stop and look out at the sea. Sometimes, when the light falls in a certain way, she says, its as if the sea has a skin on it and if you were to jump onto the water, you'd never be able to get through the skin.

I watch the meagre light the cloud-ledge has allowed through from the sky, spill on the surface and scatter outwards like a coating. It has a fine pattern of wrinkles on it, as if poured by a shaky hand. The sea surface is shivering, in the light wind.

We follow the path, round by the Priory, turn off into Tynemouth. I imagine myself clad in water-skin. I would like someone's hands to define it. Not remove it; but define it. But they would need to be hands made of light.

# James Robertson

## The Bluidy Sark
(A Poem in Six Voices)

### Old Woman in Residential Home (September 1998)

I wish, son, I cud tell ye I wis there, that I mind it
Juist like yesterday, thon time when Buffalo Bill's Wild West,
An this auld shirt that's in the news, rowed intae toun;
But I wis eicht year short o bein born in '91. I'm sherp,
But no that sherp. Ma Uncle Jim tho uised tae speak aboot it.
He wis a polisman in Glesca – they tuik on
Muckle kintra lads like him, tae keep the keelies doun.

It wis a time o miracles: ye'd see the weirdest things
In Glesca then. No Bible stuff – the halt made haill,
The deid recawed, plagues o puddocks, water intae wine –
An no the miracles o later years, like angels in white gounies
Haudin back the Hun wi bleezin swords –
Na, Glesca's ferlies were mair doun-tae-earth,
Which tae ma thinkin maks them mair sublime:

A herd o buffalo in Dennistoun, wi bairds like shuils;
Wee Annie Oakley shootin fags oot people's mooths;
Cowboys lassooin coos; the Deadwood stage; Reid
Indians daein a war dance. Oh, hoo I wish I'd seen
*Them* in their braws. Uncle Jim had tae lift yin for assault.
He'd fetched a white man in the show a michty clour
Wi a kinna club, on the back o the heid,

Eftir getting fou wi whisky in a Duke Street baur.
The Sheriff must hae thocht himsel in sheriff heiven,
Sendin a reidskin tae the jyle for thirty days. Oh,
It wis a sin, ma uncle said: the fella'd only dune
Whit awbody else wis daein that nicht in Duke Street;
But ye canna act that wey an syne no pey for it
When ye're an Indian in a Wild West show.

The man he skelped – na, *skelped*, son – he wis
Geordie Crager, that translatit for the Sioux an cud,
Jim said, hae talked the erse aff a Hielan coo,
He wis that gallus. Jim tuik him tae the Kelvingrove,
An he gied or sellt that shirt tae Paton, the curator.
I wish I'd speired if there wis bluid on it, or bullet-holes,
But it didna seem important then. Is it important noo?

I wish that I cud see it yince afore it gaes,
Afore I gae. No that it maitters, but it's juist
The news aboot it's set me thinkin on ma Uncle Jeems.
He wis ower saft tae be a polis, sae he cam back hame
An wis a postie, an he mairrit Auntie Jean. He wis aye
A gentle man, an tellt aboot thae times wi winner,
As if in gaun tae Glesca he'd crossed continents in dreams,

As in a wey he had. But aw the tales gaed oot o him
When I wis seiventeen an baith his sons, ma kizzens
Chae an Sim, were killt in nae man's land, yin eftir ither,
On the first day o the Somme. The nicht that news cam in,
I had ma ain wee miracle masel, an it's lastit me a lifetime.
I luiked up at the burnin starnie sky an I kent for shair
That we, for guid or ill, are on oor ain, an heiven isna there.

## Woman at Public Meeting (November 1998)

Nae contest is there? – faur as I can see.
Nuthin tae argie-bargie ower, if it wis doun tae me.
I'm tellin ye, I'm maist impressed.
But wait, whit's this noo? Oh aye, might hae guessed.
Here's whaur their dignity gets gien a squeeze:
*Here, chief, a haun-oot fae the lucky bag!* Aw, please,
No a tartan scarf! I mean tae say,
These folk huv no cam aw this wey
For geegaws. Noo whit? Haud me back!
A set ae prints bi Rennie Mack?
I thocht I'd seen it aw.
But naw.
I mean, whit mair dae they huv tae dae?
Get doun on their Injun knees an pray?
It's theirs, we've got it, disna maitter
If we peyed for it or no. Naebody here needs a translator
Tae unnerstaun the situation.
We're Scots, they're fae the Lakota nation,
So dinna beat aboot the heather, dae whit's right an best:
Gie them the shirt an stuff the rest.

## Man on Radio Phone-in (December 1998)

That we, in the land o James Clerk Maxwell, David Hume
An Logie Baird, can aye be bairns an souk the thoum
O superstition, scunners me. That we shuid feed
The freits o a bygane age, simper assent tae a creed
O ignorance, because it is the PC thing tae dae,
Gies me the dry boak. I'll hae nae hokum, naw, I'll hae

The facts. The fact is, if this sark's the genuine Mackay,
Its *magic*, sae-cawed, wis aboot as magic as the wey
At fifty twa-pund shells a minute – a Hotchkiss gun spits leid:
Nae magic there at aw. Itherwise, hoo did he en up deid,
The puir mislearit savage that wis weirin it tae sain himsel?
The slauchter shuid hae blawn at least thae glaiks tae hell.
There's a principle at stake, an tae *it* we shuid be leal:
Naebody is dignified bi pittin faith in whit's no real.

If, on the tither haun, the sark wis niver near
The battlefield, but this guy Crager, ower here
Wi Buffalo Bill, spun a guid yarn tae the curator
O the 'Calvin Grove' Museum (great nomenclature
*That* by the wey, maks it soun like the kinna place
The Kirk tuik ower frae God – Eden wi a Presbyterian face)
Syne flung it in wi some ither bits o Indian gear
For a handsome forty pund – weill then, it's clear
The case for giein it back is oot the park.
That's aw I hae tae say aboot this bluidy sark –

Forby juist ae thing mair: I dinna haud
Wi ethnic cleansin, auld or new, no for God,
For land, for race or onythin. But for the luve o man
Shuid we no be giein the Sioux a helpin haun
Intae the next millennium? Insteid this is a bribe
Tae stey in the past like some noble reid-skint tribe
O Jacobites, that we can watch an pretend tae be,
But only in oor dreams, in virtual *un*reality.

### Black Elk (1931)

I didna ken hoo muckle syne wis at an en.
When I luik back frae this the heich ben
O ma auld years, I can aye see them, see
The frozent murdered fowk at Woundit Knee:
The hashit bairns an weemin juist as they had been,
Huddert an squattert the lenth o the cleuch –
I see them noo as clear as wi ma young een.
Somethin ither dee'd in that sair feuch
In the bluid an glaur, an wis smoored bi the snaw:
A people's dream, a bonnie dream, dee'd there.
The nation's gird's in shivereens, awa,
Aw skailt. There is nae centre ony mair
An the haly tree, the people's hem an heid,
It tae is deid.

## Man in the Street (June 1999)

Awthin chynges, naethin chynges.
That's an Indian proverb, an it's true.
Luik at this stushie ower the ghaist shirt.
Appearinly, there's a revisionist view
That says if it's stained wi bluid at aw
It's chicken bluid. Weill, chicken shite
Tae that. That's no a hert-felt dout
Aboot its authenticity, that's spite.
Funny hoo aw thae years gaed by
An naebody iver spottit the mistake;
Or that the ticket niver bure the legend,
*Ghost shirt : genuine, but may be fake.*
Shaw me an object that ye care aboot, onythin,
Disna maitter whit it's made o, whether it's new
Or auld, an I'll shaw ye an icon, symbol,
Signifier. That's whit this is tae the Sioux.

## Newspaper Reader (July 1999)

The day thae cooncillors set aff for Sooth Dakota,
Takkin the ghaist shirt wi them, there's me
Oot in the gairden, howkin weeds. I luik up,
An a heron, a raggie clout o a thing, is sailin
Ower ma heid, juist like some grey-gouned sowl
Gaun tae God. Awa abune it in the blue
A jet's white threid wis frayin intae oose.
I stude an watched them baith, the bird, the plane,
An thocht o fowk an things in flight, auld
An new exchanges, an that sark gaun hame.
I thocht hoo the heron fishes: like a statue o itsel,
As if the inner bird has left its birdness bi the burn
An flee'd aff for a while, but it aye flits back in time
Tae stob the fish it's waitin on. An somethin else
Cam tae ma mind: a photograph that's hauntit me
Since I wis nine or ten: a deid man in the snaw,
A seik auld man in aw-throu-ither claes,
Hauns raxt oot tae grup at naethin, ice-stiff
Whaur the bullets foondert him; still an on he lies,
Auld Big Fuit, deid a century an mair,
Aye frozent there,
Aye ettlin tae rise.

# Bright Mirrored Bauble

## *Frances Campbell*

The party is moving, the thing's in full swing, sometimes you just hear yourself over the din. And people are dancing while green strobe lights play and the pulse of the music has them all in its sway. You wend your way through to a group on the side and they pull you on easy, they pull you on in, for you're magic tonight, you don't know why it's so, it just happens that way, you've felt it before. And a few are familiars and the rest are quite nice, though there's some hostile auras to put down for the night. And the laughter and chatter it leaps to and fro like a dolphin on water with sparkling *bon mots*.

You're gorgeous, lovely, you're brimful of ease when a voice from the crowd gives you something to seize, and you catch its direction and you light on his eye and it's dark and it's tender and you think you'll just try. But he mustn't know as you wreathe him in smiles and play with the others that you're up to your whiles. So you chatter and sip and angle your chin, giving promise of good things that might be for him, and his gaze is upon you, intelligent eyes, taken in by the woman, the womanly wise.

He's yours now to play with, he's swallowed the bait, like a bright mirrored bauble you slowly rotate. But you mustn't hang on though you've hooked him for sure – let the hunted come a-hunting, let him follow the lure. The timing's important, the timing can't wait, too long in a crowd makes the spark dissipate, he'll be inured and your chance will be gone, it's time to take leave, it's time to move on.

But wandering away you're not quite detached, his eyes, you can feel them, they're burning your back, and at the food table you crumble some cake, suppress your excitement and casually wait for him to come up and close in on your bait. Look here now, he's coming. He's crossing the room. You've got him, you darling! Oh, but you've done well! And your heart it lifts up in a jubilant swell.

Now there's just you and he and you're fidgeting still. It's different now. You've nothing to say, for there's something between you as clear as the day, but it's not right to come up and come out and just say ... So you talk of the party, and the people who're there, and things flag for a moment and you're scared it will go when he puts his hand on your shoulder, leads you onto the floor. And the dance is a slow one, and you have to dance close, and that's just what you wanted, that chance to be near, and you don't have to try now, it's all up to him, no resistance speaks for you, with your breath in his ear.

And the music's all round you and into your soul, and the people are hazy and doing their thing as his arm tightens round you and presses you fast and that hand on your hipline it kindles a glow and the blood in your veins starts to quicken its flow. Then the music stops playing and you're linked evermore, like two palm trees swaying from one root in the floor.

And people move round in the light from the door and a voice from the kitchen shouts – Room for one more? – and then you must turn and look into his face and his eyes they receive you all light and sweet grace. And you smile in return when the music starts up and he bends down to kiss you and turns up your chin and you think you adore him, adore giving in. And as the music keeps playing you neither let go, but mouths pressed together, suck each other in. And you don't know how he's feeling but you think it's the same. The wide mouth of his hunger knocks you back with the force and the strength of its claim. And then the dance stops and you loosen your hold though his hands clasp your head like a bird in their fold. And when he bends down to whisper, his lips touching your ear – Woman, you're lovely. I'm taking you home – your heart it explodes and bursts forth in a grin. You're so glad that you're lovely, lovely to him.

*Illustration by Colin Dunbar*

# Fighting Talk

## *Alan Bissett*

**DOWNSTAIRS**

GonLewis, gonLewis, gonyacunt … asit, asit, hitthefucker, hitthefucker, hitthefucker … ooya … OOYAfuckinbastartye! Wooof! See that? Whitdya fuckin makey THAT?! Got a fuckin fight noo, ih? Ay Ah fuckin saw it, da no jist! Belter!

Noo …

Noo … Dinny dae anyhin stupit ….

DINNY DAE ANYHIN STUPIT!

Asright.

Aaaasright!

Nae bother … jist erse aboot till the enda the roun. Fuck it! Ay.

Asit.

DINNY DAE ANYHIN STUPIT AH TELT YE, CUNT!

Yerawright. Yerawright.          Awright …

Well done, son! Well fuckin done that man, ye fuckin deserve that round.

 Ay, wan oot the fridge if yer gawin, Archie …

**UPSTAIRS**

Yes, yeeees, oh I *know*. I know! What is Bridget Jones like? She's *soooo* funny. I mean, I can *totally* relate. She *defines* modern woman, do you know what I'm saying, with all our post-feminist insecurities. I mean … yes. *Yes!* You're *soooo* right. After feminism won us the right to reject male-dominated obsession with our weight, bust and hair, we *became* more worried about them! Fat really is a feminist issue, you're one hundred per-cent correct, Fiona. It's like Germaine Greer says in *The Whole Woman…*

Oh, you haven't read it? You *must*, you simply must! *Sooo* inspiring.

Robert? Oh he's watching the boxing downstairs. Yes, yes, barbaric. Vulgar. It makes me sick, it makes me *physically* sick. Who's playing? Oh, Lammox Lewis or somebody like that. No, I don't know the score. I think it's on cable, hang on … I'll put on the portable…

Uh … Lennox Lewis versus … someone else, can't pronounce his name. It must be half-time, they're sitting down. Oh hang on, the umpire's calling them back up …

**DOWNSTAIRS**

Right Lewis, montay fuck. This round, this round.

Intayum. INT-AY-UUUM!

Nawnawnawnaw, Gawin the wrang wey! Take the fight tae HIM, take the fight tae HIM.

Fucksake. Naw son. Nut! Blown it! Get aff the fuckin ROPES!

Noo! Noo's yer chance!

Fucksake, ih! Refereeeee! Ats BANG ootay order! Disqualify the CUNT!

Aw Ay. Wee talkin-tae. Handslap, yer right Archie, fuckin handslap. Biased cunt.

Noo ...                           Gon ...

FUCKYE! OOYABASTART!

AGAIN! AGAIN! AGAIN! AGAIN! ATSIT! ATSIT! ATSIT!

HITUM! HITUM! HITUUUUUM!!!

## UPSTAIRS

Oh barbaric. Bar*bar*ic! I can hardly bear to *watch!* Are you watching? Yes. Cavemen. Two grown men butchering each other in the name of sport. Typical product of a society based on patriarchal values. Don't know *what* Robert sees in it.

Hang on, Fiona ... Something's happening ... Oh dear!

Oh DEAR!

Did you see that? One of the men just-

Oh for *God's* sake, don't STAND for that, son. Hit him back.

Terrible, absolutely terrible.

## DOWNSTAIRS

Hing is, Archie...Ah've no goat that sortay special sumhin whit you an Jan huv goat. Naw, naw, Archie, come oan noo...dinnae sell yersels short ... You and Jan are *great* thegither, fuckin *great*. An that wee bairn ...

Bit ... me an oor Angie ... Ever since she startit that fuckin university, it's like ... we've nothin tae say tae each other oanymair. Like that marriage guidance cunt wis sayin: try tae take an interest in each each other's hobbies. Ah ast her earlier if she wantit tae watch the boxin wi us the night. The fuckin *look* she gied us, man! Aw ay, like *she* made a big effort, eh?

When she's no oan the phone tae *Margo*, or fuckin *Fiona*, she's giein it lah-de dah aboot Germaine fuckin Jackson or whitever her name is. She's chainged, Archie. A chainged woman, Ah'm tellin ye.

## UPSTAIRS

Oh, son! Come *on*. Don't stand for *that!* A disgrace. You're right, Fiona, absolutely scandalous. No way was it below the belt. In fact, I'm sure his belt's higher than the other man's ...

Oh!

OH!

Belt him! That's right. You're doing good, son.

Oh, for fuck's sake! (scuse my French, Fiona). Bloody terrible!

Whack him! Into him! Hit the cunt! Hit the CUUUUNT!!

## DOWNSTAIRS

Ah mean ... men and women, Archie. Men and women. We're no *built* tae get oan. Men like boxin; women like *Bridget Fonda's Diary* an aw that pish. Feminism! Feminism's tae blame, Archie. That bloody university ...

If we'd only sortay seen each ither's point eh view, me an her, tried oot each ither's lifestyles. Too late noo though. Too different noo. Absolutely nothin in common at all.

## UPSTAIRS

A *DRAW,* REFEREE? WHIT! WHO'S PAYIN THAT CUNT, YA FUCKIN CHEATIN BASTART YE ...

# Gathering Winter Fuel
## *Mary McCabe*

Shuddery clamminess, mud on her face. Jinty awoke as water seeped under the wall. She rose, moved the drier straw near the fire. After squatting at the dying embers for a moment she put the last of the wood on. This made her responsible for gathering more fuel on time.

Nearby, Chassy began to stir. Gran sat up and stretched. Jinty thrust the papers at her.

"Hey, Gran. Read us some more before we start work."

"Wait. My eyesight isn't what it was."

Chassy hugged his knees and sang:

> *My eyes are dim I cannot see*
> *I have not brought my specs with me,*
> *I have not brought my specs with me.*

"I'm surprised you like this stuff." Gran held the papers at arms' length, towards the firelight. "Where was I?"

"'Two screens ...'"

Two screens in a plastic wall. Public and personal windows out of Catriona's cosy home. The business screen filled with the list of Working Places vacated in the past day. Details of each were keyed in and a dozen names appeared, eligible by education and time in the Availability Pool. Catriona put the monitor on hold while she accessed her personal screen.

"Stuart. Kirsty's over here. Fancy meeting for eats?"

"Not now," said Stuart. "I'm off for a walk."

"In December?" yelped Catriona. "The park's four junctions away!"

Stuart shrugged and disappeared from the screen, leaving Catriona's saver – a series of unidentifiable mammals, all jaws and no body, swallowing each other in a symbolic binge of voracity.

"Have you considered Stuart?"

"Nice personality. Don't know about the genes."

"Gran," said Jinty "The way these women talk about men..."

"Jinty," said Gran "before, women could choose if sex should lead to babies."

"No babies for me. Not after how Ma went, and for a dead thing with no ..."

"Ssh, child, you're young. Many girls think like you, but eventually ..."

"Not me. I live and die a maiden lady!"

On the screen – thin-faced, hollow-chested, melancholic...

"I've been allocated WP798 and I don't want it."

Catriona ran WP798 through. Calculating tax on imports.

"What's wrong with it?"

"I hate figurework. I had a Place before that was all about money and I was bored."

"What's your Pool number?"

"AV80037." Catriona ran AV80037 through. "You did accountancy at college."

"They needed me to meet their targets. Didn't want it then. Don't want this now."

"It's only six months."

"Six months is one hundred and sixtieth of my expected lifespan. A precious, irreplaceable fraction."

"All Places involve staring into some terminal and pressing keys. Who cares what the keys mean?"

"I want an Outdoors Place."

"A *what?*"

"Had one in a park, once. Cleaning graffiti off walls. Checking out the swans. Enjoyed that."

Catriona accessed the global directory.

"Closest for that kind of Place is Cumbria. But, well, I suppose you know the Pool Allowance system in England is diff ..."

"I'll stick with Scotland, thanks."

"There's nothing like that here just now."

"Then I'll take nothing."

Not melancholic at all. Defiant.

"While the State is supporting you, you must contribute when called."

"That's okay. My family'll share theirs."

Catriona ran AV80037's family through.

> Mother – four months into Place in a mall eatery.
>
> Sister – five months back in the Pool.
>
> Nephew – in education.

"Your family must be getting little enough to keep themselves."

"They'll forgo extras."

Defensive, not defiant.

"You don't mind sponging off your family?"

"Not at all."

Kirsty leaned over and clicked Secrecy. "Look, Catriona, here's another bloke just as suitable for WP798." She ran AV63954 through for Catriona's benefit. "Get it over with. Then we can mosey off for eats."

Catriona clicked to AV80037. "You're back in the Pool. I'm cancelling your Allowance until a further suitable Place comes up and you accept it."

"Thanks for sticking your neck out." The unemployee smiled warmly.

"How could they contact people as fast?" snorted Chas. "How could they have as many life stories to hand?"

"The publisher accepted that all right. It was the attitudes he found hard to credit."

"Attitudes?"

"I originally targeted it at a fem... at a women's rights magazine. The magazine closed down before publishing my story. The next publisher I approached couldn't accept the altered relationship between the sexes."

"How did you justify it?"

Gran's murmur drifted round the shadows on the walls. "In those days, work was becoming more casual, training more superficial. Then we underwent major changes to our government. I'm sorry, this is complicated …"

"Go on. I like listening. It's … restful."

"I thought: the relationship between Scotland and England has changed. What if this is a catalyst for changing other power structures?"

"Catty … what?" said Chassy.

"When primeval men …"

"Evil men?"

"After men discovered fatherhood, they invented marriage to gain control over their offspring. Unmarried mothers were ostracised; girls set in competition for husbands."

"Ostriches?"

"In my story, by controlling reproduction, women got men competing for favours from *them*!"

"Favours. That's nice."

The eatery area swept down to the Clyde, under glass, exposed to the weak winter sun. Celtic music wafted over the tables, while the back murolograph showed teenagers stripping an endless willow. Catriona clicked on the autoserve for Indonesian food, carried her food to a table. "Mind if we join you?"

Jackie's book fell and she heaved to retrieve it. Her dungarees, decorated with a bullseye, stretched over her abdomen.

"Can I see?" Kirsty glanced at the cover. "Good?"

Jackie shrugged. "Anthology of turn-of-the-century apocalypsia. Nostradamus, nuclear winter …"

"… comets hitting Earth …"

"You got it."

"Surely a bit dated?" remarked Catriona. "After all, it never happened."

"And it won't," claimed Kirsty, "now we've booted out everything nuclear and got to scanning the skies for meteors."

"Who's to say what will or won't happen? Anyway, it's fascinating in a morbid way. Stone Age living with glimpses of a better existence…"

"Heavy reading for you, surely, just now."

"When I was pregnant," Kirsty took a forkful of pasta, "it seemed more six years than six months."

"Six months?"

"A feminist society would develop incubators to shorten pregnancy."

"When's it set?"

"Let's see. I wrote it before the Catastrophe. Turn of the century. I set it fifty years into the future …"

"That makes it just about …"

"Fire's almost out," remarked Chassy. "Who put the last stick on?"

"I did. I know, I'm going."

"I never knew you'd had a child!"

"The sly thing," Catriona nudged Jackie in the ribs. "Won't name the dad!"

"Why honour one, when you can honour five? Actually," announced Kirsty, "I took my five from the Pool. Their genes can match anybody's. They're all graduates …"

"Sure. 80% get awarded degrees only to measure their lives in half-years."

"At least here they're awarded degrees. In England they must buy them."

"A degree! I've got that!" Jinty scampered to her recess.

She had a beautiful collection – a bit of red glass for looking at flames and sky, a broken watch for opening and her favourite, a picture showing lofty stone buildings and brightly-dressed people. On the back SAUCHIEHALL STREET GLASGOW – in loopy writing she could hardly decipher:

> *All change here. New Parliament, new millennium, Edinburgh magnificent, Glasgow hopeful., 100,000 at the Hogmanay bash in the centre.* Chi mi a rithis thu. Duncan.

"Look!" She held out a grubby page, cream and red. "Isn't it pretty?"

"You wee rascal! So that's where my sociology degree parchment went!"

"What's it for?"

"Sentiment."

"Why don't we flit back to the glen?" complained Chassy. "Then Jinty and I could attend school all year."

"Up here, the potatoes don't rot in the soil. Anyway, I can teach you better than Fergus."

"That's right," said Chassy. "You've read lots of books."

"Fergus didn't even know which was the biggest planet," said Jinty. "I asked him."

"Fergus was also born too late."

"Jinty, the fire."

"I'm going, I'm going." Jinty heaped sheepskins around her shoulders. Lifting a brand, she pushed out into the dark.

Each solstice further up the hill, the scrub was now visible in its entirety. Black wispy patch against the less perfect blackness of the moor. Scraggy branches on an indigo sky, one planet aglow. Too late for Venus, too blue for Mars. Friendly beam from a poisoned face.

"Jupiter. The biggest." Then Jinty was felled from behind. Sweaty smell, matted hair, big blurred mouth, lice crawling beside her eye. Two laughs and her light went out.

Nine months later, Jinty died in pain. Out of her corpse the midwife cut a healthy boy. However, the only nursing mother in the glen had barely enough milk for her own, and the village herd had been put to graze in a bad field. After two weeks the baby gave up. Gran and Chassy disposed of him where they had buried Jinty and then packed up their blankets, pots and hens and flitted to live in the glen. So Chassy could, after all, attend school the year round, to learn what he was there.

# Telling Yarns

## *Ian Stephen*

My mother and most of my uncles were always telling yarns. Some of these were Lewis stories of murder, tricks and intrigue but most were family stories, developed into set pieces. I'd started to tell some at family gatherings and at sessions, Aberdeen way, when I was a student. Someone told me about this Festival at Keith run by the TMSA. Great music but it was a bit like a Mod for speakers of Scots and English. Bothy ballads, diddling and storytelling were encouraged by way of afternoon competitions in halls with bad acoustics and scraping chairs.

My landlord in Aberdeen had won the men's ballad, the previous year and Stanley Robertson, a mutual pal, was a regular at the storytelling. It was pretty foreign to me, the idea of one story after another, without too much warm-up yarning. Then the judging. I got nowhere but a few people came to talk to me afterwards. One David Campbell said I'd have to come down to the camp site for a tent-ceilidh later on. A tall man with a soft voice and a louder laugh came to say my style of telling a story reminded him of a few folk from the west coast and I had to meet …

This was the first but not the last time I experienced Hamish Henderson's way of introducing just about everybody in a given street at a given time to each other. Continuing on somewhere, leaving a wake of muckle discussions. Soon I was in a bar with Hamish and another fellow who'd told a story through a beard that could have been nicked from the Van Gogh postman. Neither Ian King nor I were drinking alcohol at the time but we were in the pub long enough, meeting Pinouelle Og and her wiry man.

It didn't take Hamish long to find that she didn't mind belting out big ballads. Frank Sinatra meets Jeannie Robertson in the Royal, Keith. In turn he treated Pinouelle to a discourse on the provenance of her name. It might have gone on but we realised we hadn't eaten since breakfast. Hamish said the sit-down fish and chips high tea was the thing at his age, not much more than a carry-out and he'd pay the difference if we were short.

David's tent-ceilidh spilled into a Renault 4 and sped for Edinburgh. Norman MacCaig was doing a reading at the Calton Studios. David introduced us and we talked about Harris. This was long pre-Castaways. Norman talked a bit about Scalpay, his mother's native Island. I'd toured it in a black cab – my father did business with the local merchant and his son was a cabby in Glasgow, home on holiday. Back in Aberdeen I went to a gallery talk, on the working songs of Carrara, without even realising this was being delivered by Hamish in a more scholarly but no less lively mode. I'll never forget the recordings, strangely reminiscent of Gaelic worksongs, echoing out from the reel-to-reel machine.

I never got to know Norman so well but found only a generous streak behind the fast sharp wit. When I returned to Lewis and did my Long Island National Service by way of editing an anthology, he couldn't have been easier. Here's some recent ones about Harris. Use what you like and I don't want a fee for anything linked to that place.

At Keith or Muchty I'd meet up with Hamish and be introduced to a hundred or so new folk each time. This is Karl Dallas, writes for *Melody Maker*. And we were on to the necessary quality of restraint in art, particularly the fiddler's art. A stage that usually came long after amassing all the techniques. As it happened, Alasdair Fraser, who'd been a bit of a prodigy, winning Mod competitions, was quietly playing in the street. The crowd was building up, recognising the qualities we'd been searching for.

I saw the BBC's alternative Remembrance Sunday programme, where Hamish was filmed revisiting the settings of the Elegies. EUSPB re-issued that fine book about the same time I published my first collection of stories and we met again as part of the First of May bookshop's Fringe programme. This was a classic fringe of the fringe event. Not in an upfront venue and not at a peak time. Hamish led the half-dozen round to Sandy Bell's and we did a round-robin. He sang in Scots. Barbara sang a Brecht song. A woman who happened to be married to Adrian Henri was a fine singer. The next guy happened to be Adrian Henri. There may well have been poems but we all sang. A pretty routine evening in the big guy's company.

*Poetry London* had a second coming, I think for one issue only. The cover was an Ian Hamilton Finlay poem, in colour. It came with a wee flexi record of Alan Ginsberg wailin awa. Hamish's songs were published alongside some stuff from the Beatles. Another time he introduced me to Sidney Graham. I'd been to the reading, arranged by *Cencrastus* to coincide with Faber's publication of the *Collected Poems*.

W S Graham was swaying at the lectern. He picked out MacCaig in the audience and had a wee go at him –

"Is he as good as they say he is…"

After this I wasn't desperate to meet the great exiled bard who seemed to be a second cousin of Dylan Thomas but it was like being able to time-travel to days when poetry was urgent. We were in East Nicolson St but it could have been Soho, with combatants home on leave and before I knew it the big man was saying, Now Sidney you really must hear a story from …

I couldn't do it. OK we were now in the pub but it was still really a literary do. In Hamish's world there were no divisions. All his own reputations belonged together. He was visibly shaken when he saw we hadn't hit it off. But a pint or two later he and Sidney were in full flight and I was able to slope off to another table. I bought the book and sensed the parallel with MacCaig's self-suppressed apocalyptic days. Except in *The Night Fishing* which might well have been the Daffodil, a Scalpay drifter. Norman's standpoint had become clearly defined, though not detached. The trick of perspective was pursued with constancy livened by wit. W S Graham was an expressionist.

So was Iain Crichton Smith but it took me longer to realise it. I'd met him before knowing he was a writer. He was Donalda's new man. My mother and Donalda had been great pals, both displaced Gaels in the

Central Belt, joining choirs and supporting each other. Then I'd gone to a reading at the Aberdeen Arts Centre and been asked back to Charlie King's place. Iain found it strange that I could contemplate going back to live on Lewis. For his generation, the ascendancy of the boys in the black hats stifled creative expression. I told him I didn't find it like that.

So later, going to visit the Nicolson Institute in Stornoway with Iain was great crack. These kids thought they were in for a slow tough hour, with old women and death. They were amazed by his zany humour and moved by his implicit concern. I used to think that Iain's poems were inconsistent and I still think his prose writing is. The direct way he was able to communicate with just about anybody is the clue. Dogma was dangerous to him because it threatened the power to express what is inside. For me the key is his translation, "You are at the bottom of my mind." He dares. And look at the range of reference to colour through the poems, over the years. Donalda told me Iain seldom missed the chance to look at paintings. Yellow and orange occur a lot.

MacCaig's conversation was never so poised it was detached but the wit and structure was elegant. The few times we met, he always came over as friendly behind it all. Hamish's talk was eclectic, sonorous, driven and yet also structured. Iain's was the nearest I've come to being on a bobsleigh ride. At a great event, staged by Thom Nairn in Dingwall, I had to force myself to leave the table to go for a piss. Tom MacGrath also cracked. We left Iain and Michael Marra with a head of steam. I remember Tom saying, at the urinal, Hell, we'd better not be too long about this. That conversation could go some distance in a couple of minutes.

The last time we met it was courtesy of Citylink. The Glasgow office gave me duff gen on connections to Oban to get me in time for a project on Mull. Then came the smart move – the Inverness office wouldn't sell me a through ticket to Oban because they realised they'd be liable to get me there when the bus stopped at Fort Bill. I wasn't going to get to Mull that night so I explored connections and got on an alternative range of buses at driver's discretions which took me through Taynuilt. Iain and Donalda were in and wouldn't let me me get a later bus to Oban. The dinner topics ranged from Shakespeare, through the West Coast of Scotland Pilot to holidays which included all you could drink of own-brand liquor.

They dropped me at the pier in the morning but it wasn't quite goodbye. A year or so on, Kevin MacNeil and I hired a car to take some of the luck out of getting to the memorial service. I think he'd have enjoyed the range of personality and topics of conversation, following the service. I saw big lads last seen in short breeks and Ian King, with an inch or two on the beard. Then Kevin and I got back in the car and unknowingly set out to pay true homage. When you're off the island, with wheels, who cares which road, how many miles. So we drove by the settings of so many poems, not stopping but knowing Luss Churchyard was down there and we were going through Dumbarton. In one of these schemes was the woman who urged the young man, "And now you'll take a bath."

I'd learned that from Iain. If the words are the right ones they don't have to include the marks of rhetoric to have resonance. But no-one was at home at the flat we were going to stay at or at the house with the telly we were supposed to be collecting. We parked outside Kevin's former des. res. while a heavy frost was settling and I thought of it, through glass, through curtains, idling, probably with power going to it but no picture.

A conversation with George Mackay Brown seemed more in control though the range of subjects could be eclectic. Have you read Flannery o Connor? And what do you think of Borges? Of course you had to go and see him. You wouldn't meet at any literary dos off Orkney. In contrast to Iain's work, I found some later poems too formally crafted. But I'd never forget the image of the old guy at the helm of a yole, going down but still sucking at his pipe. And I loved the stories in *A Time to Keep* – a hammered hardback on my shelves. The themes and symbolic weight, the span of history – all these were there but just happening within a simple narrative drive. I returned to *Greenvoe*, chosen by a Scot Lit discussion group, meeting in afternoons in downtown SY and found it compulsive and deep.

I only met George twice. When you think of all the students, critics, readers and aspiring writers who called at his door (outwith the sacred morning writing period) his generosity with his time was amazing. The pace of his talk appeared measured, even slow but the pauses were more than punctuation. He took the time to read some of my stories and pointed to one he thought worked. This was nearer a spoken voice.

It's taken a few years for the hints to sink in. The old guy who's cooking smoked haddock in milk, thickening the liquid, and the young guy who's got to get to the dogs, get the bet in – there's a hell of a lot in common. Orkney and Glasgow, Brown and Kelman. It shouldn't need saying because it's so obvious. The vernacular voice is strong. But I found, when I became a Civil Servant, organising maritime rescue within a paramilitary organisation, that the vernacular voice had inferior status. To carry weight, spoken and especially written statements had to be made within formal conventions. I realised I'd grown up in a culture which valued spoken language on its own terms. That wasn't just a Lewis thing or an island thing or a rural thing, but very strong strand in Scottish literature.

Latterly, I sensed a shift, even within the Coastguard Service. The last course I attended, in Search and Rescue Planning, was really one long seminar, compiling experience. When it came to allowing for tidal influence on drifting targets we should talk to the fishermen. Lift our gaze from tidal diamonds – these were only keys to controlled sampling at particular places and times. But guys trying to get a livelihood in there, every day of their lives – we should ask them, on the VHF radio what they reckoned the tide was doing. The detail between the salient points. Hamish and George and a whole tradition in Scottish literature would like that. Talk to the guys, don't sound bloody official. Then feed what they tell you into the computer plot with the rest of the data. Then speak back to them, when you've got the area and you're sharing out the sea you've got to search.

# George Gunn

## Four Points of the Saltire

### First

& foremost the North
the Pictlands & the skerries
where the cat has its province –
Take heed of your son

### Second

the South, in the ballad land
of Eildon & the clash
of horsemen –
Take heed of you son

### Third

the broad Buchan East
where the plough
sings to the sky –
Take heed of your son

### Fourth

the kyle cut West
Mannon Mhic Lear
Hebridean sea gatherer
Take heed of you son

Today into Scotland you go,
Ghillie Mor
Tomorrow, songs
will flow free again, and new voices
be borne on the carrying stream

*This poem was composed in Blairgowrie on the morning of Sunday, 5th of May on the occasion of the ashes of Hamish Henderson being interred on the summit of Ben Gulaben, his beloved 'Hill of the Whaups', in sight of his mother's house in the Spittal Of Glenshee. The poem was read out by the author as a banner bearing a likeness of Antonio Gramsci was unfurled. It was a truly beautiful day. The last verse, obviously, is quoted from Hamish's own poem, 'Into The Earth I Go'.*

*The following six essays first appeared in* Chapman *16, 1976. The authors were asked to answer three questions: What started you writing? What keeps you writing? What is your relationship with poetry or the Muse?*

# My Way of It

## *Norman MacCaig*

A man, whether he likes it or not, can't climb down from his genealogical tree and scramble up another of his own choice. To go back, then, only two generations, three of my grandparents were Gaels and the fourth was a Border Scot from Dumfriesshire. She's the one who gets me to places on time.

I am, that's to say, a three-quarter Gael. Now, Celtic art is not at all the romantic, not to say sentimental thing of popular belief. Its extreme formality is to be seen in all the forms it takes in its carvings and sculptures, its personal ornaments, its poetry and its music. (Think of pibroch.) All those genes I carry about, therefore, incline me strongly towards the classical rather than the romantic, the Apollonian rather than the Dionysian, and this inclination was both revealed and supported by the fact that I took a degree in Classics. By some, sloped in the other direction, my work has at times been criticised as being, to their taste, too cool, too restrained, too controlled. Naturally, this doesn't bother me at all. My defence, if I were to make one, would be restrained murmurings about the distinction between passion and emotion and a smug re-telling of Mallarmé's answer to the lady who asked him, "Do you not, then, ever weep in your poetry, Mons. Mallarmé?" "No, madame," he said, "and I don't blow my nose in it either."

This means, too, that I have always had a great and to some degree an exploratory interest in prosody and rhymes. Until about ten years ago, or less, I wrote only in stanzas that were metrical and used rhymes. But I was aware of the bullying authority of the compulsively iambic nature of English and particularly of the danger of adding to the thousand miles of banal iambic pentameters. But my way of "breaking the neck of the iambic" was not, for many years, the Poundian one of flopping into free verse and deserting the basic element of the metrical foot in favour of the looser, and more variable (and more difficult) basis of the cadence, or phrase. I tried to rescue my metrical lines from a rocking-horse humpty dumpty by using off-beat stresses – but not so off-beat that the ghostly paradigm of the iambic pentameter (for instance) was not to be noticed behind the frailer metrics I was using. I also began to indulge more and more the ancient practice, publicised as 'sprung rhythm' and often overdone by Gerald Manley Hopkins, of taking liberties with the number of syllables in the foot – but, again, still preserving the fundamental iambic movement of the line.

In much the same way, I very soon became bamboozled by the apparent assumption of many people then that the only rhymes were those in which the final vowel, or vowels, and the final consonant happily chimed in consort (sin, begin; sorrow, tomorrow; Proteus, hello tae us) and I was soon writing what many people would say weren't rhymes (road, red: mud, fur: full, pale: backs, taxi). I say "then", because this sort of thing has now become common enough practice. All this was nothing new: Gaelic poetry has been assonantal for centuries and I believe Irish Gaelic poetry exploited about every kind of rhyme you haven't thought of. At any rate, anyone interested in such fascinating delicacies need look no further than the Irish English verses of that insufficiently recognised poet, Austin Clarke.

There came an evening, however, eight or nine years ago, when I broodily sat down to write a poem and to my surprise the little thing was fledged in free verse. I of course produced more of the same and got very interested in the techniques of this, to me, new form. Whoever it was – was it Graves, or Auden? – who said, in contempt of free verse, that it was like playing tennis without a net was talking through a hole in his own practice. The formal structure of a metrical, rhymed poem may be in some respects a restricting straitjacket, but it also keeps you from flailing your arms about in meaningless, shapeless gestures, and it's my belief that to write a formally good poem in free verse is more difficult than to mosaic away with iambs and feminine rhymes. How many free verse poems are ruined by the lack of a through-going rhythm to articulate the whole and by line-endings which are purely arbitrary and serve no functional purpose whatever.

The thing is, art, whatever else it may be or do, is concerned with form, and that's to say, with order. I don't know whether artists see an order in the chaos of experience that other people don't or whether they impose an order on that chaos. But that order must be there. To defend formless and chaotic writing on ground that it's an enactment of the chaotic times we live in is to commit that aesthetic sin, the fallacy of imitative form, and to renege from the primary duty of any artist, in whatever mode he is operating.

I also hatefully reject the limiting notion, bannered and free-floated most spectacularly by A Alvarez, that, the times being what they are, the only poetry possible is a poetry of extremes, scribbled frantically on your way back from a mental hospital to commit suicide. Of course there is poetry to be written from the far edge of consciousness, of suffering, of despair. But into my, and your, five ports of knowledge come many cargoes and we should unship the lot. If art is to be concerned only with the tragic or, even, only with the huge concepts of death, alienation, love, loss of Eden, and what the devil is time anyway, a vast amount of the great art of the past will have to be rejected as 'irrelevant'. There's conceit for you. I also detest the notion that all art is a therapeutic expression of inner, psychological tensions, of the quarrel with ourselves whose expression Yeats thought produces poetry as opposed to rhetoric. Of course that is true of a great deal of art. But what about the other great deal, whose cause, purpose and effect is pure celebration of a woman or a chair or a landscape? Are we to dismiss these as trivial? If so, I have written a good many trivial poems, and here's one.

## Ringed Plover by a Water's Edge

They sprint eight feet and
stop. Like that. They
sprintayard (like that) and
stop.

They have no acceleration
and no brakes.
Top speed's their only one.

They're alive – put life
through a burning-glass, they're
its focus – but they share
the world of delicate clockwork.

In spasmodic
Indian file
they parallel the parallel ripples.

When they stop
they, suddenly, are
gravel.

In my self-belittling way I call poems of this kind (they're really celebratory) "snapshot poems", a bad habit I keep meaning to break.

I said poetry involves order. It has to submit to the control of the rational mind – it's not enough to lift the trap-door to the subconscious and lasso whatever crawls out. I say this, blushing with guilt, for there was a time in the thirties and early forties when that is pretty much what I did. Poem after poem was a splurge of hardly related images, sloppily bound together – and it wasn't enough – only by the blessed formalities of metre and rhyme. An odd thing is that men from Cornwall to Edinburgh (and Glasgow), who didn't know each other or what the others were up to, found themselves writing in this same, foolish way. They became known as the New Apocalypse and serve them right. I was rescued by the only critical remark that was ever any use to me, when my second book came out and a friend, having read it, handed it back to me, saying, "When are you publishing the answers?" This took me several steps back towards my senses and I started on the long haul towards lucidity. Some years later I read, in a novel by Peter de Vries, a nice remark made by a woman to her husband about a friend of theirs: "He's profound on the surface but deep down he's shallow," and I greeted that with a fanfare. The label 'Apocalyptic' stuck, as labels do, long after it was contravening the Trades Descriptions Act and even yet I occasionally hear it and am reduced to shuddering fits and grittings of teeth, for it's long since I decided that poems which are wantonly or carelessly obscure (not difficult) are bad art and bad manners.

I don't remember being unusually interested in poetry at school (perhaps because so much of what we were given was romantic?), but what started me off occurred there. When I was in the fifth form at the Royal

High School, the English teacher, Puggy Grant (a nice man) said that by next Wednesday we were to write an essay on something or other, or a poem. Well, I thought, a poem is shorter. So I wrote a poem – to the tune, interestingly enough to those who know me, of a Gaelic song, which I would name if I could spell it. It was, naturally, awful.

From then on I wrote a tremendous number of 'poems' of an elaborate and increasing awfulness that culminated in the Apocalyptic riddlemerees I mentioned above. I think one reason for this was that it never entered my head to try to get them published. Since I had no audience, the fact that they were incomprehensible seemed to matter little. My friend's remark, however, jolted me with the realisation that a poem is a form of communication, and what can you communicate in gobbledygook?

All the same, my writing habits haven't changed much. When I feel like writing a poem, I sit down with a blank sheet of paper and no idea whatever in my head. Into it, where there's plenty of room, enters the memory of a place, an emotional experience, a person, or, most commonly, a phrase, and the poem stalactites down the page from that. This means I'm into the poem, various distances, before I know what it's about. In fact I don't know what the whole poem's about till I've finished it. This sounds daft, but I believe it's a common enough experience with poets.

Sometimes, even, I think I've written a poem on theme A and when I read it I find I've written a poem on theme B or, more commonly, theme A + B – as, for example, in this one

### Birthdays

In the earliest light of a long day
three stags stepped out from the birch wood
at Achmelvich bridge
to graze on the sweet grass
by the burn.
A gentle apparition.

Stone by stone a dam was built,
a small dam, small stone by stone.
And the water backed up, flooding that
small field.

I'll never see it again.

It's drowned for ever.
But still
in the latest light of a lucky day I see
horned heads come from the thickets
and three gentle beasts innocently pacing
by that implacable water.

While writing this, I took it to be a "snapshot poem" only, and it was nearly finished before I realised that it was not only a description of that place and those events, it was also about time and memory. It could be, I think, that each stone in the dam is a year of my life (hence the title) and the water is time, drowning what was known and now exists only in the memory.

Many poets polish and refine and eliminate and add, making version after version of the original attempt. I can't do that. The poem, whatever its worth, generally comes easily and quickly and pretty often with no correction at all, and once it's on the page, that's that. This hit or miss way of writing means that I write a lot. It also means I write a lot of unimprovable duds. I reckon at least half, probably more, of what I write I put in the bucket – an act I relish almost as much as writing the things. It's a wasteful form of production which I recommend to nobody.

My notions about the value of poetry and the ways it is produced are, I've come to notice, fairly low-falutin'. I never met a White Goddess in my life and when I find myself in the company of singing robes, hieratic gestures and fluting voices I phone a taxi. The pleasure in making poems lies in making them and seems to me not different from a true craftsman's pleasure in making a table, or a meal to put on it, or a boat that marries the water as a boat should. The pleasure in making something that was never in the world before, with our gifts and abilities at their farthest stretch, is surely one that is common to everybody.

I'm not, of course, denying the special, unique and practical importance of poetry and the other arts. The nub and centre (pith if you like) of my thinking about that is this: An adult physique with the intelligence of a child is looked after as potentially dangerous. But an adult intelligence along with the emotional equipment of a child is even more so. Intellect and sensibility – the arts develop both. Poetry teaches a man to do more than observe merely factual errors and measurable truths. It trains him to have a shrewd nose for the fake, the inflated, the imprecise and the dishonest. So, it compels him to resist stock responses, because it compels him to examine the emotional significance, as well as the rational significance, of whatever comes under his notice. To have unexamined emotional responses is as immature, as dangerous, as to have unexamined beliefs. And what proportion, I wonder, of the misunderstandings and miseries in the world are due to no more than the stock use of big words – liberty, patriotism, democracy and all their dreary clan – and the stock response to them?

*Norman MacCaig as Laureate* by Alasdair Gray, cover *Chapman* 45

# Not Like That, You Bloody Fool

## *Tom Scott*

I suppose the direct, terse answer to this three-part questionnaire would be: 1. Compulsion Neurosis; 2. the same plus cultivated habit; and 3. that of the lover to the beloved. But let's see if I can fill out and orchestrate that simple melody a bit.

There is something in the old dictum that the poet is born and not made: though if he is not 'made' as well as born, he's been born in vain. There really is a constitutional basis to the poetic sensibility, a nervous system of a more complex and finer sensitivity than average. This constitutional factor provides the compulsive force which drives a man, however much against his will, to seek in versifying a musical expression of his heightened sensibility which can find no outlet in ordinary life. Whether this is true of other artists driven to paint or music proper or sculpture or whatever I know not: but for me the compulsion has always been to two kinds of singing – vocal and literary. The vocal singing was never enough for me because I have to express, wrestle with, something too complex, visionary, and difficult for the simple lyricism of the vocalist. I have always been susceptible of feelings, powerful and even ravaging, for which I could find no adequate equivalent in formal expression – whether words or song, but which was always related to words and song. How do you give social expression to ecstasy? To despair? To a longing for the Infinite? To mystical feelings of which you know neither the cause nor the aim? To a vision of social perfection patently not of this world but constantly critical of this world? Out of such emotional storms and possessions, having an early noticeable talent for writing, I began compulsively to write, as for dear life, about the age of eighteen – at first poems, stories, a novel, but more and more finding satisfaction only in verse.

I have three strings to my bow – I can make words sing, tell a story, and argue. I am not a philosopher and frankly ransack original thinkers for ideas which help me to understand my own feelings, to understand my world, to express my social vision and the all-in vision of life by which the social vision is contained. I am indebted to Marx, Darwin, Freud, Jung, C H Douglas, Sartre, Plato, Aristotle, Coleridge and Eliot (as poetry critics), Fraser, Schweitzer, and scores of others for one or another intellectual tool, and to Dante, Villon, and many others, Henrysoun and Dunbar, for much of my poetic technique. No poet is or should be an original thinker: but he has to be a discriminating critic of original thinkers from whom he borrows and to whom he is indebted for his own eclectic scaffolding of ideas upon which, plus his own original perceptions and evaluations, he builds his poetry. Thus Dante built upon Aquinas; Lucretious on Epicurus; Whitman on Emerson. Good philosophers make bad poets, and good poets bad philosophers: yet the poet and the philosopher cannot live with but each other. Of the two, it is the poet who is the practical man, the maker, the artisan: the philosopher is the visionary. And for me, Yeshua of Nazareth has always been the supreme visionary – Marx, the best of Marx (not his prophetic futurism but his critique of capitalism), and of all the others who have influenced me except, perhaps, Darwin, fit into my vision of Yeshua (not to be confused with Christianity): whereas he cannot fit into them.

One goes on writing only because one can't really help it. I speak as one who has tried hard at times to give it up, to come in from the cold (and by God it's cold out here) and draw in to the couthy social fire, go straight as it were, lead the comfortable life of ordinary men at one, more or less, with God and his fellow men. It's no good – you just get into a mess, you are still included out, you fall ill, nobody is deceived that you are one of them ... and out of the ensuing mess and even illness you come back to scribbling again as to a destiny. Success or failure have nothing to do with it, are irrelevant, in the worldly sense: the only success is to go on writing, the only failure to stop. Nor is it possible that one day, by dint of effort, dedication, the long slog of the Everest climber, at last you are there on the top of the world, you have said all you had to say and can retire into decent, happy obscurity: those day-dreams of a cottage on the river, salmon in the spring and autumn, trout in the summer, grayling in winter. The last word can never be said, the well is no sooner empty than it fills up again, you come back to the constitution which grants no rest. Eliot was wiser than any other man known to me on this matter of the endlessness of the literary vocation, each new start a new failure, only undefeated because one goes on trying. Not just Tom Scott – Dante, Shakespeare, Michelangelo (look at his 'spoiled' stones in Florence). Yet in that unhappiness is our happiness: in that non-salvation is our salvation: in that dissatisfaction is our satisfaction. Our footprints in the sand show that a man passed here.

My relation to poetry and the Muse. In youth I sought a pure poetry, a pure music of words and imagery: that led to the work which (plus other factors peculiar to time and milieu) seemed to fit in with work by others of my generation and for which (significantly in 1940), the theory of the New Apocalypse was mooted: the theory was bad, the practice much better than has been acknowledged even by those most influenced by it, including older writers vociferous against it. The movement published early work by Dylan Thomas, Norman MacCaig, Vernon Watkins, W S Graham, Henry Treece (who found himself chiefly as a children's writer), myself and several other stubbornly individual writers. This was no mere sport but a force of social nature, of history. But for me pure poetry was a dead end: language is by its nature corrupt, impure, of the earth earthy, not inhabiting the spheres like the heavenly music of great mathematical talents like Bach and Mozart, but down in the fury and the glaur of human life.

At first I tended to separate prose and poetry as much as possible. in that 'pure' period. Now I feel the opposite. I want to see poetry once again taking over much of the territory lost to imaginative prose: in particular the story and the drama. A purely lyrical poetry is almost totally unsuited to our age, to major work in any age. We need to rediscover epic and drama, the larger, composite forms which have the stature. guts and power to struggle with the complexities of real life, the battle between life and death for the human species now being decided in our time. We need a poetry that assumes evolution, history, anthropology, religion, psychology, economics. politics, money and credit, the arts – all that is relevant to human life. This need of course comes first from inside, from dissatisfaction with what one actually sees on the page, its inadequacy compared with the turmoil inside oneself. I am always impatient with an art that expresses only part of me, part of my vision, my feelings: I want everything in that's relevant, warts and all, the kitchen sink and all. The great poets of the past took that for granted – Chaucer, Villon, Henrysoun, Dunbar, not to mention the two supreme poets. There is no such thing as a non-poetic subject, given that it's part of human life as lived. There is nothing the novel can do that the poem can't: but there is much that the poem can do that the novel can't - it can sing, for instance, as Homer and Virgil sang. It is interesting that the most poetic of Scottish novels is called *Sunset Song:* it would slip easily and triumphantly into Scots symphonic verse such as I used in 'The Ship' and some of my Brand poems. I do not say that we should turn our back on the lyric and other short forms (though they lend themselves to amateurism and the usual plethora of poetasting pedagogues and other weekend versifiers) but that we should add also the major forms in which Scots poetry is so lamentably lacking. In all this MacDiarmid is a pioneer all serious poets should be following up, each in his own way, according to his own gifts. I have written many epigrams: but I have also written 'The Ship' and *The Tree.*

The Muse is a mysterious figure who comes and goes in one's dreams and is always about one in waking hours. Graves has gone into the history of the Goddess more than most. but every poet has his own personal experience of her which is no more historical than the women in his life. Edwin Muir used to say "what Graves calls the Muse I call Imagination". For me there is a clear distinction between my dreams of the Muse (rare and holy) and those of other anima figures – the Young Girl, the Wife, the Mother, the Old Woman. She is a priestess or even a goddess, one with Authority, her attitude to me always commanding, mine to her one of humility and subservience. It's like being briefed by one's commanding officer – often in bullying, hectoring manner. Apart from one dream in which I went through a sacred marriage ceremony with a young Muse figure of awesome beauty, they are never sexual dreams: and even the marriage dream was religious ritual, not erotic, and it was understood that I was but one of many men being so honoured by the Muse, who has many husbands, each privileged to be her husband, and petty jealousy quite impossible. She can possess us but we can never possess her. To me she is Nature on the one hand and the patroness of verse on the other: she is not the craftsman – I am that. But she is the critic of the craft. Sometimes she orders destruction of a work or works (my early poems for example): other times she intervenes to say, in effect, not like that you bloody fool, like this. But always such a dream closes one door and opens another, is purposive, instructive: and however obscure some of the instructions seem at the time, I soon read the code, and the orders are carried out in the work. We poets are her spies among men and vehicles of her advice to men on necessary adaptations, criticism of the idiocies of their anti-natural society. At the core of her teaching is *Do thus and live: do other and die*. And she is not only *for* life: she *is* it.

# Tom Scott

## *Apologia pro amor suo*

Hou mony queyns have speiled the stair wi me
And gane doun lippnan i the bed o love
Hou mony times a bonnie boat's gane wrack
On the rocks o a makar's weird! Some o them
Had bewtie, seelness, virtue – aa had love
And guidness tae, some gied their aa or mair:
Yet maugre my ain will, I saw ilk ane
The last time throu the door and doun the stair.

It's no I didnae lue them – I lue them yet
Ilk for her ain byordnar gift and grace
For they are aa the guid I've kent in life
But that there aye hes been anither Queyn
Ane I've anerlie kent in my mudes and dreams,
whase bulk alane can fill my saul's tuim space.

## *Murgeon*

The Muse can charm with every sweetness known
To verbal music, whether said or sung:
But she can also scorn, and flyte to the bone
And turn on vice the rough edge of her tongue

## *Epstein's Adam*

In ma haunds Lord
domenion
ower aa that grouws
aathin on the aerth
domenion
in ma haunds Lord.

In ma haunds Lord
the weasel an the laverock
the reid tod an the auld hen
rabbit burra, eagle eirie

the trout in the burn the flee in the air
the worm an the throstle
in ma haunds.

Aathin binna ae thing.

In ma haunds Lord
the herrin an the sword fish
plankton an whale
aathin fra the twathirds seas
the flean fish an the albatross
dauphin trundlin throu simmer seas
bull amang the dauwits
aa in ma haunds.

Aathin binna ae thing.

Under ma haunds.
the Mither's redwuids faa
rivers dry up an flush
deserts are made an flourish
touns are biggit an bombed
the world becomes a village
the sun himsel yields up his pouer
his horses, chariot.

In ma haunds Lord
domenion
ower aa that breathes –

Aathin binna masel.

*Note: the originals of these poems are lodged with the National Library of Scotland.*

Tom Scott photographed by marc marnie

# A Terror and an Adventure

## Iain Crichton Smith

When did I start writing poetry? When I was eleven years old or even ear-lier. The first poem that I have a vague recollection of composing (I use the word advisedly since I didn't write it down) was one about Chamber-lain coming back from Germany with his umbrella and Peace with Honour. I woke up one morning and I poured out this effusion to my astonished family. I don't remember any of it now. But I think it was meant to be comic since Chamberlain with his umbrella was a figure of fun at that time. I must therefore have taken some slight interest in politics then though I haven't written much purely political poetry and I am not committed to any ide-ology. I think the fact that the poem was recited orally is interesting since it links me with Gaelic poets (though the poem of course was in English).

After I had left my village school and had begun to attend the big school in Stornoway – seven miles and yet a world away – in the Nicolson Insti-tute I bought in Woolworths a big red exercise book in which I wrote all my poems. I didn't show them to many people and certainly not to my teachers. Nowadays of course creative writing is all the rage in schools but I don't know whether I would have benefited from that or not. Poetry is a very private thing for young poets.

All the poems I read in those early days were in English and I think, look-ing back, that they were either sad and languorous or resonant and ornate. I liked reading poems about people who had died interesting deaths or about countries which were distant and old. For instance I liked reading that poem by Wordsworth about the Lucy whose footsteps stopped at the bridge and who was never seen again. I liked poems by Keats and Shelley and never tired of reading the latter's poem about the Skylark. I remember also that I was very fond of Shelley's elegy for Keats. Curiously enough I also liked reading sonorous poems such as Kipling's 'L'Envoi', "There's a whisper down the field where the year has shot her yield and the ricks stand grey to the sun". I loved reading poems aloud. It wasn't till many years later that I could read a poem silently and gain any pleasure from it. As well as reading poetry I also liked books such as those by P C Wren, books about deserts and the Foreign Legion, abandoned romantic men.

My tastes, I think, were really very heterogeneous. For instance as well as reading P C Wren and Dickens' *Oliver Twist*, in particular, which was one of my favourite books since I seemed to identify with that waif of the streets setting out to find his identity – I also used to devour pulp detective stories, in the tradition of Black Mask. There was a series called the Phantom and another called the Spider which I used to borrow from a friend in the next village and which I read omnivorously. I can still remember the smell from their yellow pages. And of course I read Western stories featuring people like Wild Bill Hickock. Also in those days there was a small library in the classroom of my first school and after we had finished our arithmetic problems we could go and take a book from one of the boxes on the floor. I read all the time. I used to go up to the attic of our house and find there old copies of *Chambers Journal* – in double columns with Edwardian-looking illustrations – and read these as well. There was nothing that I wouldn't read except for factual books. And I wrote a lot of poems in the style of Keats and Shelley and sometimes in the style of Sir Walter Scott.

During a crucial period in my schooldays too I fell in love with geometry and in some strange way this also seemed to be connected with my poetry for in the same way as I used to have flashes of illumination which produced poetry so also I was able to see solutions to geometry problems instantaneously. I got into trouble in my fifth year in school for producing for the school magazine a series of mock obituaries on the style of the ones in the local paper. This was considered to be in bad taste. All this time I never met anyone else who wrote poetry.

After leaving the Nicolson Institute I went to Aberdeen University in 1945, when the war had just finished, and there entered, for me, a very exciting world. I was fortunate to find myself among a number of people who were writing poetry and genuinely cared for it. They were mostly older than me, people who had come back from the war and were resuming their studies. I was in fact in an ideal position for, as they knew far more than me, I could learn from them. Yet they weren't too distant from me in age and I wasn't overawed by them as I was by my professors. Among these students were Alexander Scott, Derick Thomson and Kenneth Buthlay. Scott was running a magazine called *North East Review* and was himself writing in a prolific manner, both poetry and plays. Kenneth Buthlay edited *Alma Mater* and like Scott gave me much encouragement. I remember those years in Aberdeen as years of discovery and happiness in a city of light and granite which seemed to glitter all around me. I felt totally free and my happiness consisted in discovering new writers and writing my own verses. The following is a poem that I wrote then (I suppose I must have been about eighteen when I wrote it). It is composed I think of an Eliotish obscurity combined at the end with a certain simplicity. (In those days Eliot and Auden were my heroes. I was attracted to them by my puzzle-solving faculty and also by their mysterious ability to fuse the past and the present in a new way). The poem is called 'Bookworm'.

> To know oneself is to face unexpected peril,
> to walk beneath the ladder and to hear
> the cocks quarrel in a sun-shrouded afternoon:
> to be assaulted at the dark corner
> by the stiff stranger with the folded knife.
> To know oneself is the ultimate terror
> that comes from the slanted mirror and the dream.
>
> All this he knew not and he never bothered
> to lift his muffled eyes from the crabbed notes:
> his pen scraping by the winking candle
> he pondered Yeats and pencilled minor comments

in the bare ragged margins and heard nothing
of the last tramcar leaving its damp stance
caught in a web of lights and the rain
drumming on roofs condemned by pert inspectors.
Footsteps stirred along the silent corridors
and the hopeless man was dragged from the brown canal
drowned with the bottles and the slimy canisters,
and always the scratch of the pen and the guttering candle,
the false maidens and green tumultuous islands,
the misty legends and man-created deaths.
He watched the hawk wheel in a doomed midday,
the dog howling on the dark sea flats,
and huddled in his study still more closely
till his bleared eyes forgot the moon's red claw
the spring corn and the fertile valley:
behind the shaded light and the green room, the storm
confused with spears of rain and the wind whistling.
Perhaps he thought of an old man lost on the moors
of time and Fate and calculating foes
warmed by philosophy in a madman's cave
and penned his reasons for unnatural fellness.
Quite suddenly the final summer came
and flowered beneath his window in the dawn,
the swallow's shadow fell across his books,
the sun whirled on the clock's white dial,
and there before him in a calm perspective
he saw his life objectively and clearly,
a bookworm inking on the virgin jotters
his notes in second hand. The grey lark
plunged in the impossible summit of heaven.
After the loud clamour came the stillness,
the pure unclouded vision and the dread.
Recoiling from the inadequate quotations
the pencil dropped from his white withered hand.
He died his own dead not another's.

As well as Eliot and Auden, Yeats is also strongly visible in that poem.

After leaving Aberdeen I did my National Service (not very productive of poetry though I did write one or two short stories: but privacy was hard to get) and then lived for some years in Dumbarton. My first book belongs to this period of Dumbarton and Helensburgh though it would be difficult to see much real evidence of their physical existence in it. It was called 'The Long River' and is composed of lyrics not very closely anchored to a recognisable reality, aching for meaning and 'beauty'. They have lines like:

Those elemental ones who have
burned the black grave away.
Catullus Shelley Burns
Sappho Blake and Clare...

Among the council houses of Dumbarton I was crying to the people I thought of as my ancestors, searching among mythology too for subject matter since I found Glasgow and Dumbarton opaque and poetically unmanageable. I could hardly bear the sheer ugliness of the area, and what appeared by that very ugliness to be a contempt for beauty and therefore for poetry. I remember always running away from the ugliness to Helensburgh and the Lomond area: I was, I think, thirsting for water and the sea.

It wasn't until I went to Oban that my poetry, I think, began to gain depth and lock itself to a certain extent with the real world. It was as if this town, outwardly beautiful, was necessary to me by being neither wholly Highland nor wholly Lowland: it had a certain cosmopolitan feel about it because of its tourism. Here I began to write about the Highlands again, about my obsession with discipline and freedom, about the 'black and red' elements in human nature. Here also I began to bring poems together to form groups such as in my book *The Law and the Grace* and *From Bourgeois Land*. And here too I was visited by strange moments such as led to my longish poem 'Deer on the High Hills'.

So far I have written about how I began to write and how I continued writing. And I have also been asked to say something about my approach to poetry. Poetry to me has always been a necessity like breathing. If I didn't write poetry I would feel that my life was meaningless and without excitement. I can't imagine a life without creativity. It is true that with me as with every poet (I suppose) there has been some willed poetry but along with that there have also been poems which arose quite naturally and without strain. These usually are the best poems. and they are also the rarest. The poem 'Deer on the High Hills', for instance, was not a willed poem: it wrote itself to a great extent. I believe that a poem like 'Hallaig' by Sorley MacLean is a poem of this kind. True poetry is not a matter of the will.

Much of the poetry that one writes is not very good, and I have written a lot and a lot of it isn't very good. But I prefer to search for the good poem by making my way through less good poems than to wait patiently for the good one to come along. I don't have the kind of patience that waits eternally for a 'masterpiece'. Poetry may be a search for harmony, for perhaps a primeval harmony. I have always been attracted by ideas of harmony such as, for instance, I found in geometry. This may also come from my Highland background since Highlanders in their work (as in Celtic designs) have been interested in patterns of style. This is shown in a sonnet (the last of a number of sonnets) in an early book called 'The White Noon'.

> And lastly I speak of the grace that musicks us
> into our accurate element till we
> go gowned at length in exact propriety.
> I speak of the glowing light along the axis
>
> of the turning earth that bears the thunderous sea
> and all the chaos that might learn to wreck us
> if the chained stars were snapped and the huge free
> leonine planets would some night attack us.

> I speak of the central grace, that line which is
> the genesis of geometry and of all
> that tightly bars the pacing animal.
> Around it build this house, this poem, this
> eternal guesthouse where late strangers call,
>
> this waiting room, this fresh hypothesis.

In my early poetry 'grace' is a keyword though not so much so in later work.

To me poetry is an adventure of the mind, an adventure of the spirit. It is used to solve problems, it is used sometimes for its own sake, it is used to explore humanity. I like poetry which, though graceful, is closely connected with the human. I do not, however, like Robert Graves, have any romantic ideas about the Muse. There is I think no fatal goddess I am trying to placate. I do however believe that at certain privileged moments some silence may descend on the spirit and out of it the true poem speaks. But I do not believe that this is in any way supernatural. For that the origin of poetic discoveries and scientific ones are the same according to the writings of those who have created them. My first book was called *The Long River* and in it a poem which says much of what I think about poetry.

> That masterful persistence of the spirit
> that wears like a long river through the stone
> has such a vigorous force that time which married
> the ponderous cloud of flesh to the weight of bone
> has little power with little things to stir it:
> till to a patient inspiration grown
> we hear the swallows we had though had flown
> return upon the season of our merit.

And I find also that this image of the long river recurs through my poetry.

As far as the actual writing of poetry is concerned I am not a great reviser. I would prefer to throw away a poem that didn't come right and start again. But if I know that a poem is right, though not yet quite right, I am willing to work on it, though often a great deal of work is not necessary. When I am revising, however, it is not a simple question of changing one word for another. I change the word and then read the poem over and over with the new word in it – I keep rereading the poem aloud – so that the word finally takes its place in the poem, which I think of as an organism. It's got to be able to breathe in the whole poem. I suppose, really, it's like fitting a part in the human body, a heart, for instance: it's got to start beating, and if the whole poem doesn't beat then it's no good. I never type the first drafts of poems, I only type out the completed poem. I would type a story from the beginning but never a poem. In fact, sometimes a typewriter can create a rhythm for a story but never for a poem. What one looks for in a poem and rarely achieves is a new cadence, a new sound. But often this doesn't happen because the mind may be too much in control. There is of course no question but that the mind must have some control but it must not have too much. There must be room for the accidental, and the courage sometimes to accept the accidental, on the part of the poet. I have a far greater regard for poetry than I have for prose. There has never been a prose writer who has had the same impact on me as poets like Auden, Eliot, MacDiarmid. These poets have at times illuminated the world for me in a way that prose writers haven't been able to do. When I was reading poetry in my youth I read for the sound and the taste of the words. I didn't really bother very much with the actual meaning of what I was reading. Thus for instance it would never have occurred to me to criticise Kipling for Neo-Fascism or whatever, since that wasn't what I was concerned with. Similarly I was very fond of Swinburne, his 'Garden of Prosperpine' for instance, with its languid rhythms. I was enthralled by the music and wasn't particularly interested in the content. Later, I was attracted to Anglo-Saxon poetry for the harsh craggy sounds that it made. For I suppose really it is not the content of poetry that is important but whether the poet has created a new cadence, whether he has brought a new music into the world.

I suppose there will come a time when I shall cease to write poetry. When that time comes I know that it will be a death of the spirit. For the writing of poetry is one of the most difficult things that a man can do and also one of the most exciting. I remember once walking down a street in Aberdeen chanting a line from *Othello*, "put up your bright swords or the dew will rust them". (That I wasn't interested in the content is shown by the fact that I thought of the swords as being up in the air whereas they are of course to be thought of as being put back in their scabbards). This was in Aberdeen of the granite and I have always thought of *Othello* with its marbly imagery as being in some way suited to Aberdeen. Also when I read *Hamlet* I was enchanted by the lines,

> Absent thee from felicity awhile
> and in this harsh world draw thy breath in pain
> to tell my story.

What I love is the sound of the lines. University professors would tell me that the power of these lines comes from the combination of long words derived from the Latin with simple Anglo-Saxon words. But one hears the music without knowing how it has been created. And as long as one hears that music or can recognise a new authentic music when it appears, one has not lost one's perception of what poetry is.

There are times when one brings a poem home like a bucket full of water making sure that none of it spills. There are other times when one fights to bring a poem into existence. There are times when one needs all one's courage to be true to one's inspiration. There are times when one writes a bad poem without recognising that it is bad. There are times when continuing to write poetry is a frightening thing, as if one's personality is being opened out with a knife. So poetry can be both a terror and an adventure. In one of the romantic poems of my early days I wrote this:

> For beauty has to be earned
> in terror, lightning and calm:
> the diamond-browed one stands

horizons and seas beyond
the habitable land,
armoured in moon and sun:
and where she strikes there is stone
or fire. These saw her often and dared
her face keen as a bare sword.
And one less great than these
has an image for this toil,
on a night of terror and storm.
Most terrible here at pause
to wait, the breast being dark and dull
with heaven's milk turned sour.

The poet I am referring to in the closing lines there is the Gaelic poet William Ross. But though I would still go along with the terror and the adventure. I wouldn't express what I think of poetry so romantically nowadays. And I would be less sure about using the term 'beauty'.

## Aig an Abhainn

O abhainn a tha ruith ann a Hades
far a bheil an asphodel a' fàs
far a bheil fear a' bhàta
ag aisig nan anaman a-null,
far a bheil Eachdraidh 'na tàmh,
tha cuimhn' am mi fhìn is Daial
bhith 'nar scasamh aon latha
ri abhainn eile.
'An leum thu tarsainn?' ars esan
is leum e
's thuit e a-measg nan asphodel
is chaidh e à sealladh
gam fhàgail-sa anns a' ghaoith.

## At the River

O river, running in Hades
where the asphodel grows
where the boatman
ferries the souls across,
where History sleeps,
I remember myself and Daial
standing one day
beside another river.
'Will you jump across?' he said
and jumped –
and he fell in among the asphodel
and vanished,
leaving me there in the wind.

## An Coinneachadh

Chan eil cuimh' am air d' ainm
ged a bha thu còmhla rium anns an sgoil.
Tha sinn uile a' fàs càm.

Ciamar is urrainn dhomh a bhith sgrìobhadh,
a bhith bruidhinn air ròsan is samhradh,
mur a h-eil cuimhn' am air d' ainm?

A bha còmhla rium bliadhnaichean air ais
air an aon chlas
a-measg na cailc is an ince.

Tha thu mar chnoc ann an dealanach.
Chì mi thu airson mionaid
's tha thu a-rithist a' dol às.

Na bruidhinn air ròs neo neòinean tuilleadh,
arsa mise rium fhìn,
seach gun do chaill thu cuimhn' air ainm

a thàinig le a nighean thugad
airson gu sgrìobhadh tu anns an leabhar aice
d' ainm fhèin cho truaillidh, fann.

## The Encounter

I cannot remember your name,
though you were at school with me.
We are all growing stooped.

How can I write,
or talk of roses and summer
if I can't remember your name?

You who were with me years ago
in the same class
among the chalk and ink.

You are like a hill in the lightning.
I see you for a moment
and then you disappear again.

Do not speak of roses or daisies again,
I say to myself,
since you can't remember his name,

he who has come to you with his daughter
that you might put in her book
your own signature so pathetic and weak.

(from *Na h-Eilthirich* by Iain Crichton Smith, translated by Kevin MacNeil)

# The Supreme Companionship

## *Kathleen Raine*

I do not remember a time when I did not compose poems. Before I could write my mother wrote down my poems, and as soon as I could write, poems were what I wrote. This may prove that vocation is innate; or it may prove only that my mother, herself full of unwritten poetry, used me as a medium for her own expression. Whether by heredity or by early training, therefore, I owe my poetry to my mother. To my mother also and to my grandparents and aunts on my mother's side, who were Scots, I owe my early memories of poetry as something said or sung, with a deep and immediate emotion, as though the words of song or ballad had been just that moment created to express the feelings of the speaker. Poetry for my mother and her family was part of life, not part of education. So although I have never had a permanent home in Scotland I have always felt myself a part of my Scottish inheritance (as a poet) far more than of my English.

Yet to my father also I am deeply indebted for my education in English language and literature. He was English master at a County High School, and books were always at hand, and my father would read Tennyson and Shakespeare to me in his beautiful cultured voice. He taught me the structure of English metres and also Latin, and the Latin and Greek verse-forms. I regret only that I have not made more use of these beautiful structures.

To both my parents and to the old-fashioned schools I attended I also owe the habit of learning poems by heart; the only way, in my opinion, in which poetry can be completely experienced. Better by far to learn 'real' poetry at the age when memorizing is relatively easy, even if the full meaning of the poems only reveals itself later. It seems a cruel waste of time to learn 'children's poetry' that we outgrow rather than psalms and Shakespeare and Border Ballads that will be with us always. Not that some children's poetry – traditional nursery rhymes, Stevenson and de la Mare and so on – is not real poetry also; but thank God I learned *L'Allegro* at an age when nowadays children are either 'expressing themselves' or reading rubbish. I was a child before the publication of trash became commercially profitable, and therefore my generation received perforce either a good education or none at all. Bad education was relatively unknown.

I keep writing because only in writing am I able to come close enough, to enter experience fully, to explore some vision whether of the visible or the inner world. The writing (as to a lesser extent the reading) of poetry is a way into the reality of existence – of my own existence or that of the seemingly external world. It is the most serious activity I ever undertake, and the hardest work. It is also a form of contemplation that is at the same time action. In it I forget myself completely while at the same time realizing myself most fully; or I become a channel for a mind beyond myself. In either case it is the greatest happiness known to me -reason enough surely for practising any art or skill. I write, I suppose, for love and for pleasure.

I see in my work mainly its faults and shortcomings and failures ever to quite coincide with the unwritten something seeking expression. Very occasionally the two seem to coincide absolutely – and that is what one works towards always, the perfect embodiment. As I work it is as if the area of my consciousness expands and I know and perceive more, and become instantaneously aware of relationships normally unperceived. This imaginative expansion is often accompanied by some rhythmic pattern which lays the foundation of the poem before words come. Words then fly into place like iron-filings in a magnetic field. In this lies the great happiness of working on a poem. It is hard work to raise oneself into this degree of imaginative attention, but the writing becomes increasingly easy as one proceeds. Often I make a dozen or twenty drafts of a poem before getting it right. Only occasionally, usually after a spell of concentrated work, is the poem 'given' with the effortlessness of Kubla Khan. I imagine such poems arise spontaneously only in the highly trained mind of a Coleridge.

I believe that such creative activity is the greatest happiness known to us; in whatever art or craft, and above all in working on life, in human relationships, in bringing up children, even in our own solitude. What is my relationship with the Muse? In my case, the daemon. I have all my life been aware of this 'other', the inspirer, as an Ariel-like figure, not feminine; an ever-living companion, immortal, free, not at all human. This relationship has for me been the deepest in my life. When I have turned away from poetry I have lost this ageless companion, sometimes for years. Some might call that 'other' the Collective Unconscious, but to my experience that presence has been like a living person, bringer of sometimes lines or phrases, sometimes sudden magical glimpses or realizations. A part of myself – another self – impossible to say; at all events objective to the ego. In that companionship I am never lonely: it is the supreme companionship.

*(The Collected Poems of Kathleen Raine is published by Golgonooza Press, 2000.)*

Kathleen Raine

# Writer's Shop

## *George Mackay Brown*

I first began to think I might have ability as a writer when at the age of seven or eight we had to write compositions for our teacher, Miss Garson, in Standard One of Stromness Secondary School. I found to my astonishment that I always wrote the best composition. I say astonishment, because in all other subjects I was only average or below average. At drawing, I was the worst in that class of fifty. I was poor at geography and arithmetic. I did like history – maybe because it touched my imagination. Miss Garson would say "George Brown has the best composition this week, again. That's because he reads good books. If you all read good books, you would write better compositions." But, as a matter of fact, I didn't like books at all. The only literature I read was stories – hardly models of their kind – out of *The Wizard* and *The Rover* – the magazines that all boys read in those days.

There was another reason why I was astonished at my success with composition, and that was that the phrases, and sentences, and paragraphs came so easily. Anything so effortless must have small value, but apparently in Miss Garson's estimation, not so. There were other aspects of classroom English like parsing and analysis, and much later, interpretation, that I loathed – I'll speak about poetry in a minute. Writing compositions on subjects like 'A day in the life of a beachcomber' or 'The last day of the holidays' or 'A night out of doors' – that was all I shone at in the dark prison of school.

I believe with scripture that every person has a talent of some kind, a creative gift, and he must spend the rest of his life trying to perfect it. I don't subscribe to the modern snobbish heresy that the creative gift is only operative in literature and music and art in general. The man who makes a table or bakes a loaf of bread is being equally creative and is in some ways more important. Where would we be without the satisfaction of our daily necessities? What the artist tries to create at the centre of his life and time is a place of order, a place of remembrance, a place of vision, to which he returns again and again in times of difficulty and confusion, in order to have things made simple and meaningful once more. It is the workshop of the imagination that fills the world with beautiful shapes.

So then, I did have this gift with language. It is a gift you do not ask for nor work for. It is a grace given for no apparent merit, but once you know you have it the rest of your days are spent perfecting it as well as you know how, in order to try to understand yourself and the world you live in.

I was brought up in a small seaport called Stromness in the Orkney Islands. Children have no awareness of beauty in their surroundings. To me at the age of ten or so, Stromness seemed an ordinary place. The magic places were elsewhere and unobtainable, Edinburgh, China, the planet Mars. And the folk who came and went about the piers and closes moved in the light of common day – fishermen, shopkeepers, whispering gossips and sybils tongued like seagulls, farmers on a market day smelling of the earth. We spend the last fifty years of our lives raking among the treasures that to our childhood seemed ordinary as pebbles, shells, seapinks, stars.

The talent once you are given it must be constantly nourished and used, or else it will wither. I have known instances of young people with the gift who have let it pass from them, through neglect or lack of faith in themselves or maybe disinclination to face the poverty and neglect that is the lot of every young artist. The way the gift is nourished varies no doubt from writer to writer. I was never a bookworm in the sense that I devoured every book that I could lay hands on. At most, about a hundred books read in maturity have influenced my art in any deep way: Thomas Mann, E M Forster, Brecht, T S Eliot, Hopkins, Yeats, Keats. In those early days, the nourishment came spasmodically, through *Grimm's Fairy Tales* and such stories from the Old Testament as Joseph and his brothers, David and Jonathan, Samson, Jacob and the Angel. I learned from these stories, without realising it, how narrative is shaped and given rhythm. Other influences came later from Border Ballads and the Icelandic Sagas. These confirmed that a well-told story is conceived in simplicity and grows surrounded by silences. Later of course these seminal stories became still more precious as I grew to understand that they are, as well, fables of the human condition.

The way we were taught in school in those days to appreciate poetry was enough to put anybody off. We had to learn by rote a stanza every week and then stand up one after the other and utter the meaningless jargon. Yet from time to time, about the age of ten, a stanza would open like an oasis in the desert.

> There sometimes doth a leaping fish
> Send through the tarn a lonely cheer,
> The crags repeat the raven's croak
> In symphony austere.
> Hither the rainbow comes, the cloud
> And mists that spread the flying shroud,
> The rainbow, and the sounding blast,
> That if it could, would hurry past;
> But that enormous barrier holds it fast.

I think it is important to stress those early impulses because they set the rhythm and tone of one's whole life. A biography of an artist is really a pattern of those moments, that, once realised, appear and re-appear over and over again in his work. The imagination hoards from the ruck whatever it needs. How I hated arithmetic in school and later geometry and trigonometry, but later these disciplines taught me to reverence form – the beauty and mystery and inevitability of numbers, all of which proved useful in the workshop when I came to serve my apprenticeship.

I realise now how lucky I was to have been brought up in the Orkneys. There could be no better setting for an artist. Not only are the islands beautiful in themselves and layered with history and pre-history, but here lived the food providers, the farmers and fishermen whose work keeps the breath in us all. I don't need to go in search of themes. Rhythms and images and legends are everywhere. To utter a name or a word is to set the whole web trembling. The farmers and fishermen are more than workers. They take part in basic rituals that give a meaning to the labours of all men. They are caught up with the elements in a grave, beautiful dance of fruition.

I think that the work of some writers is shaped by a few over-mastering images. One image I discovered when I was just beginning to write stories and poems and was having some trouble sorting out important matters from trivial matters was that part of the gospel where Christ speaks of man's life as a seed cast into a furrow. Unless the seed dies in the darkness and silence, new life cannot spring from it – the shoot, the ear, the full corn in the ear, and finally the fragrant bread set on the tables of hungry folk. That image seemed to illuminate the whole of life for me. It made everything simple and marvellous. It included within itself everything. From the most primitive breaking of the soil to Christ himself with his parables of agriculture and the majestic symbolism of his passion, death, and resurrection. "I am the bread of life. This is my body that is broken for you." That image has a universal meaning for me, especially when I can stand among ripening fields all summer. You will find it at the heart of many of my stories and poems – *A Spell for Green Corn, A Treading of Grapes, A Time to Keep, Greenvoe*. A poem called 'Stations of the Cross' in which Christ's passion is counterpointed with the work of the crofter is I think a key poem for anyone who is interested in my writing.

*Stations of the Cross*
(for a chapel in the fields)

Pilate
Our winter jar of grain and malt
Is a Lenten urn.

Cross
Lord, it is time. Take our yoke
And sunwards turn.

First Fall
To drudge in furrows till you drop
Is to be born

Mother of God
Out of that mild mothering hill
And that chaste burn.

Simon
God-begun, the barley-rack
By man is borne.

Veronica
Foldings of women. Your harrow sweat
Darkens her yarn.

Second Fall
Sower-and-seed, one flesh, you
On stone and thorn.

Women of Jerusalem
You are bound for the kingdom of death. The enfolded
Women mourn.

Third Fall
Scythes are sharpened to bring you down,
King Barleycorn.

Stripping
The flails creak. Golden coat
From kernel is torn.

Crucifixion
The fruitful stones thunder around,
Quern on quern.

Death
The last black hunger rages through you
With hoof and horn.

Pieta
Mother, fold him from those furrows,
Your rapt bairn.

Sepulchre
Angel, shepherd, king are kneeling, look
In the door of the barn.

Finally a word about the way I work. I don't believe in waiting for inspiration, if there is such a thing. I toil in the writer's workshop for three hours every morning come rain or shine. Sometimes all the sweat is for nothing, but occasionally a passable piece of narrative emerges or a pleasing line, what Yeats called "the articulation of sweet sounds".

George Mackay Brown by Gerald Mangan

# Gaelic Singer Manqué

## *Sorley MacLean*

I have been asked to keep in mind three questions: what started me writing; what keeps me writing; and what I see as my relationship with poetry or the Muse.

In my early teens, that is from about 1924, I realised that I was a traditional Gaelic singer *manqué* for I was born into a family of traditional singers and/or pipers on all sides, and that in a Free Presbyterian community, of all the most inimical to such 'vanities', my Matheson grandmother, my father's mother, lived with us until she died, when I was between 11 and 12. Her Matheson great-grandfather had come to Staffin in Skye in the 18th century, after his family had been "rascally deprived" of their land in Glas na Muclaich in Lochalsh by the Earl of Seaforth. She lived first in Staffin, then near Portree and latterly in that dumping ground of the cleared, the Braes of Trotternish. Although in her seventies when I first remember her, she had still a very fine voice, and early collectors of traditional songs, especially my maternal uncle Alexander Nicolson used to come to her for old songs and for the Gaelic names of all animate and inanimate things. Her family must have brought to Skye and preserved many fine old songs of Lochalsh and Kintail, and she had in her head a great deal of the folklore of the larger range of Trotternish. When she married my grandfather, Malcolm MacLean, she brought those with her to Raasay. Malcolm MacLean had died when my father, the youngest of three sons and two daughters, was only about eight, but he, my MacLean grandfather, was reputed to have been a very good singer and a bit of a bard. From certain things that my elder paternal aunt Peggie had and which her mother did not appear to have, I deduce that my paternal grandfather must have had songs current in Raasay that his wife had not learned. My MacLean grandfather was a fairly close relative of the great Mackay pipers, through the MacLean mother of Angus Mackay, but that does not mean that the MacLean blood added to the Mackay genius. My father, however, turned out to be one of the very fine pipers who never competed, and was a great devotee of John MacDonald of Inverness, whom he used to hear at the Portree Games. The eldest of the three brothers, John, had died in his twenties and of course I do not remember him, but my father's older brother, Alasdair, was a piper too, but as he lived in Glasgow I seldom saw him when I was young.

I think that the first great 'artistic' impact on me was my father's mother singing some of the greatest of Gaelic songs, and all in her own traditional versions. Among those I especially remember from her are the greatest of the four extant laments for Iain Garbh, two of the great songs of Mary MacLeod, and the 'Cro of Kintail', but, as far as I remember, my father was better at the 'Cro of Kintail' than his mother. My father's voice was good and in some songs his timing and weight was such that I now find it difficult to listen to those songs from anyone else. He was especially striking with the 'Cro of Kintail', the lament for William Chisholm and with William Ross. My father too had a great interest in language for its own sake. He was keenly and sympathetically aware of phonological and semantic variations in Gaelic dialects and remembered well the usages of the innumerable ministers and 'men' whom he had heard expounding at the Raasay communions. The South Argyll man, Donald MacFarlane, who had been a schoolmaster in Clachan in Raasay for all the years of my father's schooling in Raasay had spoken as much Gaelic as English to his pupils even in the 1880s and '90s. His influence on my father's sense of language was immense and he had taken his best pupils to something like the modern level of fourth year Secondary. My father's interest in all kinds of Gaelic poetry was very great. Among my earliest memories are arguments between him and Alexander Nicolson, the eldest of my mother's seven brothers, on the relative merits of Duncan Macintyre. William Ross and Alexander MacDonald. Unfortunately. in anti-Catholic Free Presbyterian Raasay not even my father knew much about Alexander MacDonald, but he knew a lot about Rob Donn and a surprising amount about Iain Lom.

Both my father's sisters were unusually good singers. The younger Flora was living in Glasgow but I remember from her a cradle-rocking refrain for the 'Braes of Uig' that I have never heard from anyone else. The elder, Peggie, ten years older than my father, used to stay with us for a whole month every year. She had a mania for fishing, sea fishing of course, and I had then a mania for boats, that is from my earliest memories until I was about 20 when the Cuillins seduced me from the sea. Peggie could depend on me to take her out thrice a day. Most of the fishing was the very leisurely deep-line fishing for haddock, whiting etc. That left enough time for Peggie's singing, my listening, and many political arguments, for the First World War had made Peggie a Tory although she had been before that a Socialist, a Scottish Nationalist and a militant suffragette. I became rather a good rower for my physique, and until fairly recently I could not forget the words of any Gaelic song I liked even if I heard it only once. My ear's defect in pitch seems to me now to have been compensated for by a painful sensitivity to what I felt faults of rhythm and time.

My elder brother John was always a good singer. I remember him in his last years at Portree School being picked out by the notable Ethel Bassin as one of the three or four best male singers in the school. Later, in his early twenties, he took to Ceòl Mór and very soon had as colossal a memory for pibroch as he had for Greek poetry. Thus he was able to transmit accurately the tunes, as I the words, of the many great versions of old songs preserved by our family. In our later days at Portree School one of our greatest friends was John Mathieson from Kilmuir. He frequently stayed with us in Raasay, learned many of our songs well, and gave us wonderful versions of others such as Beathag Mhór's song for Martin Martin and the song about the MacDonalds at Auldearn. His singing of the Lament for Gregor of Glenstrae was beyond words and his 'feel' for most kinds of Gaelic poetry was to my mind always 'right'. His version of the song for Martin Martin (he came from the Martin country) was even better than the version sung by my uncle, Angus Nicolson.

Of my mother's seven brothers and two sisters, two brothers were pipers, two others were singers, one a bard, and one sister a very good singer. They had learned many old songs from their MacLeod mother, who had died before I was born, and who had a fine voice, and many old songs even though she was a pious 'adherent' of the Free Presbyterian Church. My brother John and I went to Braes for a fortnight every year and heard many songs from our Aunt Katie and our Uncle Calum, who specialised in Mairi Mhór, but Katie had also added to her songs some learned from her great friend, a sister of the late Dr Allan MacDonald. Our Uncle Angus Nicolson was in those days seldom in Skye, and more seldom in Raasay, but on rare occasions when he was at home in Braes or visiting us in Raasay we heard some of his great store of songs learned from his mother; from the incomparable Mary Macintosh, a near neighbour of theirs in Braes; from the Buchanan sisters; and from many others on the mainland. Much later his recorded voice earned high praise from a great friend of Gaelic song and Ceol Mòr, the late Professor Sidney Newman. In spite of differences in religion and physique, Angus was strangely like Calum Johnston, both rare human beings even without their remarkable sensibility. He frequently talked of his Stewart grandmother, of her intelligence and lovable nature. She was the wife of my great-great-grandfather, John Stewart, in whose house I now live. It was said that the Stewarts had brought 'brains' into our family. Two of them were among the three joint-tenants of Peinnachorrain in the rent-roll of 1733 and were relatives of exiled poet Norman Nicolson of Scorrybreck. It is said that the celebrated vagrant Gilleasbuig Aotrom would come to John Stewart to make epigrams for him. If it was John Stewart who made that on the minister and factor Souter, mentioning Neil MacLeod of Gesto, John Stewart must have had a turn of witty language.

Even to this day, I sometimes think that if I had been a singer I would have written no verse, but perhaps, if I had been a singer, I would have tried to create original melodies. I know 'original' is a relative word and I think I have always been enough of a scholar to be troubled by the question of 'originality'. It is important, very important. One of the reasons, perhaps the chief reason, why I think it is extremely unlikely that there is a poet equal to MacDiarmid living in Europe today is the complete originality of MacDiarmid's lyrics, their out-of-this-world quality, which rings true and hugely significant, moving in the extreme to whatever I have of sensibility. That, and because the lyrics of *The Drunk Man* are mostly not so original is why I would still put the book *Sangschaw* above the *Drunk Man*. But that is a digression. What I am trying to say is that very early in life I came to be obsessed with the lyric, first of all because of my unusually rich Gaelic background; with the lyric in the Greek sense of a marriage of poetry and music, and then, because I was not a musician, with the lyric in the Shelleyan and Blakeian sense of a short or shortish poem suggesting song even if it could never be sung, a concentration running or flying away from anything that could in any way be called sermo pedestris. Before I came to Edinburgh University at the age of 17, I had come to be entranced by the peaks of Wordsworth's *Prelude*, the expressions of a sensitivity to certain impressions from external nature that I found original, subtle and true emanating from the discursive sermo pedestris of nine tenths of the very long poem. I admire Wordsworth's poetry still although by the age of 18 I had come to acknowledge the half-truth of Arnold's dictum that he "averted half his ken from human fate". He did not always.

From the age of 16 or so onwards I had been writing a fair amount of verse in Gaelic and English, and reading all the poetry I could lay hands on in Gaelic and in English, but from the age of 12 onwards I was primarily an idealist democratic revolutionary and I fancied my future role in life as a politician helping to change the world, rather than as a scholar or a poet. 'Negative Capability' I understood but it was not for me. In the '30s, I used to be very sceptical of the Scottish writers who seemed to attribute most of Scotland's ills to Calvinism. What did they know of Calvinism? Not one of them had been brought up in a small island where nine out of ten of the people were adherents of the Free Presbyterian and the rest of the Free Church, which was in Raasay at any rate very liberal by comparison. Both sects believed doctrinally that not only were the secular arts dangerous vanities but also that the great bulk of humanity, and the great bulk of Free Presbyterians as well were to spend an eternity of physical and mental torture. Although my father and mother were also lax Free Presbyterians I supposed they too believed that at the level at which human beings can believe it and continue sane. One always believed that somehow in the long run one could "make one's calling and election sure", but the odds for eternal damnation were terribly high against a very high percentage of the lovable people one knew. The obvious fewness of the Elect made me anti-elitist in most ways. My mother's Braes was almost 100 percent Free Presbyterian, but rather anti-clerical. Gladstone's Irish Home Rule bills had made the clerical Elect Tories, and no matter how lovable as individuals a great number of those Elect were, they were politically discounted. This scepticism about the Church's politics inevitably loosened doctrinal holds or, if it did not, it led to questions about the individual minister's doctrinal orthodoxy. The *lacrimae rerum* seeped through the protective walls of the individual very early and made for pessimism and I believe toleration and a sympathy for the underdog. I do not think it made for self-righteousness at all, for was not human righteousness filthy rags, by-products but necessary by-products of Saving Grace? *The Confessions of a Justified Sinner* are, of course, a travesty of the Calvinism of the Scottish Highlands, and I believe of the Lowlands too. At the age of 12 I took to the gospel of Socialism, and I believe that in my later teens a dichotomy took me psychologically: my 'pure' aesthetic idols old Gaelic song and my humane-aesthetic idols Blake and Shelley.

I had read no modern English poetry before I came to Edinburgh University at the age of 17. Although I was still a devotee of Blake and Shelley, my English verse then became more influenced by Donne, Eliot and Pound. I had taken English because it seemed economically disastrous to take Celtic, and I believe it was for the best. My English verse could try to follow Donne, Eliot and Pound because I could not follow Blake and Shelley. Not that the great Grierson himself was half as pro-Donne as his undergraduate admirers or rather the undergraduate admirers of Eliot. Among them it would then have been blatant heresy to suggest that Milton was as great a poet as Donne, or Yeats as great a poet as Eliot. The first undergraduate I ever heard voicing that heresy was James Caird and that when I first met him, in 1933, my last years in the University. Caird was two years younger than I. I did not listen to him on Yeats enough to get past the early Yeats, but I did listen to him on MacDiarmid, to whose poetry from *Sangschaw* to *Scots Unbound* Caird and [George] Davie soon introduced me.

The intellectual stimulus of Davie and the literary stimulus of Caird was very great, but the lyrics of Hugh MacDiarmid might very well have destroyed any chances I ever had of writing poetry, had my reading of them not been immediately followed by my reading of *The Drunk Man*, 'To Circumjack Cencrastus' and *Scots Unbound*. To me, the best of them were, and still are, the unattainable summit of the lyric and the lyric is the summit of all poetry, but they could not be followed even 'afar off' by me or anyone else. In them I saw a timeless and 'modern' sensibility and an almost implicit 'high seriousness' and an unselfconscious perfection of rhythm that could not be an examplar because it was so rare. *The Drunk Man*, the greatest long poem of the century that I have read, is more accessible because, along with the subtlest and most daringly imaginative, the most organic and marvellously sustained use of symbolism, it has the variety that has something for most natures. It converted me to the belief that the long medley with lyric peaks was the great form for our age. I know it did not have the 'viscoma' at all, but it made me want to write a long medley with as many lyric peaks as might grow out of it. Hitler had come into power in 1933 and with the prescience of the pessimist, I saw that the political task of our generation, or of the '30s decade, was to save what could be saved of a bad state to prevent an infinitely worse of long duration.

By 1932, before I met Caird, Davie or MacDiarmid, I had written a Gaelic poem about a heron, and I thought it worth preserving it and some other Gaelic poems which I thought much more true to myself that anything I had done in English. Later a translation of the poem earned very great praise from Edwin Muir. So I was committed to Gaelic poetry before I had read a single poem by MacDiarmid; but the Spanish Civil War, the increasing likelihood that the Fascists would conquer Europe, my private family circumstances, the facing of questions that I long after came to be familiar with in the writings of French Existentialists, changed the directions indicated by 'The Heron', increasing urgent tensions, and from 1936 to 1939 I became, if a poet, very different from what my pre-1936 writings indicated. It was significant that the English poems produced by the Spanish war that impressed me most was John Cornford's little 'Heart of this Heartless

World'. Compared with it, Auden's 'Spain' seemed superficial, and still does. From 1939, almost till I went away to Egypt and Libya in late 1941, I was faced with a terrible personal dilemma, and from August 1941 to 1944 I could not decide whether the situation was really tragical or a farce.

Only in very rare moments, and never at all during the years 1936 and 1945, did I think of the poet primarily or secondarily as virtuoso or craftsman, nor has my practice implied that he should be a 'committed' propagandist even in the very best sense. If 'committed', the poetry must be in some way confessional if it is to be true to the perpetual dilemma of the 'Existentialist' choice. Iain Lom's famous words to Alasdair MacDonald "You do the fighting and I'll do the praising" I consider disgusting, however expedient they might have been to the exigencies of the situation, and however wise they might have been in the long run. I could not have been an Iain Lom at Inverlochy or an Auden in America in 1939.

My mother's long illness in 1936, its recurrence in 1938, the outbreak of the Spanish Civil War in 1936, the progressive decline of my father's business in the Thirties, my meeting with an Irish girl in 1937, my rash leaving of Skye for Mull late in 1937, and the events of Munich in 1938, and always the steady unbearable decline of Gaelic, made those years for me years of difficult choice, and the tensions of those years confirmed my self-expression in poetry not in action. I have to admit with shame that it was not until the early fifties that I realised the great significance for Gaelic of what Donald Thomson and other school teachers were doing in Argyll, that is teaching it to those who did not know it already. Munich and the unparalleled heroism and self-sacrifice of Communists in the Spanish Civil War almost made me a communist in 1938. I think Mull had much to do with my poetry: its physical beauty, so different from Skye's with the terrible imprint of the clearances everywhere on it, made it almost intolerable for a Gael, especially for one with the proud name of MacLean. Just after Munich, indirect approaches were made to me to accept a Territorial commission in the Eighth Argylls. I was tempted, but replied: "Not while this government (Chamberlain's) is in power."

It was in Mull in 1938 that I conceived the idea of writing a very long poem, 10,000 words or so, on the human condition, radiating from the history of Skye and the West Highlands to Europe and what I knew of the rest of the world. Its symbolism was to be, mostly, native symbolism. I started it in Edinburgh in the summer of 1939. The idea came from *The Drunk Man*. It suffered interruption after interruption, especially the beginning of the war in September '39. The final interruption stopped it abruptly in December 1939. Events in Poland in 1944 made me question its 'commitment' and at any rate much of its symbolism is not in proportion with its theme.

The long poem was always to me a *faute de mieux* as compared with the lyric but I have come to regard it as a necessity if poetry is to deal adequately with much of the human condition. By 'lyric' I mean something far removed from the semi-pedestrian short poems that now pass for lyr-

Sorley MacLean by Gerry Mangan

Iain Crichton Smith by Alasdair Gray,
cover *Chapman* 73

ics, in short poems like many Gaelic songs and the lyrics of Blake, Shelley, MacDiarmid etc etc. I think two of the reasons for my long silences and burning of unpublished poems have been my long years of grinding school-teaching and my addiction to an impossible lyric ideal. During my 16 years at Plockton the burden of school teaching was aggravated for myself by my starting of the teaching of Gaelic there and that to pupils who did not know it already.

I think I have indicated my 'relationship with poetry or the Muse'; whether I am a first or a 42nd cousin I leave to others who are not of the Gaelic establishments cherishing comfortable ultra-Minch ideals.

What keeps me writing nowadays is a question I cannot easily answer, nor could anyone else in my position. I have always had long silences, periods of no writing, but these have generally been accompanied by frequent burnings and long delays in publication because I could not get round to type things or write letters, or because an English translation was required by all publishers, except Caithness Books, who would publish my work. Besides, it has been difficult for me to abandon my lyrical ideal, even when I thought that the non-lyrical was, to paraphrase Wordsworth's language, the product of long and deep thought 'carried alive into the heart by passion', or if I could recognise it as subtle, delicate and true. I had for long been fascinated by Yeats' and Màiri Mhór's power of expressing common 'thoughts' barely and as if a common truth had come home to them for the first time. In spite of MacDiarmid, the 'full-time' professional poet is not for me and never has been. If I have time to do it, I brood over something until a rhythm comes as a more or less tight-rope to cross the abyss of silence, I go on it, as far as I can see, unconsciously. Nowadays I shun 'free verse' because so very little of it in others satisfies me and because its rope is so often so slack as to be loose bits of Chopped-up Prose, even if courtesy gives them the name of rhythm. I could not be primarily a Gael without a very deep-seated conviction that the auditory is the primary sensuousness of poetry. The invention of convincing new rhythms that are not primarily prose 'rhythms' is so rare that I can think of no-one who has done it convincingly in Gaelic this century except Campbell Hay and two others in a few poems. There may be more but, if there are, their rhythms have not impinged on me, or I have not read them. By saying that they have not impinged on me means that I felt their wheels were poor for their loads. Gaelic poetry that is published with English translations cannot be assessed on its translation alone even by the most honest and perceptive of critics who do not know Gaelic.

Some say that the habit of writing grows on one and that, once it is formed, it is not easy to eradicate. That may be true of most writers, but I think its truth depends on the chances of life. The chances are very much against the 20th Century Gael, who has always to make a living in other ways, and too often he has to do it by what must be one of the most exhausting of all ways, school teaching.

Hugh MacDiarmid by Gerry Mangan

# The Inaugural MacDiarmid Literary Lunch & Lecture

## *The Shinin' Streams –*
## *A Salute to MacDiarmid*

Speaker:
### Scamus Heaney

Buccleuch Hall, Langholm
Saturday, 17th August 2002

Tickets – £20 including lunch
Available by Phone from Mary Carruthers on 01387 380230

# George Bruce

## 93rd Birthday Interview, 10 March 2002

### Lucina Prestige

*The sea trembles – voiceless*
*It is a rare moment*
*when a word is sought*

George Bruce, man of letters, poet, critic, teacher, BBC producer, Saltire Prize winner (1999) poet laureate of Fraserburgh, publisher and editor of numerous books, anthologies and magazines. Eyes sparkling with a rare intelligence, a voice full of warmth and welcome – this was the man I interviewed just before his 93rd birthday.

We met in his book-lined study, in a Georgian house on the edge of Edinburgh's New Town. I was told that George had been ill recently, but I found him in much better form than I expected. Lively, and with eyes that smiled at me over the top of spectacles (regularly lost) – he entertained me with stories and anecdotes from his past. Small, agile and bent slightly with the stoop of years, he still lives in his own home with a little help from family and friends.

His house looked fresh and clean and I was told by George that his son and daughter had recently helped him do some redecorating. His book-lined study was warm and cosy: papers scattered everywhere, over chairs, filing cabinets, his desk and the floor – exactly the environment you would expect a man of letters to inhabit, words being so much more important than tidy surroundings! George lives in his head and his mind constantly works away at some literary activity.

George Bruce (b. 1909) was born and brought up in Fraserburgh, that rough-hewn town on the North-East coast of Scotland leaning into the wild north sea. The town where the bravery and sorrow of the fishing community was stored in the heart of the young George Bruce. And later, the tragedies and joys of the tough fisher folk were used to represent the universal in his poetry. No small town mind for Bruce, doyen of Scottish poets, one time school master, and then twenty-five years producing Arts and Features programmes for the BBC. At the same time he was also Theatre and Book Critic for *The Sunday Times*. All the while he was acting as literary editor for many international publications, as well as writing and publishing his own volumes of non fiction and poetry.

After his retirement at sixty, a new career beckoned – academia, beginning with an appointment as first Creative Writing Fellow at Glasgow University. After Glasgow he was much in demand as an international lecturer, this included a year as a Visiting Professor in the Department of English Literature at Wooster College, Ohio, USA. He made further visits to other universities in the United States and to the University of New England, New South Wales, Australia where he was the Scottish Creative Writing Fellow in 1982. Throughout these years George continued to write and publish his own poetry – Ninety-three years filled with more productivity and creativity than many of us mere mortals could produce in ten lifetimes! Fifty-nine of those years were accompanied by George's beloved wife Elizabeth Duncan whom he met as a student at Aberdeen University. Elizabeth died in 1994 and I wondered how he found the strength to go on after a loss of such enormity?

"It was my own work that kept me going after Elizabeth died," he said. Even now George is working at his desk most days and still composing new haikus and poems. His most recent book *Today Tomorrow* was published in summer 2001 and contains his collected poems, 1933-2000. Last year he also produced an art/poetry collaboration with the painter John Bellany, *Woman of the North Sea,* in a hand-printed and limited edition. And, unlike most people his age, he is busy completing a book of haiku in collaboration with artist Elizabeth Blackadder. He is also working on a book of new poems – almost all written since his 90th birthday. George told me: "I think I shall probably call this book *The Singing of the Foxes* after a poem I wrote of that name – the foxes really do sing you know, at night with such beauty and anguish."

Since his 90th birthday, George has won the Saltire Prize for the Book of the Year 1999; this was awarded for his book *Pursuit: Poems 1986-1998*. He was also awarded an honorary degree by the University of Aberdeen in the summer 2000. He has published three books, broadcast, and given readings of heart-stopping emotion at the Word Literary Festival in Aberdeen, and at the Edinburgh International Book Festival in August 2001. The poignancy of his later poetry has been known to reduce half his audience to tears! His poetry is sparse, lyrical and lovingly hewn. The whole is presented with a restrained emotional depth.

There were so many more questions I wanted to ask George Bruce, not least of all about his motivation. I began by quoting one of his haikus … 'On Hearing Yehudi Menhuin'

> *Suddenly but gently,*
> *you stopped time.*
> *There was no before or after*

**LP**     George Bruce – is this what your poetry does?

**GB**     Some of it does this, it moves into such a position. But there are other poems that are intensely lively which have a different objective. Ultimately there is a seeking beyond whatever is achieved on paper, as if the space between the words was as important as any word.

**LP**     This almost like painting with words.

**GB**     Yes, that's right.

**LP**     George, it is your ninety-third birthday, most people would put their feet up, relax and enjoy their retirement, it is extremely rare for people to continue to be creative into their nineties. I would like to know what keeps your zest and motivation going?

**GB**     It is not my own motivation. It is a motivation which grows a poem

*Illustrations by John Bellany*

in the mind. And when its bloom has been near-reached, it becomes a question of copying it.

**LP**     So your poetry comes from within. You don't need conscious motivation?

**GB**     Yes, that's right. For a short time after my illness, I thought it (my motivation) might not come back, but happily the imagery began to present itself again in its own way. In recent circumstances I have feared an insufficient contact with the ordinary external world. The quality of roughage is of importance. The contact of the hand with the boat or pen seem to me to guarantee a continuity with the writing of my poems.

**LP**     Has your writing changed from when you were young to your most recent writing in your old age? Does it come from the same source?

**GB**     My early poems were factual for example 'My house is Granite'. My writing changed in 1952 – the change was evident in a poem called 'A Gateway to the Sea'. The reason was because the war had finished. Consequently there was not the same intensity or demand being made. This gave me the chance to find a way of expressing the sensation of the thing itself. I discovered a way of saying the truth. However, it is generally thought that my later poems are demanding, although I was not aware of this – I just thought I was writing in a childlike way. I aimed to purify the language and for clarity and did not appreciate the implication of my descriptive writing in connection with the town of Fraserburgh – in fact it was John Bellany, unconsciously I think, who took me back.

> *... and you send me this great gift.*
> *At least it's given to one who*
> *fifty-eight years ago wrote these*
> *words about another place.*
> *Did once the sea engulf all here and then*
> *at second thought withdraw to leave*
> *a sea washed town?*

'A Birthday Gift from John Bellany')

**LP**     You've been very interested in art/poetry collaborations recently. Last year you produced *'Woman of the North Sea'* with John Bellany the painter, a limited edition art/poetry book of six new poems and six new Bellany prints. At the moment you're working on a book of haiku with Elizabeth Blackadder the artist. What has led to this development?

**GB**     First because my mother was absolutely determined that I would be associated with the visual. She used to make me copy Dutch Paintings when I was a child. To be more particular, the two artists to whom you refer (Bellany and Blackadder), lead to two sides of me. Delicacy and a sense of fragility which went with the delicacy – which suggests that things would not last.

Secondly, the awareness that the town (Fraserburgh) and the characters of the town and the sheer resistance to nature of the people

– its immense robustness, brought me nearer the facts of life. So there are the two things. After that there were the great staples, for example my secure background. From an early age I recognised that the most precious thing in life was having loving parents.

**LP**     Is there a price to be paid for remaining creative in your old age?

**GB**     How can one tell? If I hadn't gone on writing I would have died in ignorance. Yet, you can't put all that energy out and it seems that the more I do, the more there is available to be done.

**LP**     Does 'memory' haunt you?

**GB**     I don't think the work 'haunt' fits my sensation about images that presented themselves to me sixty years ago – now and then they appear again with great clarity, as if repeated in the mind many times as when I wrote and quoted from John Bellany. I recognised these words as taking account of the vision and reality of what some of my poetry should contain. It's the reality of the happening; I can see it in my mind with complete clarity – for example the reality of the storm at the pier head, but I have transformed it. Two readings of a given situation – there is the simple reality of the moment itself (reported in the *Fraserburgh Herald*) – described in my poem 'Sea Talk', I don't know why I wrote it at the time (1943). Many years later it comes back to mind the same phrasing, having seen a painting by John Bellany. It's only comparatively recently that an awareness of the meaningful character of my early poems has been made to me.

**LP**     George, you are the doyen of Scottish poets. You've known all the finest Scottish Poets from William Soutar, Iain Crichton Smith to Edwin Morgan. You have known all the greatest poets of your generation. Sorley MacLean, Hugh MacDiarmid, Norman MacCaig, and George Mackay Brown. A number of them, apart from poetry, were famed for their drinking abilities! You have never been known for this activity!

**GB** To be honest, although I enjoy the occasional glass of wine, I don't like quantities because I like to keep a clear head, so that I can think and write with ease. There was a saying when I worked for the BBC: "He's in Studio 5". This meant that the person in question was either in The Abbotsford or drinking in Milne's Bar (Rose Street, Edinburgh)! MacDiarmid was famous for his drinking capacity – drink before he set out, drink on a train and when he arrived he'd be unable to speak! In 1970, I did an interview with MacDiarmid and slotted in his poems at the end of it. When the interview had finished, I drove MacDiarmid back to my home and offered him a whisky (kept for such occasions), but to my enormous surprise MacDiarmid said he would rather have a cup of tea!

Norman MacCaig was also a great supporter of the drink and a regular attender at Milne's Bar. MacCaig often restrained MacDiarmid, but couldn't always restrain himself! I didn't like ordinary whisky – but I liked Neil Gunn's (the novelist) – it was like a fine wine! They were all passionate poets and the drink oiled their poetical activities!

**LP**   In some ways during that time you were less well-known than the other poets of the Scottish Renaissance, why was this?

**GB**   I just worked on my own, I went my own way. I couldn't be identified as a Scots Nationalist or Marxist for example. MacDiarmid was thrown out of the Scots Nats because he was a Marxist. He was then thrown out by the Communist Party because he was too close to the Scots Nationalists! MacDiarmid didn't like that because he liked to identify with a cause. I worked in a different way. I felt that my vision was universal and didn't belong to cause or creed.

**LP**   What is your view on the current state of poetry in Scotland today?

**GB**   It is as it should be – complicated. It doesn't know where it's at. It is driven now with anxiety and less concerned with standards than I would have it; but I am insufficiently knowledgeable about the work of the youngest people – I have some knowledge about those in the middle way, whose work I greatly admire - these poets include people such as Edwin Morgan, Seamus Heaney (an honorary Scot!), Stewart Conn, Kathleen Jamie, Valerie Gillies, John Burnside, Aonghas Macneacail. There are many others also doing good work.

**LP**   I understand that you prohibited the reading and broadcasting of your own poetry while you were working for the BBC – why was this?

**GB**   Because my job as a BBC arts producer was to present other people's work and not my own. I felt it would be improper to use BBC funds for my own poetry.

**LP**   Do you think there will come a time when you will want to stop writing?

**GB**   I thought there was such a time, but I was proved wrong. The doctor told me that I couldn't expect to go on writing as I did before. However, there is no doubt that I shall prove him wrong. I think I will go on writing until I die.

**LP**   I like this haiku (still unpublished) very much …

> *In his age he waxed*
> *lyrical. He saw the*
> *whole thing was fable*

Is this a reflection of your view of life?

**GB**   Absolutely!

And so I left George Bruce quietly celebrating his 93rd birthday. As I departed from the house, I turned and listened – all I could hear was a rustling of paper and a tap-tapping of the word processor keys.

*Pursuit: Poems 1986-1998,* Scottish Cultural Press, Edinburgh 1999.

*Today Tomorrow: The Collected Poems of George Bruce 1933-2000.* Ed. Lucina Prestige, Polygon/Edinburgh University Press 2001.

*Woman of the North Sea:* an art/poetry collaboration by George Bruce and John Bellany, produced by the Printmakers Workshop. Edinburgh.

# Derick Thomson

## *Sgrioban*

Nuair a chrìonas an làmh,
an fheòil air seacadh, is an fhuil
air sìoladh,
is gun dad air fhàgail
ach an cnàmh,
dh' fhaodadh gum mair
cuid de na strìochagan
a dh' fhàg i air iomadh pàipear bàn,
is beagan tachais
a' siubhal bho na meuran luasganach
a bh' air an gluasad
leis an inntinn gu h-àrd.

## *Scratchings*

When the hand withers,
the flesh subsiding, and the blood
drained away,
with nothing left
but the bone,
perhaps some of the scratchings
it left on many white papers
will survive,
with itchings
moving from the restless fingers
that were impelled
by the brain above.

## *Feannag*

Feannag a' coiseachd na stràide
a' piocadh closach eun eile a bhàsaich,
no ann an aonranachd na mòintich
a' sealg am broinn caora
a chaochail, car coltach ri na daoine
bhios a' marbhadh 's a' truailleadh
an co-luchd-dùthcha
ann an Kosovo 's an Africa
's air feadh an t-saoghail.

Agus anns an t-saoghal sin
tha Glaschu is Obar Dheadhain
is Sasainn is Eirinn,
ged nach eil sinn air ar glasadh
ri borbalachd ar sinnsearan
ann an Gleann Comhann
's ann a Lunnainn,
's ged a tha Bùidsear Chumberland
air a bhith còrr is dà cheud bliadhna
anns an ùir.

Ur?
Tha rudan ùr gu leòr anns an t-saoghal againn
ach cha bu chòir dhuinn ar sùilean a dhùnadh
ris an fheannaig
a tha fhathast a' coiseachd ar stràidean.

## Carrion-crow

A carrion-crow walks the street
nibbling the carcase of another bird that died,
or in the loneliness of the moor
searching the innards of a sheep
that died, rather like the people
who kill and violate
their fellow-citizens
in Kosovo and Africa
and round the world.

And part of that world
includes Glasgow and Aberdeen,
England and Ireland,
though we are not locked
to the barbarity of our ancestors
in Glencoe
and London,
and though the Cumberland Butcher
has been for over two hundred years
in the earth.

New?
There are plenty new things in our world
but we should not shut our eyes
to the carrion-crow
that still walks our streets.

## Saoghail

Saoghal is saoghal a' tighinn gu crìch:
bochdainn nan Afghan
is mulad Africa,
bomaichean a' togail dusd
's a' leagail beatha,
gunnaichean gan cur fon talamh
an ceann-a-tuath Eireann,
ach a' losgadh fhathast
thall 's a-bhos,
tuiltean an Sasainn
's an deigh a' leaghadh
gu tuath is gu deas,
cànanan a' leaghadh cuideachd,
is cuideachd a' dol á cuimhne,
cràbhachd a' crìonadh
is cràbhachd ùr a' fàs
's a' breothadh.
Saoghal ùr, an dùil an è,
no an seann saoghal fhathast beò?

## Worlds

World after world coming to an end:
poverty of the Afghans
and Africa's misery,
bombs raising dust
and toppling lives,
guns being buried
in Northern Ireland,
but still firing
all around,
floods in England
and ice melting
in the north and the south,
languages melting too
and community being forgotten,
religion withering
and new religion growing
and crumbling.
A new world, is it,
or the old world still alive?

# Alan Riach

## *The Banks Business*

On the crossing, on the ferry, I read *The Business* by Iain Banks.
He doesn't really bother any more, but if people keep buying his books,
good luck to him. Having read it, and having it in my hand
on the helicopter deck of the *Port of Bilbao,*
I was seized by the impulse to hurl it into the Bay of Biscay, which,
a nearby notice about whales (and how to spot them) informed us,
is over 3,000 metres deep in places.

This impulse was creative, rather than critical.
I was suddenly taken by the image:
The neat, dry density of words – to be hand-held,
to be read in the light – suddenly spun out above the sea
– the ocean – to look for an instant like a badly designed seagull, flapping
its white covers like disabled wings. Then the splash,
the thirst of dry pages for water – transformation – literature in the drink,
as the black and white of its design blends and loses
in the endless, receding white and wash of the ship's wake …
Into my mind came scraps of Phlebas,
*The Tempest,* Byron, they bob about, and churn, and sink again …

Once, at the age of about nine, during a summer holiday,
I found myself standing, as I often would, at the quay's edge in Tarbert.
My hand was in my pocket, jingling pennies.
That seizure of impulse.
I took one out and flipped it away,
down to the deep-green slick of the harbour water.
It winked and winked beautifully, catching the sun
until at last it just disappeared, disappearing
beautifully, too.
I repeated the process with the other coins in my pocket.

A month or so later, back at school, I was called to the front of the class.
My act had been observed. Information had been passed.
I was held up now as a salutory example of some kind of badness –
mainly betrayal of that cardinal virtue, 'thrift'.

I still have the novel.
It is now neatly shelved
with the other Bankses, with their matching black and white design.

Thus there are those who always
seek to arrange an evil
on the innocent shelves
of the minds of children.

## *Mahler 10: Adagio Transcription for Piano by R S*

It starts where everything begins to say goodbye, like that last night
before you had to leave. You go to your grandparents' bedroom,
to say goodnight, to try not to leave, to stay awake, stay up,
extend it all, hold time, make it last. Last things always all too quickly over
far too fast. It starts with one touch, one finger then another,
                              precise, poised, exact,
strong, one key then another, a cadence, a chord, a magical concurrence,
                              the sound holds on,
subsides, the texture and movement grow stronger, heightened,
more intense, rising to extremity, and then the hardest loneliness of all –
after the company, after the sounds of the world and all the world,
all that is older and lonely, attached to it all by exactness and warmth
precision and love, unsentimental, present, fact. To occupy the air,
                              like time,
like silence, after you've gone, with this, like this, like this. Like this.

## *The Recollection*

Like chaos on the past horizon, thrusting
intelligent twists, turns of dark
intellect, pressing the rock,
the fire turning porous, frictive for handhold and foothold,
limestone to marble, sheer there
and cold as the slabbed rock-marble mined in that quarry down there.
Intense as that, and hot, the memory like mountains
on the past horizon, sawing the sky with their fists and their cries:
irregular, serrations, hoarseness, dimensions and depths.
But could they be held like a possible energy rising, as if, not with regret,
but full in the knowledge of pain, the price that is paid?

Yesterday was an easier climb over hills from which to look back:
the Black Cuillins rising like some malignant ocean turning towards you,
receding, advancing in black and intelligent waves,
their solid afflatus, a low subterranean breathing,
like literatures, sentences, judgements,
open for longer than our words could measure.

Yesterday, we walked up Beann na Cailliach,
then looked down on a curving ridge, like a ropebridge leading over
to Beann Dearg Mhor, and then, from that summit swinging
around and lower, to the peak of
Beann Dearg Bheag ...

It should have been easy, but breathless and slow, unsuited
to the scree-slopes descending more sheer than

we thought, I was looking back on
lean brown curves, with neither fat nor breathlessness on them.
We followed the ridges, sky-lined, round,
from peak to peak, coming back in a broad curve,
back, to the car and the drive to the house.

But we drove right on to the point,
to Elgol, to look back.

And there on the horizon, far beyond the circle of our walk,
the Black Cuillins rose within the several sweeping colours of the wind,
on a cloudless early evening, turning, now,
as we were turning, had been turning, in a
way I cannot exactly say how, or more
precisely than this, how, turning from
the storm of that chaotic thrusting into
something not ever again at rest, like hands that are cupped,
and the necessary water, held in them tremblingly –
or turning from that violent range
through some kind of furnace whose memory holds you, trembling –
into what, at this distance, now,
is another kind of cradle, like a rocking,
a rocking, over
desolation mountain, maybe just
another day, gone down in evening's
mackerel skies,
with something like solace,
or something, at least, at last, like hope.

## *Odysseus*

Here's the ice, Ben. Have you got that
cocktail-shaker? There's bears on it.
It's dark among this, the snow outside,
the Southern Cross, the mast, these ropes.
I'm bound to it, Ben, and the song
from behind me, behind my eyes, the door,
the song from back of the door, I can't
turn my head from the mast I'm bound to,
hold my eyes staring ahead: but
there's the ice, Ben, there it is, the bowsprit
points to the Pole, will swing away
down there, and I'm going back,
away from the ice, Ben, I'm going
back, to knock on that door.

# Mary McCabe

## *Sperr Chinge, Please*

Then, they were old
Tale long told.
Worn retreads
Brown trailing shreds.
Fighting, on the long way down:
In world wars
The bosses
The means test
Publicans and sinners
The polis
Other alkies
Personal demons
The winter freeze.
Hunched, they stood,
"Sperr chinge, please."
Frayed bonnet gripping
Proffered for pity
Rheumy eyes dripping,
Gumsy mouth champed
Chanting some ditty.
Mouth-organ vamped
Tootling a tune
The warm bottle brought peace in a cowp
Under the moon.

Now, they are young
Race half run.
Wiry weasel strays
Seasoned past the rays
Of easy mother love.
Fighting, on the short way down:
Step-parents
The teachers
The Benefit Agency
Peddlers and pushers
The polis
Other smackheids
Personal demons
The winter freeze.
Cross-legged, they sit
"Sperr chinge, please."
Plastic cup, curled dog
Acne-scarred

Eyes in a fog
Scrap of card
Awaiting the warm high
Peace in the lee of a gravestone
Under the sky.

## Eòrpa

Sàilean, bhiorachan, a'toirt gliong
air na clachan-mhuila
Fo drochaid dorcha, iarainn
air taobh an Seine, a' Bhltabha,
an Danub donn, còinneachail
Nebha dubh, gleansach.
Cracaireachd is gàire
Cruinnichidh air na sràidean
Fad na h-oidhcheannan geala
aig Petersburg
Cafaidhean òraich ann am Budapest
's Alba fhuar, fhliuch,
Ghleansach le ola
Streap, slaodadh
Leantainn ris am balla an iar-thuath.
An urrainn fear-sam-bith
a bhith gam cluinntinn?
A bheil cuideigin deònach
Leigeil dhomh a-steach?

## Scotland into Europe

Court shoes clacking
on cobblestones
Under a dark iron bridge
by the Seine, the Vltava
the brown mossy Danube
the glistening black Neva.
Crack and laughter
gathering in the streets
In the white nights of Petersburg
The golden cafés of Budapest.
And Scotland, cold, wet,
gleaming with oil
trauchling out and up
clinging precariously to the north-west wall.
Can anybody hear?
Will somebody let me in?

# Thom Nairn

## *Old Tall Men Moaning*

The bamboo
are a cluster
of tall Chinamen

complaining bitterly
to each other about
how annoying the winds are

## *After Paradise*

(For Viola)

On lush and wild islands
they prepared and watched and felt
the colour and beauty of destruction.

Later two cities perished in white fire
a jumble of vanished corpses
black silhouettes on the remnants of walls.

Others eyeless faceless still moving and burning
there death came with the light
and decided to stay.

The beauty and colour
a flash in the eyes of blindness.

## *Initial Analysis –*

Do you feel all right? *Yes.*

Do you have any hallucinations? *No.*

Do you hear any voices? *No.*

Do you perceive any images? *No.*

Do you have any problems? *No.*

Do you have any complaints? *No.*

Are there any improvements

You could suggest? *Yes;*

What?

*Would you tell the fridge*

*to stop shouting at me!*

# Limbo Driving

## *Gerrie Fellows*

Blurred lozenges of light came at her, broke up, were scattered by the wiper blades across the windscreen. She strained forward over the wheel, the heater right up but the clear place she'd made with her palm vanished, was breathed over and behind it only more mist. Ahead a green light diffuse in the fog switched to amber, red. The indicator ticked. She felt the road surface damp and slippy under the wheels.

Faint markings, the road swinging her round. She thought she could make out hedges, long blocks of flats, very pale, stucco or concrete. Rectangles of light, someone still awake. But quiet on the road, the odd flickering headlight turning off somewhere ahead of her. The car gliding.

*A yellow square of window. Someone in a room.*

Fizz of orange light, her hands like gloves on the wheel and behind her in the car just a dark hollow. She watched the dials and segments glow in the dash, the luminous red numbers of the clock flick over.

*A yellow square of window. Someone crossing and recrossing.*

Engine roar. Or the fan, like white noise. Something behind it she couldn't figure out. High-pitched, a whine, the fan squeaking maybe, because it sounded like it was right inside the car. She turned the dial back to zero, but the noise was still there and the car started to mist, the windscreen disappearing into fog. And she braked. Too fast. The wheels locked, rubber slewed on the asphalt and then she'd stopped. The car had stopped. Nobody else on the road but her face hot and the car hardly out of line she saw now. And why did she do such a stupid thing, hit the brakes like that? But the noise was still there, high-pitched like a cry.

She fumbled across to the glove compartment for tapes, flicked on the overhead light, put the car into first and carefully this time, absurdly because the street was empty, checked the mirrors, signalled, pulled out into the ochre dark, the pale blocks of flats and dark low bulk that must be hedges still running alongside the road. A light on.

*A woman carrying a baby against her shoulder. She crosses the yellow square, recrosses it, disappears.*

And the car has moved on, its driver leaning across, fiddling with the controls. The harpsichord drowned out by the fan and somehow tangled up in its roar the high-pitched whine.

*Something about her posture; she's patting the child on the back, soothing it. Sleep, sleep.*

She turned the volume up. Trees in a line at the side of the road now, darker houses behind. Left, take a left. Lights scattered through the mist. She rubbed at the windscreen. Almost instantly it misted up again, a murky fog that threw out yellow particles of street light.

*But inside the yellow square the baby is crying. His face is purple from screaming. Sleep, she tells him sternly. You've got to sleep. Mummy's tired.*

She clenched her hands around the wheel, tried to keep open a path between her eyes and the clear patch she kept making and remaking on the glass. Faint markings, the road running down. Bank of fog, bank of grass. Turn, turn. Under a rail bridge, shadowy as if the car had dived into a pond, a dampness and then suddenly the road rising again and she had to change right down, letting the motor drum on the empty hill. The houses gave way to rows of grey blocks, hedges, the road sweeping round. She heard the engine soften to a purr on the flat, the fan's whirr, the tinkling resonances of the harpsichord and it was still there.

She pulled over and stopped, turned off the tape. Turned off the fan. Windscreen wipers. Ignition. Headlights. She sat in her box in the yellow fog, just a muffled shape like a blanket.

Very faint, like someone screaming. *Let me sleep.* Over and over. Maybe it was her ears, after the driving, all the noise. Perhaps that's all it was, like thinking you still hear the fridge after you've walked out of the kitchen at night, closed the door, but the mechanical drone is still coming through the door at you and you walk into the bedroom, close the door, two doors between you now and you don't know if it's the machine you hear or a memory, an electrical whine imprinted on your brain waves. She sat in her electric box in the yellow fog and heard someone screaming.

*Inside the yellow square the child cries and cries and won't sleep. The walls jump at him. He's wide awake now. Okay then, play, she dumps him back in the cot. The painted mobile tinkles. She yanks the curtains open and screams at him, It's night-time, look! It's dark! She's knows she's losing it. She can hear someone screaming.*

She turned the key in the ignition, put her foot down hard, heard the rev of the engine, swerved out into the dark.

*Inside the yellow square the woman's scream and the baby's cry are all tangled up.*

She put her foot down into a blur of engine noise, the whirr of the fan, the music tangled around her in the car. *A yellow square. Inside it a woman screaming. A baby's cry.* The noise is a box and outside it she's almost blind, can hardly see the road now. The street lights don't seem to help, and she must be going round and round because here is the yellow window again.

*But the crying has stopped.*

*There's no sound except a sobbing.* The car floats on it.

Her hands are white gloves

and there are lights coming towards her, dazzling, out of the dark. Her lights not on, that's why. But not now, now she is dazzled and all the yellow particles are sparklers thrown out into the dark.

# National Library of Scotland

supporting Scotland's written heritage through

## The Callum Macdonald Memorial Award
(for poetry pamphlets)
sponsored by the Michael Marks Charitable Trust
and assisted by the Saltire Society

## The Robert Louis Stevenson Memorial Award
(for published writers of fiction, poetry,
travel and children's books)
jointly supported by Scottish Arts Council and NLS

## The NLS/ Saltire Society Research Book of the Year Award
(for original scholarly research in Scottish subjects)

In addition to these annual awards, the National Library
of Scotland acquires manuscripts and archives of
Scottish writing by gift and by purchase

*For further information contact the Library on*
0131 622 4807
*or email* events@nls.uk

# Aimée Chalmers

## *Peerie Birlin on the Mound*

inveesible speerits, words
whusper, whusper, whusper
ilka ane gangs its ain gate

fairspoken wyce-like angels
tryst wi the the sair hauden doon
say thegither wi the naitral-hertit
are vexed for them that tyauve

inveesible speerits, words
whusper, whusper, whusper
ilka ane gangs its ain gate

fair-faced auld mou'd deils
draw blear ower mowdiewart een
coax timmersome lugs wi haiverin jibber
wheedle intae saft sides

taen thegither, yon stalwart host
whuspers, whuspers, whuspers,
whar we've cam frae, whar tae gae
whar oor weary heids maun lay
whit we hae, whit tae dae, whit is whit an whit isnae

… and wha is ower feart tae sae
oor leid has weirdfu pooer!
Nae escape

forrit forrit
skitie weys, steep braes
backside foremaist
sideyweys
roon aboot, roon aboot, roon aboot

ae wee spider's
hail-heided endaivour
brocht hope an glory
tae the nation

but there wis naethin lik this
i the days o The Bruce
it wis mirksome, nae glancy,
i the cove o The Bruce

sair peety for me, spider
i the bathtub o McLeish
swirlin roond an doon the plug
they made a bauchle o me.

## The Cross Pairty Group on the Scots Leid

Speak in Scots! Wha, me?

Nae fiddletee-dee, it's just up tae me.

I hae the brieth
I hae the hert
I hae the inclination

I fin whit thochts
I fin whit taik
I fin whit wame is in me

I'll yaise ma brain
I'll yaise ma wit
I'll yaise ma flinty gumption

I'll raise a stoor
I'll raise a reek
I'll raise a steekit neivie

I'll dae it eence
I'll dae it ower
I'll dae it, dae it, dae it.

I am the wey
I am the truth
I am the een wi the gash gabbit mooth

## Jack's Dream o Wild Horses

atween the lichts
in hail-heided
concentration
reinin in wild horses
on rashie moss

a scad, a sklent
a blink o licht
stangs blearie een
glisterin spunk thru mirk
on rashie moss

hint o dinnle
dirl o brattle
a thunderbolt
maks thocht tak vauntie form
on rashie moss

derf and douchty
fechtie and fliskie
wild vauntie horses
whap windblawn sowel
on rashie moss

# Allan Crosbie

## *The Chapter House, Inchcolm Abbey*

*Stet domus haec donec fluctus formica marinos ebibat, et totum testudo
perambulet orbem.* (Let these walls stand for as long as it takes an ant to
drink the ocean, and a turtle to circle the world.) – *According to legend,
this was the inscription above the Abbey's original doorway.*

I want to write our *Scotichronicon*,
the legend of you saving me from the storm,
sheltering me here and sharing your one possession,
your faith, like the hermit who shared his tiny farm
of one cow and shellfish with a shipwrecked man
who was in fact the king who gave Inchcolm
its Abbey. If that sounds too pretentious, then
I'll scrap it, change the tone and start again,

but you can't deny we knew we'd marry here
when we entered the Chapter House, its perfect octagon
an ancient ring that held us like pagan worshippers
as we kissed and gently made our faces turn
so that from above we formed an eight of hair
and cheeks that crossed at our lips. If hyperbole's forbidden
I'll be as silent now as we were then
when we stopped and laughed, two nothings in ourselves again,

too scared to speak of marriage. The number eight
will lose me in its loops as I dream alone:
of two moons colliding; the snake that ate
itself; of me, aged eight, arriving home
from school to find my mother trying to tessellate
a patchwork quilt of perfect octagons
(she said you need a square to fill the gaps);
and the world that's fallen off the turtle's back …

I take it, then, you'll allow me to exaggerate!
I hope you let the sin of repetition
be forgiven, too, since I commit it – the eight
that's in everything needs double recognition.
Draw one from Porty to Dunfermline and you'll make
an 'X' across the Forth that sets its kiss on
Inchcolm Abbey so our homes when we met
are joined through this House now and we can never forget

that all of us live on someone else's horizon . . .
The empty cups of our separate selves have kissed
and left this final perfect eight frozen

and fallen on its side as if to make a toast
to infinity which fills us slowly and then spills over.
What we drink keeps filling up like this
and whether we're a shape or a space in the endless
tessellation, we are a piece that fits.

## History
### after 'Mi Pais' by Marden de Ciazo, San Salvador

My country is a book
to be read on sleepless nights.

It is a cradle.

It is a bleak plateau,
its hiding places empty.

It is a fist sleeping
in the lazy centuries.

Be careful.

Before the mountains are born
there is nothing.

## Islands

*The older I become the more
I am aware of exile.*
— 'Claiming My Inheritance', Ron Butlin

## Iona

The summer sand has a tourist brochure's gloss.
I leaf its sticky pages through my fingers.

Running my hands over the world like this
leaves an imprint. It marks me too,
gluing its microbes on my fingers like news-print
or pollen on the dipping head of a humming-bird
that cannot help tasting the flowers, moving
among them for what it thinks are its own ends.
Trying to read it all too closely distracts
from the simple skill of skimming — word
to word, flower to flower, longing to longing.

Sometimes I open my hand and where I thought there was nothing
atoms of everything weigh like eggs, unbroken.

## Leaving Coll

Hamish, think of those seals we watched from the rocks,
their bobbing heads like dark whiskered buoys,
or the others at Feall that rocked themselves away
when we approached because there were two of us.
Do you think they've ever said, in seal-barks,
*Think of the men we watched who came too near;*
*do you think when they left the island one of them said,*
Now that we're leaving I feel a pain, a sting,
like the sting of salt-water on sun-burned skin –
*I doubt it, eh?* I doubt it, eh, do you?

## At John Smith's Grave
### *An honest man's the noblest work of God*

I have walked from the Abbey, through the tourist chatter,
across the cobbles on The Street of The Dead,
on a gravel path around a new wall
built only to protect the ground where you lie,
to face Fionnphort across the pure quiet water.
From here I can read the plain words on your headstone
because they've turned it the wrong way round,
upside down, like this country when you left it.

## Fingal's Cave

The sea in its pool, lunging at the rock,
is the holy water in this cathedral.

I sit on an organ-pipe of stone
amidst the candle-flickers of cameras.

The air sighs through the cave
as if a door has thudded shut or blown wide open.

I look out at the bright swell
and see a collection-bowl of seaweed in the foam.

But when I feel the sudden need to pray
it's not because this place has left me small
but because I know too well the space I fill,
just how deep my footsteps cut,
and all the pain I've ever caused.

# Ken Morrice

## *(1924-2002)*

### *Bus Stop*

If you knew what was waiting
round the corner (so they say)
you'd turn and run for home.

No you wouldn't!
*Curiosity and bravado would win;*
you'd rush to find out.

Find out what? Louis Armstrong,
his trumpet and his All-Stars
blowing up a storm;

Or a whisky lorry on its side
and the drunken driver handing out
bottles and bottles of Macallans

Or a girl with large emerald
eyes, naked apart from a flowery
hat, smiling and saying "Help";

Or a man with a bright bow-tie
declaring, "O, there you are.
You've won a new Mercedes Benz";

Or a funeral procession where
you recognise all the mourners,
particularly the deceased?

You saw it far too late.
Travelling fast, the bus rounded
the corner to an unscheduled stop:
its and yours.

### *Itches*

Said a prim young woman from Sitges
Of course you may scratch where it itches
    On your nose or your ear
    But never my dear
At your crotch or the seat of your britches

*Note: a tribute to Ken Morrice, by David Purves, ex-editor of* Lallans, *is published later in the issue. These poems were accepted only a day or two before he died.*

# Solo

## *Kenneth White*

According to this taxi-man, Bordeaux was going down the drain: *"C'est la fin des figues"* ("It's the end of the figs") was how he put it. The place, he said, was hoaching with Bulgarians, Rumanians, Arabs, Afghans, and Zulus. They gathered there at the station, *"le rendez-vous des perdus"* ("the haunts of the lost"). They stank, he went on – "they're not particular about hygiene", and he knew their tricks; he could spot them a mile away. If one of them opened his door, saying "hotel?", he'd tell them right off to go to hell. "Scum", he said: *"la racaille"*. If they tried any hanky panky with him, they'd see what they'd get: he had a baseball bat under his seat, they'd end up in the river with a broken skull. He was a real terror, this fellow – a wee man, with a big moustache. Hot on the ladies, too. When we passed by a woman getting out of a car, "some thighs" (*jolies cuisses*), he said. "It must be great to have a harem", he went on, in a free association kind of way.

We'd left St Jean station and were rolling alongside the Garonne river making for the Meriadeck quarter, where I'd booked a room at the Mercury.

In the restaurant later on, while I sat at dinner, Louis Armstrong was thinking to himself what a wonderful world it was, and some other joker was saying that if you go to San Francisco, you should wear a flower in your hair.

I got into the lift at the same time as two women. Maybe this was their last chance before calling it a night. "In a lift at night with two dolls", said the bolder one. "The seventh heaven", I said. But I got out at the fifth. I was on a mission.

Bordeaux, capital of the South-West (France) had gone West with a vengeance, at least there in the Meriadeck Mercury. There were shots from Western films all over the place. I had Gunfight at OK Corral on my door.

I mentioned my mission. It came from Alec MacLaren. Ever since Glasgow began to think of itself as a City of Culture, Alec (otherwise known as Eck – you'll see later why I supply this information) had a bee in his bonnet. He wanted to open a wine-bar for intellectuals. "What'll we call it, Solo?", he said. Solo – that's my intellectual pseudonym, short for Solomon. I thought for a while, ostentatiously. My reputation was at stake. This was in a beer-and-whisky joint on Byres Road, and there were ten Glasgow intellectuals present. I looked up at the ceiling, I looked down at the floor, I looked round at the expectant faces. Call it *Ecce Vino*, I said. At first there was a nonplussed silence, then there was thunderous applause. At least two guys out of ten had twigged, which isn't a bad proportion for Glasgow – for anywhere, come to that. If any ignoramus thinks I'm going to do any explanation here, he can think again. I hate explaining, loathe describing processes – I size up the field, and the next act works itself out, intuitively.

Naturally, though, I had to explain to Eck MacLaren. He'd heard of Nietzsche, of course, but he'd never got beyond *The Twilight of the Idols* (in an abridged version for universities), and he'd never even heard of the man's lightning autobiography, *Ecce Homo*.

It was mainly the *vino* he was interested in.

And since, MacLaren considered, I could speak French and knew the country, he had entrusted me with £5000 to make the best purchase I could down there in the Bordelais vineyards and arrange for shipping to Glasgow.

I went to sleep that night with, in my mind, the big wall-map at St Jean station. There you have the mouth of the Gironde, with lines moving out to Canada and America, the West Indies, Senegal and Morocco, and, down below, the dark mass of the Pyrenees stretching from the Atlantic to the Mediterranean.

At breakfast next morning, as I looked out over the commercial quarter of Meriadeck, I listened to two Chinese talking, in English, to a French-man, but I couldn't make out what they were saying. Some wine deal, no doubt. Chapmen, like me.

I didn't really feel like getting down to business at all myself, though. Instead, I went wandering around Bordeaux.

They were doing a face-job on the city. The front of the St André Cathe-dral was being cleaned up. And for depth-work on the stone they'd set to work a bacteria called *bacillus cereus*. The bacteria feeds on the stone, shits out calcite, and dies, leaving cement. Bio-mineralisation, they call it. Neat.

I wound up in a back street café that had a bullfight scene daubed on one of its walls, a big plastic replica of a bottle of Desperado tequila set above the door, and loud crap coming from the local radio.

Talking about crap, I'd seen this woman several times, in one street or the other. Dressed elegantly, leading two greyhounds with black capes on their backs, she was shouting at the top of her voice: "Shit – I shit on all of you! Lawyers, politicians, churches, families – I shit on you all!" She went round and round and round like this, shouting all the time. Bad news. The pathology of civilisation. Not that she wasn't talking sense. It was just the shitty method.

As for me, my conscience was bothering me, because I wasn't getting down to business for MacLaren, but I really didn't feel like it. I still had that big map in my head, and just kept wandering around.

I never did get down to business.

I ended up taking a train at St Jean station to Marseilles, from where I took a boat to Morocco. I'm sitting now in a quiet spot down by Essaouira smoking kif.

I'll go down further south in about a week's time.

I'll probably never be able to go back to Glasgow.

At least not while MacLaren's around.

# Kenneth White

## *Lament for McManus*

It's a blue diamond evening over Lannion Bay
the sea is whispering up against the shore
and the gulls are yelling homewards

the news came through this afternoon
that you died this April morning
of the cancer that after lingering
had speeded up and reduced you
almost to a skeleton

as I walked along the Goaslagorn valley
the air was full of bird notes
some close some far
like some unfinished symphony

I was remembering
the last time we walked together
that was at Cramond, Edinburgh
along the banks of the Almond River
talking about Duncan Ban Macintyre
and about the name he gave to the Lowlands
the *Machair Alba*

when suddenly we saw a heron
standing still and so absolutely attentive
in the midst of the rippling water

the way the mind can be at its best
as you well knew, McManus
son of the celto-galatian West
always looking for the words and the music
to say that highness

it's the flowers of the machair here
whin flowers and blackthorn bloom
with sprigs of purpurine heather
I'm scattering over your grave, McManus
over by Mortonhall
at the end of your fight

but it's thinking of what your mind was after
that I'm looking at that first star
shining away up there to the North
in the clear erigenian light.

*Note: a tribute to Tony McManus by Norman Bissell appears later in this issue.*

# *Obituaries*

*courtesy of Norah Morrice*

## Ken Morrice

(1924-2002)

### Poet and Psychiatrist

Dr James Kenneth Watt Morrice was born in Torry on the south side of the Dee. He came from fisher-folk and had a distinguished career as a psychiatrist, in Scotland and the USA (Denver Colorado). He was a compassionate man who knew with Burns that: *the hert's aye, the pairt, aye, that keeps us richt or wrang.* He had no sympathy with the ancient psychiatric notion that treatment of mental illness should be a kind of punishment. His life-long experience in psychotherapy equipped him with a profound insight into the human condition.

In 1968, he came home to Aberdeen, where he developed new skills as a writer: as a poet in both Scots and English, an his muse reflected his psychiatric experience with all kinds of people. His work with criminals and sex offenders gave him a unique set of perspectives. His poems were widely published in newspapers and literary journals such as *Akros, Chapman* and *Cencrastus*. In the decade, 1985-95, several of his poems in Scots appeared in *Lallans*, and some were included in anthologies such as *The New Makars* (Mercat Press 1991), and recently, in *A Book of Scottish Verse* (Hale, 2001). The number of poets writing in authentic Scots in the last quarter of the twentieth century is not large, and Dr Morrice was a significant poet competent in writing in this register, who rightly belongs along with his peers, Alastair Mackie and Alexander Scott, who developed in Aberdeen in the same generation.

In 'Domiciliary Visit' (*Lallans* 25, 1985), Morrice seemingly drew on a poignant visit he was obliged to make to an old widow woman who had been left alone too long. These lines give the flavour of the poem:

My man's no in yet, as you can see.
Fit did you say your name wis again?
A psychiatrist! Michtie me,
I thocht it wis the insurance mannie.

O, ye maun forgie my menners.
Sit you doon, I'll pit aff the TV,
and get the money. My man's denner's
still tae mak. But dearie me, I maun be
gaun gyte! You're nae the insurance man,
are you? Fit wey hiv ye come tae see me?

I ken I'm wearin auld, but I'm nae saft.
No me! I wis tap o the class for sums
and best in the schule at needle-craft.

Apostles of the English neo-classical poetic tradition might claim that this is social commentary rather than poetry. Others might take the view that much of the verse in the abstract neo-classical tradition has really little to do with poetry, which is properly concerned with human relationships.

Ken Morrice, whose life was concerned with human relationships, was a victim of cancer. To quote his good friend, Ian Olson, he bore this "with the wry stoicism that pervades the poetry in which he had concluded, 'each of us peoples a passing landscape/ giving a moment's meaning to friends and children'". A modest conclusion from a man whose life and writings gave so much sympathetic understanding to others.

*David Purves*

# Eric Rayne Mackinnon

(1937-2002)

## Transcending Pain and Obscurity

With the death of Rayne Mackinnon in April 2002, Scotland has lost one of its finest yet most underrated poets. A poet in the same mould as John Clare, Mackinnon lived on the road for a time, and spent many years of his life confined in psychiatric hospitals. Born in Darlington in 1937, the son of a diplomat and educated in Scotland, he explored the countryside from an early age, and on hill-walking expeditions developed his deep love of nature and the reverential attitude towards God's creation that is so evident in his poetry.

While at St. Andrews University, schizophrenia struck, a disaster which was to blight a promising future. He left the university suddenly and took to the road, getting casual work, sometimes sleeping rough, on travels that took him from England to Orkney and which he later described in poems such as 'The Hitch-Hiker' and 'Spring Work'.

His deep mental disturbance, however, led to his being admitted to Carstairs State Hospital, and it was behind its grim fences that the poetic flood-gates opened, and he produced much of his finest work. While in Carstairs he read widely, studied poetic technique, translated Dante and other European poets. It was there too that he developed his Christian faith.

His poems were inspired not only by the surrounding hills and changing seasons, but also by his close and sympathetic observation

*courtesy of Silvia Graham*

of his companions. In 'The Blasting of Billy P.' he paints, with no self-pity, a picture of the bleak daily routine of such a place of confinement, yet underlying it is his compassion for his fellows, and the ability to rise above his circumstances.

… I left the game
Of football to support itself, and found
The spot, where fields spoke music to my eyes.
One moment I would see a humdrum scene,
The next would breathe a draught of God's
glad world …

His most prolific years were the 1970s, when many of his poems appeared in literary magazines such as *Scotia Review, Lines, Chapman* and *Agenda*. He published three collections of poetry at this time: *The Spark Joy* (Caithness, 1970), *The Hitch-Hiker and other poems* (Outposts, 1976), and *The Blasting of Billy P.* (Enitharmon, 1978).

But perhaps his most enduring legacy is the sequence of 21 poems *Northern Elegies*, published by Netherbow in 1986. These poems are witness to his profound Christian faith, his acceptance of suffering and belief in the possibility of redemption. From 'Resurrection':

> … Once I saw
> Christ rise and shine
> In the old woman in her withered coat
> Who fed the pigeons…

The language of his poetry is simple but highly-charged. He can take an everyday object or situation and by some alchemy of matter and spirit transmute it into something "boundless and timeless", to borrow Kathleen Raine's phrase. From his poem 'Life':

> The cold wind forms a wall around the house,
> Stars are shivering out in space. Where can
> Life be on such a night as this, when one
> Can almost hear within the leaves and soil
> The cold snores of the sleeping snakes?…

It is difficult to choose 'representative' lines from Mackinnon's poetry. His poems have a cumulative dignity and integrity which requires them to be read whole. Like the music of Beethoven and Brückner he loved so much, the poems soar free from bonds of clay and attain a spiritual dimension where the pain and anger that are part of being human are transcended by acceptance and joy.

> And when in the dull throb of death, the soul
> Sings clearer, then eternity will watch
> With patient eyes, and the low lamps of life
> Will feel a brighter light
> Shine thru Man's weakness and his ignorance.

In recent years he wrote less frequently, but his accomplished rendering of the Orpheus legend may be read in the School of Poets Series No 8. Other poems may be found in *A Touch of Flame*, an anthology of contemporary Christian poetry (Lion, 1989), and *Spring Work*, a collection of his work compiled by the Penumbra organisation under whose care Rayne spent his latter years.

Rayne Mackinnon necessarily lived a secluded life, and although he won two international awards for poetry his name is not well known in Scotland today. Let us hope that his work will live on and gain the wider recognition it so richly deserves.

*Heather Scott*

*courtesy of John MacDonald*

# Tony McManus
## 1953-2002
## A Live Presence

It doesn't seem right to speak of him in the past tense. He is such a live presence still for me and for so many others who knew him. Once you had met Tony McManus there was something about his quiet manner, his quick mind and ready wit that stayed with you forever, like some deep clear pool you found in a river when you were wee.

He would take a good long look at you when you spoke to him, and you knew that what he had to say came from a man who had thought things through and knew what he was about. He went deep into philosophy, particularly in the last years of his life when he knew he had a rare form of cancer which would be hard to beat. He studied the phenomenology of Edmond Husserl and Martin Heidegger and went much further back to those free spirits of Celtic Christianity, Duns Scotus and John Scot Erigena. Here he was not only working through the remaining echoes of Catholicism which he had been brought up in and moved away from, but exploring the essential oneness of the universe. Because he had read so deeply, his thought carried real conviction and an unquestionable integrity.

He was following the intellectual pathways mapped out by Kenneth White, whom he had come across in the 1980s when on holiday in Tarbes with his French wife Nanon and family. What he recognised in White was a brilliant poet who dealt in the big questions, who also wrote prose books of the world in which he moved, and whose essay books, only available at that time in French, revealed an original world outlook in geopoetics which went way beyond all the usual categories. It appealed to Tony's wry sense of humour that he first heard of Kenneth White not amongst Scottish literary circles but from his French mother-in-law. It was as if the Scottish litearary establishment had mounted a conspiracy to ignore this poet who had been so readily recognised furth of Scotland.

Tony read everything of White's he could get his hands on and became the foremost authority on his work: writing articles, giving lectures, organising conferences, interviewing him at length for radio, and in 1995 co-founding the Scottish Centre for Geopoetics which has inspired many working Scottish poets, thinkers and interested members of the public.. The exhibition *White World,* which he curated for the National Library of Scotland in 1996, took the life and work of this original thinker to a much wider audience throughout Scotland and continues to tour in France. Tony believed passionately that a poetics of the earth which unifies disparate academic disciplines and is imbued through and through with a sense of world could provide the kind of cultural renewal so much needed today in Scotland and worldwide.

Before his death he had almost completed a book on Kenneth White and geopoetics which, when it is finally published, will provide an indispensable handbook for realising that bold vision.

It was a vision that permeated all aspects of his life: as a dedicated and inspirational teacher of English; as an accomplished guitarist, singer, songwriter, arranger, translator and writer on music and theatre; and as an outstanding poet, much of whose work has yet to be published. He set many French poems in Scots translation as songs, and even composed a beautiful setting of a sequence from MacDiarmid's *A Drunk Man* – 'O Whaur's the Bride …'. He was also a devoted husband, father, and brother. Such was his natural modesty that even his close friends often did not know of the breadth and depth of his many talents and activities.

Because he recognised the crucial importance of the Scots tradition of the democratic intellect in education based on a broad-based and rigorous curriculum, he was determined not to let Higher Still undermine the quality of that education. His pamphlet *Sense and Worth* is both a critique of Higher Still and a radical analysis of what education should be about. It was published in 1999 by the Scottish Association of Teachers of Language and Literature, of which he became the driving force and leading spokesman. Just two weeks before he died he somehow found the strength to write his last column for the *Times Educational Supplement Scotland,* an insightful and humorous article on streaming in schools and the misuse of language.

Tony wore his learning lightly, but it was the power of his intellect, the integrity of his judgement, his quiet determined energy and compassion which drew others to him and which inspired them to think and act. The pure revitalising waters of his life and thought will flow on in the lives of those he knew and influenced so deeply, and, through his words and music, will flow yet further on in the lives of those who have yet to encounter him.

*Norman Bissell*

# Reviews

## The Third Renaissance

Once upon a time in the 1990s there was another Scottish Renaissance. Since then, no-one has been certain as to who these virtuosi were, what constituted their achievements and how best to capitalise on their advances. What is beyond question is that unlike the aureate outpouring of the sixteenth century makars or the re-imagination of Scots as a literary language at the beginning of the twentieth century, the "Third Renaissance" was predominantly obvious in the realm of prose fiction. Scottish Modernism, spear-headed by MacDiarmid, was capable of integrating the prosaic but not the novelistic, and to a remarkable extent, the movement eschewed the novel as a vehicle for literary radicalism. One can hear the sense of exasperation and relief in Antony Burgess's review of Gray's *Lanark* (1981) – "it was time Scotland produced a shattering work in the modern idiom". Other reviews confirmed the book's uniqueness within Scottish letters: critical comparisons were drawn to Joyce, Borges and Kafka, but significantly there were no parallels within contemporary Scottish writing. Indeed, Burgess himself had to go back to Walter Scott to locate a precedent for a self-aware literary novel.

There are varying theories about origin of the idea of a Scottish prose Renaissance originated: Secker and Warburg's list, Philip Hobsbaum's writing group and *Rebel Inc.* magazine are all advanced as the launch point for this phenomenon. In terms of the material produced in Scotland at present, the epochal moment is undoubtedly the publication of Welsh's *Trainspotting* (1993). Whereas *Lanark* did not generate a host of imitations, or radically alter what is considered the normative form of the Scottish novel, *Trainspotting* instituted a whole genre, which, looking at debut novels of the past five years, soon came to dominate the fiction scene.

Why should this be? Any answer to questions about the preponderance of Welshian prose must lie in the fabric of the novel itself. Both structurally and linguistically, *Trainspotting* represented a prioritisation of 'voice' over 'text' which allowed for its reiteration and replication. "To have found one's voice" is a frequently heard cliché of critical approbation, and one which, I feel, hampers the development of a mature novelistic culture.

*Trainspotting* is a monologue, and most of its successors have favoured a first person narration. Moreover, it is a monologue mannered to phonetically represent a speaking voice, which delimits the extent to which other idiolects can develop within the text. This levelling of linguistic diversity has the effect of atrophying particular possible registers. Take the scene where Renton attempts to explain Kierkegaard in court: "… bit I'm rabbiting a bit here. Ah cut myself short". That slippage from 'I' to 'Ah', the curtailing of the narrative, reveals the extent to which the language is unable to integrate the change of register. It, like its protagonist, is recidivist. This should not be construed as an attack on 'Scots' as a medium for prose fiction; rather, it should highlight that even the name of the language is plural, and that homogenising the voice leads to a lack of possibility. The oral quality of Welsh's prose foregrounds the idea that it is 'genuine' – in a sense, confessional – and as such incontrovertible. It is specific, in terms of dialect, product placement, contemporary reference; in effect, "the Great Leith novel circa 1990" rather than a Great Scottish novel. This template can then be transferred seamlessly, tweaked for local twang and colour and rehashed as the Great Coatbridge novel, the Great Oban novel, the Great Longformacus novel *et al.*

What MacDiarmid proposed as the Modernist aesthetic was the antisyzygy, the union of opposites, which could contain every register from scientific taxonomy to inarticulate howl. Welsh, conversely, promotes a 'progression towards the mean', an erasure of difference rather than its accommodation.

Suhayl Saadi, in a paper given at the 2000 Association of Scottish Literary Studies conference, was right to assert that the "liminal in literature can be approached from any direction". Given the ubiquity of this novelistic form since "the Birth of Radgedy", what other vectors towards the edge might Scottish writing adopt? Or, to return to Burgess's reaction to *Lanark*, we might ask whether Scotland can produce a shattering – or heartbreaking – work in the *post*modern idiom?

*Lanark* emphatically presented itself as a book, investing meaning in its nature as a printed artefact, an inscription. *Trainspotting* and its ilk aspire to be transcriptions. Looking at the wider world, the acclaimed works in recent years have tended to emerge from the postmodernist tradition: Dave Eggers, Michel Houellebecq, Agnes Desarthes, Mark Danielewski, Haruki Murakami, Zadie Smith, Colapinto – works whose engagement with a diversity of languages in a self-conscious, formally imaginative manner are integral to their success, critically and commercially.

The time has come for a mature debate on the future direction of the novel, on the role the novel can play in Scotland's self-definition and its relationship with developments in writing the wider world. Looking back over 100 issues of *Chapman*, there have been provocative interchanges on poetics, drama, self-identity and the canon, but not on the Novel. Attempts at such a debate have been curiously stifled: Kenneth White and Ronald Frame attempted to initiate one at this year's Edinburgh Book Festival – albeit a debate overly concerned with matters of form – which rapidly degenerated into a catty spat more concerned with personalities than issues.

So: which contemporary Scottish novelists would form my proto-canon? In no particular order: Ali Smith, James Robertson, Kuppner, Bill Duncan, Crumey, Delahunt, James Meek, Lucy Ellman, Peter Burnett and A L Kennedy. There are others, and my admiration for these authors is neither unqualified nor perpetual. But please: feel free to disagree.

*Stuart B Kelly*

# Theatre Roundup: The Recent Years

There was a time when many Scottish plays reflected back to its audiences their lost lives in shipyards, the steamie or the croft. Now there are more plays which move away from a fairly accurate but often nostalgic portrayal of the past to engage the audience in a more hard hitting examination of Scottish and human nature set in the past or in the present. Some are historically based – *Heritage* by Nicola McCartney (Traverse), *Further From the Furtherest Thing* by Zinnie Harris (Tron/RNT), *An Clo Mor* by Henry Adams (Theatre Highland) and *The Speculator* by David Greig – but most, like Isabel Wright's *Speedrun* (Tron), Douglas Maxwell's *Decky does a Bronco* and *Our Bad Magnet* (GridIron and Borderline respectively), Gregory Burke's *Gagarin Way* (Traverse), and David Greig's recent plays, are set in the recent present.

*Gagarin Way*, Gregory Burke's hit play of the 2002 Festival Fringe, is set in Fife where three employees of a multinational kidnap one of the heid yins, Frank, to find that he's a Fifer too. Not only that but their ring leader Eddie, who gives high speed, off the cuff philosophy seminars to anyone, is a Frank who didn't get the breaks to escape. After an extended run at London's National Theatre, it's now in the West End with Michael Nardone still electrifying as Eddie.

*An Clo Mor* by Henry Adams tackles the problem of presenting Scotland's languages on stage very interestingly, with conversations occurring where some speak in English, some in Gaelic enabling everyone to feel both languages are equally valid, no sly sniggers, as can often happen in some plays written here or south of the border. In other European countries the use of several languages in the same play is becoming increasingly common and indeed it reflects our own possible experience here, where our residents speak two or more of the increasing indigenous languages of our country.

Stage plays often concentrate on the White Scot in our cultural life. But there are some signs that theatre practitioners are looking at what is happening in today's Scotland and are finding actors and writers from more varied ethnic backgrounds. But it's still rare to cast colour-blind or hear accents and speech patterns from outside the Central Belt's urban centres. Often the ethnic actor is drafted in from down south. We should be developing, training and using those actors from our own increasing first and second generation Scots. Not enough teaching of Scottish accents or dialects is available in our drama schools. If the actors to do the parts aren't sufficiently available, playwrights can be steered away from truly reflecting the fascinating, enriching mix of accents and outlooks Scotland has.

After difficult years for the theatre community in Scotland, recent grant increases potentially enable at least a few more productions and enriched partnerships, both between companies based here and with theatre practitioners outside our borders, provided local authorities don't reduce their support. One such very successful collaboration in autumn 2001 was *The Seagull* which saw the resident Dundee Rep Company directed by Lithuanian Rimas Tuminas with music and design by his fellow countrymen. It was an outstanding production, full of breathtaking physical acting, joyous and moving to watch. Chekhov saw his play as a comedy and so it is – the kind where you laugh at the characters for like us, "Lord, what fools these mortals be". It toured Scotland in 2002.

The Traverse recently staged Linda McLean's version of *Olga* by the Finnish playwright Laura Ruohonen. McLean reflected the original play, the six characters a mix of rural and urban accents reflecting their different backgrounds and giving the script a Scottish vibrancy. Olga is an old woman, a bit of a curmudgeon living on her own, her daughter countries away in Spain. A young man, Rundis, arrives in her city flat to do community service as a home help. Both don't fit into the ways of the modern world. Rundis treats his girl friend and the world as a whole like dirt, a very disaffected youth.

Paul Thomas Hickey as Rundis and Eileen McCallum as Olga made special and believable the developing relationship between them, both rebels with some cause. They take off to see her house in the remote countryside which Olga's family are on at her to sell.

Though still set in Finland the parallels with our own changing country, the tensions of age and youth, country and town are brought out in a lyrical script. At its heart a moving love which you sense may well change Rundis's life. They both, distanced and disaffected, reach out to one another, despite difference of age, experience and background recognising each other's strong spirit of defiance. In Traverse 2 the set was overwhelming; in Traverse 1 it would have echoed the vastness of Finland and Scotland very well. *Olga* gave two fine actors excellent roles in a play which reflects well both its original and the Scottish version, directed by Lynne Parker of Dublin's Abbey Theatre.

Boilerhouse in Autumn 2001 toured Isabel Wright's new play *Blooded,* dealing with today's girls' passage to womanhood – a topic Douglas Maxwell tackles for boys in his rightly successful *Decky does a Bronco* and *Our Bad Magnet.* Unlike him, Isabel concentrates on her characters in the here and now – a summer spent on the beach in a small Scottish town. Unlike GridIron's *Decky,* Boilerhouse staged *Blooded* indoors always, taking place on an arena stage. Wright has a particular facility with the music of words, first explored by her in *Speedrun.* In *Blooded* the girls at times chorused, breaking up the summer's conversations, underlining how terrifying girls with hormones running rampant can be. Working well with the audience on four sides, the main characters are well drawn, Kate Dickie's Amy outstanding as the girl determined to get away.

An even younger playwright still in the making, Tim Primrose, has yet to prove how varied his structures can be, but in *Porcelain Dolls* and *this here now* he shows a considerable facility for writing Godber-like plays with varied characters and dynamic storylines. Both his plays have been mounted by Lyceum Youth Theatre whose members show a real zest and understanding. Steve Small and Colin Bradie are doing much to plant seeds of the future for Scottish theatre.

The vicissitudes of fixed term funding can mean an interesting director-playwright such as Nicola McCartney finds her own company lookOUT losing its grant, despite developing not only her own work but that of other writers such as Isabel Wright's *Tongues* which she strikingly directed and produced in 2001. Her company's commitment to other writers was clear in its final production of short plays by Kate Dickie, Matthew Lenton, Kathy McKean and Rona O'Donnell. Whilst MacCartney wasn't born or brought up here, our artistic life will be diminished if we don't encourage a varied background of talent to live and work here.

A company restored to funding initially removed is theatreBabel whose production of Liz Lochhead's richly feminist version of Euripides' *Medea* came to the Fringe in 2000 and 2001 and subsequently toured abroad in 2001 and 2002, reaching Cyprus and India in its travels. Lochhead's text has Medea English-speaking with Scottish servants and chorus making the dialogue feistily of the here and now. Maureen Beattie's Medea chilled us in blood red velvet whilst the female chorus railed in heavy, dust-coloured cloth. Later in 2001 Babel with the Tron also produced Liz Lochhead's *Beauty and the Beast*, not a pantomime but a delicious exploration of myths, fairy tales, innocence and sexuality. Full of characteristic humour and dark moments, it captivated from the moment the actors stepped out of a causally laid down suitcase. Kai Fischer's set transformed during the play and had animated furniture. Michael Marra sang his own and Burn's songs to complete a special theatrical treat for Christmas.

The Arches, which reached its tenth anniversary in 2001, is developing into a wonderfully exciting arts venue, using more and more of its unique site under Glasgow's Central Station. Andy Arnold's Arches company staged John Patrick Shanley's *The Big Funk* in its UK premiere. This vastly funny surreal play set in New York had John Kazek delight as Austin, the guy who wants to make everything right in a very misshapen world. It's a play almost spiritual in scope, reinforcing through its characters those who want to be close to someone good. In one of its many exciting spaces the company's *Playboy of The Western World* had us stand round the edges of the Irish cottage, the air reeking of peat smoke. This venue makes theatre happen partly by the clubs also run in the venue, giving us new directors and theatre experiences and making increasing use of its dynamic, one which Edinburgh too could develop in the Underbelly beneath George IV Bridge.

One company sadly is about to vanish, despite good, sometimes outstanding productions and enthusiastic audiences. Barring miracles, The Brunton Theatre company under David Mark Thompson will cease to be later this spring. *Come on Feel the Noise* devised by Thompson, P J Henry, Claire Knight, John Kielty and Jack McGowan is set in the time of Glam Rock near Pumpherston. It was the best piece of popular theatre I've ever seen, the audience reacting unrestrainedly. I just hope that Thompson's talent and vision and those he has fostered in Musselburgh aren't lost to the Scottish scene permanently. His Shakespeares have also been striking and good.

David Greig is Scotland's most prolific playwright. *Casanova*, produced by Suspect Culture, was a fascinating psychological exploration, though the production, directed by Graham Eatough, was hampered by a set which increasingly overwhelmed the stage. It did though have standout performances by Callum Cuthbertson, Louise Ludgate, Mabel Atkin and Vicki Liddelle – who showed her extraordinary chameleon ability in several roles. Along with many plays mentioned here, the text is published – a valuable asset in the building of Scottish theatre's repertoire.

Greig also wrote *Dr Korczak's Example* for TAG. Korczak ran an orphanage in Nazi-occupied Europe, and posthumously influenced the UN Rights of the Child protocol. Stewart Ennis played Dr Korczak and Susan Coyle and Tommy Mullins, the orphans Stephanie and Adzic, the rest effectively represented by puppets. This movingly theatrical piece, superbly acted by a cast of three, toured to secondary schools. This difficult-to-please age group were stilled and awed by what can happen when cultures are threatened.

Several re-produced good plays in 2001 included Sue Glover's *Bondagers* by the Byre, Nicola McCartney's *Heritage* by the Traverse and Alastair Cording's *Sunset Song* by Prime Productions. To flourish, good plays and playwrights need to be seen again. There are encouraging signs – an established ensemble at Dundee, companies touring outstanding productions within and beyond, some but not enough good playwrights getting commissions produced, and, increasingly, plays published. But there are problems. Underdeveloped but performed new plays and plays commissioned but not performed are wasteful. It's not always the fault of theatres or SAC: writers sometimes shirk rewrites. There is a shortage of rehearsal space, of large performance spaces; other venues are less used than they should or could be; and theatres are either dark or open infrequently. Theatres need to be kept warm by full productions *and* by refreshment spaces and creative events. Tourists and locals lack early information about what's on in an area, I try to remedy this on the web through listings and reviews whose growing world readership amazes me. The recent increase in theatre funding from the Scottish Executive is very welcome: before then, almost all companies were holding on by their fingertips, diminished in productions, casts and morale.

I remember the theatre of twenty years ago. We have developed and enlarged our dramatic commitment and the breadth of work attempted – not always successfully, but then the finest productions are treasured because they are so difficult to achieve. The fate of theatre always lies in the lap of the gods!

*Thelma Good*

# Cross Party Group in the Scottish Parliament on the Scots Leid

It is estimated that there are up to one and a half million speakers of Scots, yet few have knowledge of the language and most remain ignorant of its brilliant cultural legacy. Despite an establishment death wish, the Scots language is still alive and thriving. But whereas in the past it could survive on its own, like many fragile living things, it now needs help and support.

Hopes were raised that our new, inclusive, Scottish democracy would recognise the culture and speech of the mass of the people, because, for many, their desire for a Scottish Parliament was always tied in closely with the assumption that it would naturally offer direct support and encouragement for indigenous culture. While this hope has been far from realised, the advent of the Scottish Parliament has offered new opportunities. Among the mechanisms for translating ideas into long-term political strategies is the Cross Party Group, which works on the principle of involving outside bodies and individuals with MSPs of all parties.

The CPG on the Scots Leid has been in existence for just over one year. The stated aim of the Group is "to promote the cause of Scots, inform members of the culture and heritage of the language and highlight the need for action to support it". So, for the first time possibly ever, the status, condition and future of the Scots language are being given serious consideration at parliamentary level.

Membership includes those at the forefront of Scots language activism, with phenomenal expertise and talent. Our main business has been the production of a 'Statement of Principles' for the language, written in Scots, which will underpin our aim to have Scots recognised and respected. The basis of this document is the Barcelona Universal Declaration of Linguistic Rights and the European Charter on Regional or Minority Languages. Plans are being formulated for a high profile launch of the Statement with copies made readily available across the country.

The group has also organised a conference for teachers, carried out an educational inventory of the language and contributed to the debate on cultural tourism. One of the members of the group was asked to compile a Regional Dossier on Scots for the European Union. This was welcomed, because it could not fail to highlight the vulnerability of the language (as few official statistics exist) and will certainly underline the current lack of political and educational support for the language. We are also considering how to build on growing interest from school students and teachers against a background of disinterest in producing material in Scots from mainstream publishers. In terms of cultural tourism we have initiated a dialogue with Visitscotland on how to promote tourism by use of language. Discussions within the CPG are lively and productive, but we will only be making real progress when these discussions are taking place *outside* the Parliament, and in the streets and houses and schools and pubs of every village and town in Scotland.

There is criticism by activists of the Scottish Parliament and its perceived lack of recognition of Scots. Only three Motions have even been lodged in Scots – all by me – and an English translation also had to be submitted. Signage throughout the buildings is in English and Gaelic only. We have had whole debates in Gaelic with translators available. A Gaelic Dictionary of Parliamentary terms has been introduced. Nae word o sic a thing for Scots. We have a Parliamentary Gaelic Officer, but not for Scots. These omissions are significant, because recognition by Parliament is crucial for the language's survival and for the status gives to those who speak it.

"The Scottish Executive considers the Scots language to be an important part of Scotland's distinctive linguistic and cultural heritage." Despite this, the Executive has singularly failed to come up with any commitment to the language – far less, the (comparatively) high levels of state endorsement and funding which Gaelic has enjoyed. This is to take nothing away from the efforts of the Gaels. The success of the Gaelic lobby results in part from its ability in recent years to present a united front, its clear view of its aims and its resolution and resources to pursue its goals. Scots speakers would do well to learn from this. Largely, of course, the CPG knows what needs to happen to improve the status of the Scots language. The twin elements of education and the media are crucial. In general, the media in Scotland behaves as if the Scots language does not exist, although the majority of the population understands and employs some Scots every day.

For many teachers, the Scots Language component of English Language 5-14 curriculum did not cause them to change their provision of Scots language. A Scots poem to be learned by heart around the start of term 3, with very little explanation of what the words mean and where they came from, is still in 2002, the only Scots language provision offered by many primary schools.

As an indication of the fragility of the language, a teacher told me recently that he visited primary schools whose names comprised basic Scots words, such as "burn", "bonny" and "brae" – words not recognised by the children. Many pupils are unable to pronounce the "ch" sound, using "k" – lock for loch, for example. But there is an appetite for Scots in schools, and a general feeling that at last the opportunity exists to effect significant change in the attitude and allocation of resources to Scots, through the political process.

Wishful thinking may not yet be consigned to the midden of history, but requests for political action, via the CPG, particularly towards improving the treatment of Scots, can now be made with greater confidence that they will not fall entirely on deif lugs.

In this new Scotland, there is no doubt that Scots is still subject to the same tired old prejudices, but now, maybe, we have the where with all to encourage the establishment into greater commitment to Scotland's neglected Lowland tongue.

*Irene McGugan MSP*
*Convenor of the CPG on the Scots Leid*

# Pamphleteer

*The Missing Tree* (Kind Red Spirit, PO Box 20859, London, £5) written by Cameron Fox for designer Meredith Swan, follows the first six months of the co-authors' love affair, each short poem intensely conveying through eloquent language and metaphor ('I want to live inside your skin, become a floating swan with eyes made of the night') the intense experience of falling in love. The poems represent the conflicting emotions the lovers' experience when together and apart, and the purity of feeling expressed so honestly in his work makes Fox's writing very moving. However, once it is revealed that the two are still with other partners, the authors' anguish seems rather adolescent and selfish. Described in the blurb as a 'star-crossed passion', one begins to wonder if this is a romantic excuse for indecision and cowardice.

*Skin Balaclavas* by John Easton and Sheena Blackhall demonstrates a different view of romantic love, with the cynical 'Glaciation', ending in the paradoxical line 'Love's for ever, while it lasts.' Easton demonstrates a contrasting love of his native city, Aberdeen, in poems such as 'Aberdeen' and 'River Dee, at Night' with conflicting themes of alienation in 'Portlethan', a critical look at the poverty and weariness of spirit often to be found beneath the surface of such semi-urban northern Scottish towns. Sheena Blackhall's remarkably good poetry in Doric is reminiscent of Violet Jacob, with poems such as 'The Bawd': "I am the bawd, the fuspert in/ The barley's beard, the barley's beard./ O sud ye drive me frae the lan/ Derk be yer weird, derk be yer weird!" Her simple use of language and repetition harks back to traditional forms, such as ballads but her Scots is not confined to themes of nature, as has tended to be the case in the literature of our nation.

Valerie Thornton, Glasgow poet and short-story writer, has produced her first collection of poems, *Catacoustics* (Mariscat Press, 3 Mariscat Rd, Glasgow. She is an accomplished writer, and the deceptively cosy images of domestic cats and birds that recur in her poetry often present us with the unexpected, like the narrator in 'The Other Side of the Coin' being endowed with feline qualities such as double-jointed suppleness which masks crippling back pain. Cats are represented as comforting domestic companions in 'The Familiar', with the narrator and her cat seeming to merge into one. Humans may also take on avian qualities, offering the possibility of flight or transcendence, as in 'Above Daldowie, 1990', describing the gradual paring down of an old woman's physical form until at death, her bones appear birdlike, and she has "spread her wings/and flown away/free as a wraith of blue smoke/free as a bird". In 'Kestrel, Conic Hill', however, we are reminded of our lumpen, earthbound nature when the narrator, finding a dead kestrel and detaching its wings, stores them 'next to the cat food' and pathetically hopes to emulate its flight by tethering them to the dashboard of her car.

Perhaps one of the most disturbing and morbid collections of poetry I have ever read is *The New Bride* by Catherine McPhail (Smith/Doorstop Books, The Poetry Business, The Studio, Byram Arcade, Westgate, Huddersfield, £3). Full of relentlessly black humour, McPhail's poetry, comparable in some ways to Lochhead's, is permeated with images of loss without hope of redemption. Its sly, subversive gaze pokes fun at stereotypical images of romantic love, as in 'Marcus', with a woman falling in love with a shop dummy she rescues from a skip and plies with champagne. 'The New Bride' and 'Resurrection' respectively give voice to the (not so dearly) departed, and reveal the unspoken fear of the bereaved that their loved one might return: *"listen, it is not finished"*. In 'The New Bride' a dead wife observes the rituals of mourning and laughs bitterly at her husband's new courtship ("And a year to the day since I shrug off the yoke/ of life, you meet the new bride. In group therapy.") and marriage, "a riot of white nylon". The vindictive last three words, 'the simpering bitch', are nevertheless shocking.

Edwin Morgan's description of Gael Turnbull's work: "Clean-cut lightness of touch and glancing insights and humanities"; may be apt, but at times this collection of small prose poems (*Might a Shape of Words and Other Transmutations*, Mariscat Press, £5), despite their brevity, is verbose. The bright snapshots of everyday life, revealing glimpses of individual uniqueness and depth of emotion beneath an ordinary surface, are sometimes lost in the complexity of Turnbull's language.

*Going to the Island* by Miriam Scott (Spout Publications, The Word Hoard, Kirklees Media Centre, 7 Nothumberland St, Huddersfield, £3.50) weaves a spell of mist and mystery, of clear island light. Filled with a sense of the past, Scott poignantly contrasts the continuity of old ways and the harmony of land, sea and islanders, epitomised perhaps in the tales of selkies she relates, with the loss of a culture forced by poverty to embrace 'modern ways' and the mainland and yet with a silent, enduring core embedded in the island itself, so that the island, and the poetry, become a mythology in themselves. Her work seems almost timeless, and yet embraces the entire history of an island, coming full circle and presenting a microcosm of a society, reflecting in turn the microcosm of the island and its community, inextricably connected to the landscape.

*Frae Glasgow til Manila* includes poems by European and Latin American poets, such as 'Piedra Negra Sobre una Piedra Blanca' by Vallejo and 'Cementerio de la cuidad' by Cernuda, translated into Scots by John Manson. Manson has aimed to "reflect the language of the north coast of Caithness of earlier decades". Considering the difficulty of representing a non-standard spoken dialect in literature, Manson appears an able translator, but I am not sure how accurate his representation of the dialect is. The difficulty of his task is added to by the fact that he appears to have mingled Caithness dialect with MacDairmid's literary Scots. With David Craig, Manson edited the Penguin edition of MacDairmid's *Selected Poems*, and is a life-long supporter of his aims. Manson's translation work appears dedicated to the objective of continuing MacDairmid's intent to break the "hegemony of English Lit-

erature in Scotland and to extend Scottish interests outwards to world literature".

Manson also edits *Recuerdo de Espana: Memoirs and Poems of the Spanish Civil War* (Corbie Press, 57 Murray St, Montrose, Angus, £2). This collection of souvenirs of the war was brought to London in 1937 by an unknown member of the International Brigade (Manson suggests Glasgow engineer Peter Kerrigan, 1900-77). There are ten 'recuerdos', each comprising an illustration and a poem or proverb to match, all by Spaniards. They offer an insight into the ideology of the anti-fascists, fighting for freedom and the continuation of their culture. The most succinct, by Jose Mas (Madrid), says simply: "Nothing is as dishonourable and monstrous as pursuing weak and defenceless beings".

*Four Play with Words: A First Anthology*, by four new writers (Ian Graham, Jane Grounsell, Lesley Scott and Valerie Walker) is published by 4P Publications, 3 Palmerston Place Lane, Edinburgh (no price given). The product of an Edinburgh writers' group, the four contributors show real signs of promise. Ian Graham and Lesley Scott particularly stand out as strong short story writers with a seam of black humour running through their work. Jane Grounsell's poetry is daring: she experiments with different structures and her imagery is vivid and striking. Valerie Walker's writing also shows potential, despite the inclusion of what is obviously (even without the accompanying note) an evening class exercise. 'Goldfinger' is a continuation of Ian Fleming's story, and while amusing, is probably the weakest contribution.

*Jewelled Tree* by Louise Cole (Spout Publications, £3.50) is a series of 25 poems and a journey through bereavement and the process of recovery from the death of a loved one. Intense and honest, Cole's writing openly confronts and wrestles with the sheer pain of grief and the multitude of emotions that accompany it, such as confusion and anger, in searingly vivid language and imagery. This is an impressive debut for a young poet.

*Deborah Kilpatrick*

# Catalogue

*Across the Water,* ed. Donny O'Rourke, is a landmark anthology of Irish writers or Scottish writers with Irish roots, developing the already strong cultural connections across the Irish Sea. Many *Chapman* regulars appear – Rody Gorman, Brian McCabe and others. Preambles from the writers set the work in context and give potent continuity. Sustained fiction and selections of poems also lessen the traditional scatter-gun focus of such an enterprise, published by Argyll Publishing, £10.99.

An entirely different theme connects *The Gay Times Book of Short Stories* (ed. P-P Hartnett, Gay Times Books, £9.95). With a laudable aim of breaking out of the ghetto that gay and bisexual writing has been forced, by wrong-headed sexual and cultural politics, to inhabit, the book has definite highlights, not least in Amardeep Gill's sensitive portrayal of an Asian gay. We look forward to future volumes which, thanks to this, may reach the mainstream market they deserve.

Any book that takes in St Columba to Norman MacCaig by way of Robert Louis Stevenson cannot be accused having a narrow range. *Scottish Religious Poetry: An Anthology* (St Andrew Press, £14.99) covers all these and then some with a mighty dollop of Gaelic thrown in. 'Religious' is interpreted widely, to include expressions of what might be called 'a religious sensibility' by professed atheists. However, there are surprising omissions such as Tom Scott's 'Villanelle de Noël'. For a country so melted in the pot of religion, this is nonetheless a seminal volume.

*Sir David Lyndsay: Selected Poems* (Association for Scottish Literary Studies, £12.50) highlights the work of a writer previously better known as a playwright. His use of metre in Scots makes for an illuminating viewpoint of the 16th and 17th centuries. Although lay readers may have to trawl through the glossary, they will be amply rewarded. Few writers are more important to the Scottish literary canon, and we need the more rounded view of his production this volume provides.

There are a few problems with *Scottish Art* by Murdo McDonald (Thames & Hudson, £7.95) – not content, which is comprehensive and thoughtful, as with layout. The book is too small for what it tries to be – it needs to be larger to do justice to the treasures inside. Colour throughout would mean that all works get full visualisation. Ironically enough, its cover features *Poet's Pub,* an imaginary convening of Scottish makars by Alexander Moffat. An informative and definitive volume.

Artistry is not confined to the paintbox or sculptor's chisel as anyone who has heard bagpipes outside of the environs of Edinburgh's tourist area will attest. *The Highland Pipe and Scottish Society, 1750-1950* by William Donaldson (Tuckwell Press, £30) is crammed full of detail and event on the development of this maligned instrument. Perfect for the piper in your life.

*Into a Room: Selected Poems of William Soutar,* a shorter reworking of W R Aitken's selection of his work is published by Argyll (£7.99). Although a fresh book is more than welcome, Carl MacDougall and Douglas Gifford expand the selection of poetry from Aitken's original – a missed opportunity, especially since Aitken omitted poems which more than merit the light of day. Heidelinde Prüger, however, gives a sensitive and sustained insight into Soutar's work with *The Righteousness of Life: William Soutar: A Poet's Scottish Predilection for Philosophy* (Peter Lang,). But Soutar's work is not only in the adult arena – *Seeds in the Wind: Poems in Scots for Children* (Bibliothek der Provinz through James Thins Booksellers, Edinburgh) is beautifully bound and illustrated; *A Bairn's Song and Other Poems* (published with RLS' *Poems for Children,* and J K Annand's *Bairn Rhymes: Scots Verse for Children,* Mercat, £6.99) gives a child-friendly format and an early introduction to a great Scots writer.

Margaret Elphinstone's novel *The Sea Road* (Canongate, £6.99) tells of one Icelandic woman's encounter with 'Vinnland' and the Nordic explorer Eirik the Red. Redolent of the far north, Elphinstone is still on top form.

Speaking of Icelanders, Magnus Magnusson's magisterial tome *Scotland: The Story of a Nation* (Harper-Collins, £19.99) thumps onto the *Chapman* desk with full force. But it seems curiously hollow – although Magnusson has huge ground to cover, surely some reflection beyond the blow-by-blow accounts could have been included. The title would be more convincing as '*A* Story of a Nation' since it concerns itself solely with the affairs of royals and other high heid yins. In similar vein, Jonathan Hearn's *Claiming Scotland: A National Identity and Liberal Culture* (EUP, £16.99) has its moments, but its canter through its 'Movement', 'History' and 'Culture' is a little too dry and dusty.

The Saltire Society brings us Alexander Broadie's *Why Scottish Philosophy Matters* (£6.99). This rummage through the country's philosophical pantry fetches out some of the usual ingredients – Hume, bestriding the scene like a Caledonian colossus – but there are less familiar names too, like John Duns Scotus and John Mair. This small volume celebrates the sheer litany ideas that Scotland has brought to the global philosophical table.

Philosophy will come in handy if Tom Nairn has his way. In *After Britain: New Labour and the Return of Scotland* (Granta, £15.99) Nairn gives an impassioned demand for independence as a cure for Scotland's ills, not least for ridding it of racism against the English. The anthology *What a State!: Is Devolution the End of Britain?* (ed. Alan Taylor, Harper-Collins, £8.99) also sees the political construct of 'Britain' crashing down. It is worth it just for Angus Calder and Alasdair Gray's entertaining and informative conversation on land ownership – Gray's response to the statement that feudalism might be retained: 'If I ever ingest mango juice, it will be with extreme caution' (Calder has a well-known affection for mango juice).

Gray also features in Canongate's collection of Scottish literature's 'greatest hits', all in pocket-size volumes. Short helpings of Burns, Scott, Hogg, RLS, Muriel Spark, James Kelman with a survey of the field by Gray (priced at an attractive £12.99 for the set) means that a toe can be easily dipped before the plunge into a full-blown novel.

Works don't get more full-blown than Scott's Waverley novels. Edinburgh University Press has undertaken the mighty task of publishing the lot with *The Monastery, The Pirate, Chronicles of the Canongate* and *Quentin Durward* in this batch – all, naturally, with the highest degree of scholarship. All handsomely presented, they make a fine addition to any library. Of a similar standard, also by EUP, is a reprint of James Hogg's *The Private Memoirs and Confessions of a Justified Sinner* in his Collected Works series although, at £35.00, still a little on the pricey side.

A roundup of other notable achievements: *Men and Beasts*, a collaboration between Valerie Gillies and Rebecca Muir (Luath Press, £15.00) is an interesting project. The two subjects are evidently interchangeable: see the celebration of Edinburgh's 'Tam the Gun' for example. The photaes are no bolt-on; they compliment and inform the words around them. An unusual and fun book.

Local endeavours are represented by *Love's Laeback Sang: Selected poems, Lollie Graham* published by the highly active Shetland Library (£7.95). Often funny, by turns satirical (see 'Auction Sale') but always interesting. Also by Shetland Library is *Stones in the Millpond: Reflections on the First World War* by Christian Tait (£8.95), a moving collection that shows the personal can be more affecting than grand sweeps of history. The era of World War I is also the frame for Bill Harding's history of Perth, *On Flows the Tay* (Cualann Press, £12.99), an illuminating examination of the town during one of its painful periods. Finally, a tiny opus from Robin Bell entitled *Le Château des Enfants*. Measuring less than four inches by three, this set of word pictures is nicely presented, with the merest outlines of a setting, leaving the rest for the reader to fill in (Perth and Kinross Council, £3.95). A brief note: these last two did *not* (allegedly) get in because the editor comes from Perth!

*Edmund O'Connor*

# Chapman

4 Broughton Place, Edinburgh EH1 3RX, Scotland
Tel 0131–557 2207 Fax 0131–556 9565
E-mail: editor@chapman-pub.co.uk
Website: www.chapman-pub.co.uk

Editor: Joy Hendry
Assistant Editor: Edmund O'Connor
Volunteers: Paula Cowie, Ann-Sophie Klemp,
Heather Scott and Rosemary Whelan

Information about the contributors is available on request

---

ISBN 1-903700-05-1          ISSN 0308-2695          © Chapman 2002

## Chapman
### Subscription Rates

|  | Personal | | Institutional | |
|---|---|---|---|---|
|  | 1 year | 2 years | 1 year | 2 years |
| UK | £18 (£13 conc*) | £34 | £24 (£18 conc**) | £45 |
| Overseas | £24/ $38 | £45/ $70 | £30/ $45 | £52/ $84 |

Single issues £6 inc P&P
* Applies to students, DSS, etc
** Applies to writers' groups and similar artistic organisations
US Dollar cheques, and Donations to help the work of Chapman welcome.

---

### Submissions:
*Chapman welcomes submissions of poetry, fiction and articles*
*which **must** be accompanied by SAE or International Reply Coupons*

---

---

Production: Scotprint, Gateside Commerce Park, Haddington, East Lothian